THE RHYTHMIC LANGUAGE OF HEALTH AND DISEASE

Mark Rider, Ph.D.

MMB MUSIC, INC.

THE RHYTHMIC LANGUAGE OF HEALTH AND DISEASE
Mark Rider, Ph.D.

Cover design: Mary Haas and Mark Rider
Cover Photo: Mark Rider
Typography: Bruce Ross
Printer: John Swift and Co. Inc., St. Louis, Mo.
First printing: November, 1997
Printed in USA
ISBN: 1-58106-000-9

For further information and catalogs contact:

MMB Music, Inc.
Contemporary Arts Building
3526 Washington Avenue
Saint Louis, MO 63103-1019

Phone: 314 531-9635, 800 543-3771 (USA/Canada)
Fax: 314 531-8384
E-mail: mmbmusic@mmbmusic.com
Web site: http://www.mmbmusic.com

CONTENTS

PREFACE

This book is dedicated to the "woman in the red dress." Years ago, I came across a local newspaper column reviewing a religious revival which had passed through town a few days earlier. Some 10,000 people, one-tenth of the local population, had attended. At one point in the revival, the featured charismatic preacher had reportedly had a vision of a woman in a red dress in the audience with an incurable cancer. She appeared from within the crowd, he "zapped" her on her head with his hands, she reeled and convulsed, and he declared her healed.

This story, commonplace by current television standards, might have passed from my mind as quickly as it entered. But, then about a week later, the skeptical journalist published a sequel to the review which this time etched its way into my memory forever. The "woman in red" had paid a visit to her equally skeptical oncologist, who had just viewed the tumor on X-ray weeks before. You could tell from the interview that the doctor really didn't want to admit it, but on the basis of her current medical exam, she now showed no signs of cancer. The physician went on to remark about the incidence of spontaneous remission in a way highly suggestive of science's blindness to the unexplainable. If a theory or mechanism can't be found to account for some event, the event may as well not have occurred. This is what I call science's principle of "out of mind, out of sight." Without a place to understand the event in our mind, science suggests that we forget it.

But the emotion surrounding magical, unexplainable events prevents us from forgetting them. Freud tried to disregard music because he could not scientifically explain its profound effects on the human psyche. Yet, he found he couldn't deny the emotions stirred within him by music, so he developed a phobic-like avoidance of music.

This book is about transforming yesterday's magic into today's science. Many facets of healing still appear magical because of their mystery. No system in the body is probably more mysterious than the immune system. Diseases of the immune system, ranging from cancer to the common cold and AIDS to autoimmunity, continue to perplex us.

Yet, as I began to search in some unconventional ways, I made some fascinating new discoveries about the mind and brain during illness and health. In this book, I will provide evidence that we already have important tools that can screen people at risk for certain types of illness. Furthermore, these tools can be used to facilitate healing from any kind of disease or illness.

A theory will be unfolded in this book which allows the health professional and health consumer alike to understand mind-body phenomena from a new perspective. Evidence will be presented for homeodynamic mechanisms in all living organisms. Homeodynamism, in some ways a complementary mechanism to homeostasis, suggests that the healthy body is in a normal state of periodic flux, and that stress and even disease are produced when these cyclic variations are prevented from occurring.

However, homeodynamism goes further than homeostasis by postulating that mind, brain, and body are organized in identical ways. These organizational patterns will be presented as evidence for a unified bodymind that help explain the commonalities among a wide variety of healing therapies.

In Chapter 1, I will present two novel approaches in the study of disease which demonstrate that homeodynamic shifts are necessary for health. The applications of inductive reasoning and EEG analysis indicate that proper immune functioning is related to increased variability within the nervous system. The cardiovascular and muscular systems also exhibit optimum functioning only in the presence of these same mental/brain wave shifts.

In Chapter 2, I will demonstrate that mind, brain, and body are organized not only identically, but also harmonically, allowing a homeodynamic state of total communication to exist—the bodymind. New evidence will be shown that persons with disorders affecting the immune system display non-harmonic frequencies in their EEG, which distorts bodymind communication. Other disease processes likewise are accompanied by a lack of harmonic organization.

In the next four chapters will be documented a collection of homeodynamic healing techniques which produce 1) bodymind shifts and 2) increases in harmonic organization of the bodymind so that total communication and health can exist. These chapters are arranged to cover, in order, physical, emotional, mental, and sociospiritual techniques. Most alternative medicine techniques accomplish their healing ends through the induction of homeodynamic shifts.

In Chapter 7, I will explore the first of two homeodynamic hypotheses. The first one demonstrates the clinical use of "symptom as metaphor" through case studies in which homeodynamic changes have been made. Having the patient consider the bodymind as a single entity creates mental shifts which allow for physiological changes to follow.

In the last chapter, I consider the importance of rituals in modern and ancient culture as homeodynamic behaviors designed to aid survival of the culture. In this organizational approach, the culture is viewed as a macroscopic organism capable of healing itself through institutional rituals collectively engaged in by its members.

I

HOMEODYNAMISM INSTEAD OF HOMEOSTASIS

INTRODUCTION

Shifting is such a normal part of life that there is nothing in the universe which does not vibrate at some rhythm. Even inanimate matter vibrates at the atomic level. The field of chronobiology is the study of the rhythms of living organisms. Circadian rhythms are those rhythms which have an oscillation of about one day. Microrhythms, or ultradian rhythms occur more than once a day; macrorhythms, or infradian, less than once daily.

Disturbances of health are associated with terminations of these rhythms. For an example of each, our normal circadian sleep-wake cycle is about 26 hours. Because this cycle is close to the 24-hour solar cycle, we are easily entrained into the solar cycle. Individuals who eliminate this cycle through sleep deprivation experience an increase in physical and emotional problems.

The human menstrual cycle, an infradian rhythm, is approximately entrained to the lunar cycle of 28 days. Severe physical stress (such as through marathon running) or emotional stress is sometimes associated with interruptions in this normal rhythm, known as dysmenorrhea and amenorrhea.

An interesting, but little known, ultradian rhythm is that the brain likes to shift cerebral hemispheres back and forth about every 90 minutes. If continuous activity is engaged in with only one hemisphere, then health problems usually ensue. For example, if you spend an entire workday in primarily one type of activity (whether it is making calculations, painting, or making managerial decisions) you will probably have a headache by the end of the day. In other words, stress can be caused by too much homeostasis.

There are an endless number of these rhythms pulsing away in this organic symphony called the human bodymind. Furthermore, the shifts embodied within these rhythms enable us to cope with the life changes, or stressors, which are thrown at us. These dynamic shifts are in essence a form of healthy exercise. Within certain limits, the greater the variability, the greater the health.

Apparently we need these dynamic shifts to stay healthy physically, mentally, emotionally, and spiritually. It is as if we were marching to the tune of some cosmic drummer, entraining our personal rhythms to those in both the atomic and the celestial worlds. Researchers have concluded that such entrainment to other rhythms conserves energy, much the same way as in the effort required to board a moving train—it is much easier if you are running along at the same speed as the train. This book will explore healthy shifts in each of these areas.

Before embarking on our discussion of the health benefits of shifting, an introduction will be made to some of the basic concepts discussed in the next few sections. When discussing the importance of dynamism, or shifting, I shall be referring to mental, emotional, physiological, and even spiritual shifts. Shifts can therefore include thoughts, feelings, perceptions of connectedness, and electrochemical changes measured on the skin's surface.

As seen in the Figure 1, feeling relaxed is associated with slower brainwave rhythms of greater amplitude (voltage), increased mental focus and increased connectedness, while the converse is true for feelings of active alertness. The construct of connectedness is used here to refer to the spiritual domain without reference to specific theology. Connectedness may be with one's God or other individuals. The topic of connectedness will be addressed in more detail in Chapter 6 (Sociospiritual Techniques and Physical Healing).

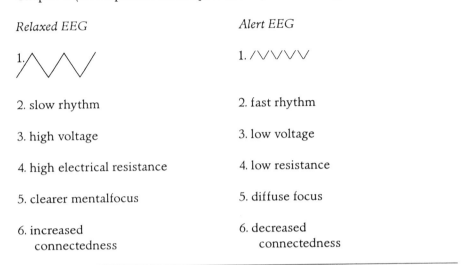

Relaxed EEG	*Alert EEG*
1.	1.
2. slow rhythm	2. fast rhythm
3. high voltage	3. low voltage
4. high electrical resistance	4. low resistance
5. clearer mentalfocus	5. diffuse focus
6. increased connectedness	6. decreased connectedness

Figure 1. Association of mental, emotional, physiological and spiritual events.

The basic tenet of homeodynamic theory is that no physical changes occur without these mental/electrical shifts occurring. Furthermore, health is associated with a particular rhythm of shifting which is related to normal human and cosmic rhythms. Disease states follow conditions in which this healthy rhythm has been altered or eliminated altogether.

The second concept of homeodynamic theory is that mind and body are organized in the same way, permitting total bodymind communication. As we shall see, this communication is two-way, allowing us to gain information about our body from behaviors such as imagery and dreams. Furthermore, these and other techniques can be used to create homeodynamic shifts which lead to healing.

In this book, body health will be explored primarily through the immune system. When the resonant properties between the body, brain, and mind are revealed in Chapter 2 the immune system will again be spotlighted. This is because the immune system preceded the vascular and nervous systems on the evolutionary scale.[1] Furthermore, the immune system laid the electrochemical blueprints which guided these phylogenetically newer systems into their present architecture. Finally, when looking at disease and health, the immune system plays a major role in both the etiology and management of most diseases. Chronic pain and the principal damage due to strokes and heart attacks are mostly caused by the immune system's inflammatory response. Ulcers are now known to be caused by a weakened immune system's ability to eradicate certain bacteria. Atherosclerosis occurs when antibody complexes form at tears in blood vessels initiated by vascular spasms. And, the "unknown origin" of essential hypertension has most often been found to be previous infections or diseases of the kidneys.

It is fascinating that the immune system is, on the one hand, perhaps the most important biological component within the bodymind, and yet so enigmatic and poorly understood on the other. The only system within the body to escape direct, real-time monitoring capabilities, thus preventing biofeedback control, is the immune system. The field of psychoneuroimmunology is rapidly pursuing a wide array of monitoring techniques to assist in the conquest of the immunological threats to our civilization.

In Carl Sagan's novel, *Contact*, an alien message was received and decoded, only to lead to another message (within the message) when scientists put it through an entirely different type of analysis. Homeodynamic theory is just such an analysis. When different systems in the body, such as the nervous, endocrine, and cardiovascular, are monitored in their traditional way, they reveal one set of data about these systems. However, when analyzed through such homeodynamic dimensions as rhythmic and harmonic organization, these systems reveal a new type of information about this most mysterious entity called the immune system. As we shall see, important clues to health and disease can be found within the rhythmic language of the bodymind.

CHAPTER ONE

The Dynamics of Health

Physical Health Benefits of Shifting
Multiple Personality Disorder: Origins of Homeodynamism

Our journey begins somewhat like a puzzle. The first clue comes from one of the most enigmatic of all mental disorders called multiple personality disorder (MPD). Multiple personality disorder is a dissociative disorder almost always brought on by severe physical abuse. Early in life these individuals learned to dissociate, or escape into a hidden world with a completely separate consciousness, to cope with the physical and emotional pain of their abuse.

Years ago I was asked to consult on a case of multiple personality disorder (MPD). Over several sessions I became amazed that as this individual would shift to his other personalities, or alters, that dramatically different physical manifestations would accompany each. For example, one alter might be sick with an intestinal virus, another completely healthy, another colorblind, and so on. One alter could even reproduce welts on a part of the body where abuse had occurred twenty years earlier! A different emotional state seemed to be represented by each alter as well.

Becoming highly intrigued with the potential healing mechanisms that were being employed by this patient, I began to explore the scientific literature for help. Comparison studies between persons with multiple personality disorder and normals has indicated that MPD's have greater variation among alters on physiological measures of central and peripheral nervous system activity.[1] Normals usually cannot fake such differences, especially on an electroencephalogram (EEG). The EEG waveform is made up principally of four frequency bands, from slowest to fastest—delta, theta, alpha, and beta. In adults, pure delta is found only during deep sleep. Theta is found during drowsiness and intense emotional states crucial to an organism's survival. Alpha is found during dreamy, passive states of relaxation. Beta is indicative of active thought and alertness. Thus, the faster the brainwave frequency, the more alert the individual.

Heretofore, no experimental studies of immune function have ever been conducted on MPD's. Clinically, however, MPD's have been found to have marked changes in allergies, respiratory and gastrointestinal disorders, dermatological reactions, and pain—all of which involve immunological mechanisms—following

5

sudden shifts in personality.[2] In fact, one interesting conclusion was consistently made in the MPD literature: Rare and unusual instances of physical alteration and healing were very common among these individuals! Suddenly, I began to wonder if somehow the high variation in the EEG of persons with MPD was the factor which enabled physical healing beyond that normally found in the rest of the population.

In particular, it appeared that the beta frequency band (or the fast frequencies) of electrical brainwave activity was the one which exhibited the most variability in this clinical group.[1] This made sense because in the alert state these individuals usually don't experience simultaneous awareness of each of their alters. Only in hypnosis (which we will see in Chapter 5 elicits shifts to alpha and theta) have I seen these alters begin to share consciousness. Thus, the EEG profile in the "day in the life" of a person with MPD is to experience a dramatic series of frequency shifts to a wider range of frequencies. While this may help protect the person with MPD from physical types of illness, there are certainly psychosocial and cognitive costs such as the bouts of amnesia and the constriction of personality within any one alter.

This first piece of evidence became the kernel of a new theory of psychoneuroimmunology hypothesizing homeodynamic rather than homeostatic mechanisms. Consequently, homeodynamic theory emerged as a mechanism complementary to homeostasis. According to homeodynamic theory, the immune system functions at its optimum level with increased variability in the nervous system. Some of the ways in which this variability is observed in the MPD is through different EEG frequency bands, different personalities, and different emotions.

Finally, one might speculate that one of the costly disadvantages to the psychological healing of MPD's is an increase in physical illness. In my clinical experience I can definitely corroborate this relationship. Those MPD patients of mine that have begun to "integrate" and consequently experience less dramatic personality shifts (as well as EEG shifts), also have increased physical complaints ranging from autoimmune disease to infections. To effectively manage illness at this transitional stage of therapy, MPD patients then have to relearn to create new brainwave shifts, this time on the conscious level. These techniques will be expanded upon in Chapters 3–6.

Schizophrenia and Immunity

Our next puzzle piece takes us to a clinical syndrome called schizophrenia, meaning "split-personality," as opposed to multiple personality. Again, like MPD, schizophrenia is a disorder in which skills involving communication and thinking are disturbed. Rather than developing different emotion-specific alters as in MPD however, schizophrenics usually have a very flat affect. As a response to stress, schizophrenics often develop delusions or hallucinations.

Yet, also like MPD, schizophrenia is a clinical syndrome which has endowed itself with protection from certain immunological diseases—namely cancer.[3] At least one physician has commented that physical illness is absent in schizophrenics.[4] Was there some common link between multiple personalities and schizophrenics that afforded protection from physical diseases?

As I suspected, the answer probably was to be found in the profound behavioral response each group displays when significantly stressed. A group of researchers had discovered that schizophrenics experience brainwave downshifts to theta during hallucinations.[5] Other research indicated that the variability of EEG amplitudes within practically all frequency bands was significantly higher in schizophrenics than normals.[6] Here it was, the second puzzle piece. Somehow, it seemed that the more dynamic activity that occurred in the brain, the more the immune system was boosted.

Hence, the data with the clinical population of schizophrenia seemed to suggest that as disruptive as hallucinations can be to the normal thinking and communication process, there seems to be some adaptive advantage to these mind-altering cognitive changes, and apparently this advantage is found within the immune system. In other words, homeodynamic mechanisms within the nervous system appear to be essential for an enhanced immune system.

Interestingly, this same shift to the slower frequencies found in schizophrenics has also been found in normals during creative thought.[5] Maybe this is why no cultures have ever been discovered which did not participate in the creative arts. Creativity may be an adaptive, survival-linked behavior for two reasons. First, creative expression through the arts enables healthy communication of repressed feelings. These repressed feelings become harmful to the body if not vented through the buildup of stress hormones. Secondly, however, creativity also promotes physical health through the brainwave shifts, not only from one frequency to another, but between right and left hemispheres as well.

Suddenly, I realized that this new understanding of the physical health benefits of brainwave shifting could help explain some of the recent results we had achieved in enhancing the immune system through music listening. In one study, I had used music as a placebo control treatment in a study of the effects of mental imagery on the immune system.[7] Music was common to both groups, but in the placebo control the imagery treatment was eliminated leaving only the music. During the first week of testing, the imagery and music groups both experienced increased immunity as defined by production of salivary antibody (immunoglobulin A). Now I was beginning to realize that what may have happened was that subjects in both groups experienced a brainwave shift which was responsible for the immune boost. Music and imagery in immune enhancement will be discussed in more detail in Chapters 3 and 4.

As with the MPD population, the physical protection afforded by schizophrenia also seems to follow a U-shaped curve. Schizophrenic patients of mine who have "positive" symptoms (hallucinations and thus EEG shifts) in addition to "negative" ones (flat affect) seem to get physically sick less often than my less psychotic schizotypal patients who have only negative symptoms. The curve of physical wellness increases again as emotional expressiveness and connectedness become integrated on a conscious level within one's personality.

Mental Retardation and Immunity

To continue this inductive research into the mechanisms of physical health, I began to search for other diagnostic groups which were associated with exceptional immune functioning. A colleague of mine, Jeanne Achterberg, mentioned that studies she had conducted of state institutions indicated that the mentally retarded also have a reduced incidence of certain immunological diseases, in particular, cancer.

From my EEG studies I remembered that the mentally retarded often have abnormal brainwave patterns consisting of a predominance of slow-wave activity. At first, nothing about their brainwave patterns seemed at all similar to the two clinical groups we just considered. But then I returned to my experience with the retarded and recalled the training I had received on administering first aid to these children because of the high incidence of seizures. Many of these same children were also on dilantin or phenobarbital to reduce seizure activity. Instantly, I felt this was the clue I had been searching for. In terms of brainwave activity, seizures are characterized by large (high voltage) spikes in the brainwave pattern. It seemed paradoxical and yet amazing that these spikes, as destructive as they were in causing further brain damage, may also have an adaptive purpose in creating a brainwave shift which boosts the immune system.

Once I knew what to search for, I felt it would be only a matter of time before evidence corroborating my suspicion surfaced in the medical literature. I had to go quite a few years back, but in a study conducted over forty years ago, seizures were demonstrated to occur in epileptics when their eosinophil subpopulation of white blood cells got too low.[8] Following the seizures, the eosinophils began to rise. Apparently, the electrical current from these seizures acted as a homeodynamic on-off switch for the immune system.

Physical Health Detriments of NonShifting
Depression, Alcoholism, and Immunity

Through inductive reasoning I was beginning to build a case for immunocompetence featuring clinical syndromes which manifested a greater-than-normal degree of mental shifting. It wasn't long before I began to consider whether the inverse relationship was true—that clinical syndromes characterized by a lack of brainwave-shifting activity had suppressed immune systems.

Several years ago I was attending a workshop on an innovative use for electroencephalographic (EEG) biofeedback in the treatment of addictive disorders. In comparing the brainwave patterns of alcoholics with normals, a reference was briefly made by the presenters to research confirming that alcoholics and depressives had significantly less alpha activity and more beta activity than normals.[9-11] In other words, a greater percentage of time with these individuals appears to be spent in active thought, usually ruminating on personal issues. Alcohol, being a physiological depressant, has a role in decreasing the brainwave frequencies from beta to alpha. In depression, as well as with alcoholism, the brain is constantly engaged without sufficient rest in the form of downshifting to lower brainwave frequencies.

This became one of the most exciting answers to my puzzle yet. I instantly made a mental connection with the well-known high incidence of cancer in depressives. In a well-controlled study of personality in individuals before disease onset, depression was associated with a twofold increase in the odds of death from cancer.[12] Other psychological studies have corroborated this finding of a correlation between depression and decreased functioning of the immune system.[13-16]

So homeodynamic theory fit the data regardless of whether EEG variability was higher or lower than "normal." Depressives have decreased variability in their EEG, characterized by an overabundance of fast wave activity and a paucity of slow wave activity. Furthermore, their incidence of immunological illness is higher.

Suddenly, I wondered about a diagnostic group which was closely related to depression—bipolar disorder (or manic depression). I postulated that manic depressives should experience immune systems which were more suppressed than normals, but less so than their depressed "cousins." After all, manic depressives experience marked shifts in mood (hence the name) which, although undocumented, undoubtedly are accompanied by brainwave changes to some degree.

Indeed, the literature confirms that manic depressives, apparently through the mental shifts accompanying their mood swings, do experience less compromised immunity than their unipolar counterparts.[17-19] I have even confirmed this in my own patients. My bipolar patients have a much lower incidence of viral and bacterial infections as well as cancer than my patients with only depression. Thus, affective shifting to alternate moods by a manic depressive, as in the personality shifting in a multiple personality, affords some immunological protection.

Chronic Fatique and Immunity: Experimental Evidence for Homeodynamism

As my clinical examples of "brain-shiftiers" and "non-shiftiers" were beginning to accumulate, my search for EEG studies of patients with immunological disorders was going nowhere. The only studies it seemed I could find were of patients whose immune disease had invaded the brain, such as in Alzheimers, AIDS, and multiple sclerosis, and the EEG was only being used to pinpoint neurological problems caused by the disease.

However, due to the controversy of a disease called chronic fatigue syndrome, some researchers had used electroencephalography to investigate this disorder. Chronic fatigue syndrome (CFS) is a malady which has received more and more attention in the 80's and 90's for which no known cause has yet to be found. Going also by the names fibrositis, fibromyalgia, and myalgic encephalopathy, CFS is usually diagnosed once everything else has been ruled out. The common symptoms include flu-like symptoms of fever, sore throat, headache, muscle weakness and soreness, and fatigue. Laboratory tests have indicated immunological abnormalities as well. In fact, CFS was initially thought to be caused by the Epstein-Barr virus, also associated with mononucleosis. It was this finding that made me investigate CFS in greater depth.

The good news was that I had finally found the only EEG studies conducted on immune disease noninvasive to the brain. The bad news was that these

EEG studies were conducted only during sleep. The result however turned out to be a homeodynamic goldmine. The major finding of these studies was that fibromyalgic patients experienced a lack of slow-wave, or deep, sleep. Slow-wave sleep is characterized by delta waves, the slowest but largest voltage brainwave rhythm. These researchers found that the delta brainwave rhythms in individuals with CFS were replaced by alpha waves.[20] Studies have even been conducted on normal subjects in which they were deprived of slow-wave sleep by awakening them when their EEG registered delta. As expected, these slow-wave-deprived subjects developed symptoms similar to those of CFS.[21]

It was with fascination that I found that the delta-wave component of sleep (deep sleep) is the restorative phase of the circadian rhythm for the human body. During this phase, immune system productivity is at its peak.[22] Interleukins, which initiate a cascade of subsequent immune responses, are mass-produced by the neuroglia in the cortex during delta sleep. Lymphocytes seem to be their hungriest also during delta sleep, as evidenced in their increased ability to respond to antigens such as concanavalin A (Con-A) and phytohemagglutinin (PHA).

This new finding meant that it was not necessarily the presence of alpha or theta which accounted for enhanced immunity. The similarity to the other puzzle pieces was that the low-frequency range of electrical brain activity was constricted. In the case of CFS, it was delta which was missing. In the case of depression, it was alpha. I felt that the puzzle was becoming clearer, especially when I pursued the relationship with delta rhythms and the immune system.

Attention Deficit Hyperactive Disorder and Immunity

As the puzzle pieces were beginning to fall into place, an explanation for the differences in immunity in the various populations was emerging. It seemed that the lower frequency, higher voltage brainwave patterns (alpha, theta, and delta) were responsible for the operation of the immune system. These large voltages were somehow required to turn on the power to the immune system.

As I was becoming more sure of this "on/off switch" hypothesis to the immune system, a colleague of mine at Texas Womens University, Daniel Miller, Ph.D. was collecting data on individuals with attention deficit/hyperactive disorder (ADHD). One night I inadvertently booted the wrong data disk into the computer and onto the screen appeared the brainmaps of some ADHD patients. I scanned these brainmaps with curiosity for awhile when I noticed that the eyes-open EEG for these individuals seemed to have a prevalence of theta activity. Beta activity should have been present. Not long after this I heard at an EEG workshop that others were reporting this same phenomenon—people with ADHD were manifesting too much theta and not enough beta.[23]

When I got my chance, I asked the presenter about the physical health of these ADHD patients. Not only, the presenter reported, did ADHD individuals experience more illnesses and infections than normals, but that with EEG biofeedback to correct the brainwave frequency imbalance these patients became more attentive and improved in physical health.[9] I immediately went to the medical literature and, low and behold, ADHD children had been found to experience more otitis media, upper respiratory infections, asthma, and allergies than normal children.[24] Could the absence of any EEG band—in this case, beta—lead to reduced immune functioning?

Some groups of researchers have looked at the ratio of the amplitudes among the various frequency bands with different populations. The ratio of beta-to-theta power for attention deficit children and adults has been demonstrated to be as low as one-seventh that of normals.[25] After brainwave training to increase the power ratio to 1:1 (beta-to-theta), decreases have been found in 1) drowsiness, 2) inattentiveness, and 3) physical illness.

Homeodynamic theory was beginning to appear more and more valid. The data from the ADHD population suggested, however, that it wasn't necessarily "downshifting" to lower EEG frequency bands that was immune enhancing, but rather any EEG shifts which led to the best immunity.

Aging and Homeodynamism: The Fountain of Youth

It is common knowledge that our immune systems deteriorate as we age. We become more susceptible to viral and bacterial infections as well as cancer. What I didn't know until I stumbled across a pertinent reference one day, was that the elderly also experience reduced variability, or complexity (in chaos terminology), in a host of physiological behaviors.[26] These include first and foremost a restricted range of EEG signals. The list continues with less variable heartrate and blood pressure, and less variable diurnal rhythms for hormone release and immune secretion.[27] This was not direct, causal evidence, but nevertheless an important link in showing that decreased immune responsivity was at least related to reduced variation in brainwave activity.

Perhaps one can even draw a homeodynamic conclusion that maintaining the variability in our nervous and cardiovascular systems can increase our physical longevity. The two most obvious ways of accomplishing this variability is to maintain our emotional support and our interests and activity levels through our old age. Emotional support in a therapeutic setting has been found to increase cardiovascular variability.[45] Keeping up our interests and activity levels has long been associated with health in old age. The reasons, however, are speculated here to be the homeodynamic shifts which different activities would afford. Consequently, the fountain of youth may possibly be reached by never losing the beat of this psychophysiological symphony.

Immunological Health and Brainwave Shifting

I felt excited that so many puzzle pieces were coming together in an inductive way regarding the validity of homeodynamic theory and health. There was still a hole missing when it came to direct evidence of brainwave shifts and the immune system. What we did know was that there were nightly rhythms of immune production which correlated with phases of sleep, each of which were associated with a different electrical brain rhythm. Evidence from chronobiology, in fact, had demonstrated that the immune system fluctuated more rapidly than any other system in the body. This is why the immune system is the system within the body which is the most fragile to electromagnetic radiation. Becker has discussed at length the high incidence of cancer following exposure to different types of electromagnetic radiation.[28]

Because cancer has its own unusually high DC electric potential, electromagnetic fields have entered into the arena of cancer therapies.[29] One particularly exciting cancer therapy has been developed by the Swedish cancer surgeon Bjorn Nordenstrom. Treating the body as an electrically-closed circuit, Nordenstrom has explored the use of electricity as a way of dehydrating tumors, which cannot survive without water.[30] In the process, it was discovered that white blood cells are also electrically charged and could be guided toward cancerous areas by placing the appropriate electrodes near the tumor. But if the body's own immune cells are attracted and repelled by electricity, then wouldn't the DC potentials manifested by the brain and body allow for this process to occur naturally from within?

To my delight, several groups of researchers had just conducted some studies in the last fifteen years which confirmed the relationship between brain electrical activity and the immune response. In these experiments, mice and rabbits had been given an antigen (a substance foreign to the animal which would evoke an immune response) while having their brains electrically monitored. In each of the experiments immunization led to increases in the firing rate of neurons in the hypothalamus.[31-34] Interestingly, in each of the experiments, the complete immune response was accompanied by several frequency shifts over several days. In other words, normal immune functioning apparently required an ability to engage in a dynamic range of electrical brain wave activity. Homeodynamic theory regarding the necessity of dynamic shifts for optimum immune functioning was gathering more and more evidence. The only puzzle piece missing now was the confirmation through clinical evidence that patients with immune disorders displayed a lack of homeodynamic variability in their electrical brain wave activity.

EEG Brain Mapping and Chronic Disease

If electrical dynamism in the brain was at the seat of immune responsivity, was it then constricted variability of human brainwaves that caused illness? This question wasn't tabled for long when an opportunity opened up which allowed me to find an answer to this question.

A cross-disciplinary brain mapping lab opened up for what was to be only several years at the University of North Texas. After hearing of the lab, I went to talk to one of its directors, psychologist Daniel Miller. I left him a copy of my initial paper on homeodynamic theory and asked if he had any suggestions to complete the bodymind puzzle I was working on. This meeting turned into the beginning of a working relationship which was to bring home the missing pieces I sought.

I began soliciting patients with chronic immunological disorders, noninvasive to the brain, to participate in an electrical brain mapping study using standard EEG protocols. After collecting data from only eleven patients (with cancer, autoimmune disease, or fibromyalgia) and four immunologically-healthy controls (all women), significant differences had already begun to emerge in many of the protocols.

For statistical purposes, all patients were ultimately collapsed into one group due to the similarity of their EEG profiles. Even with the cancer patients it did not matter whether the data were collected during or after their course of active malignancy. The same EEG profiles seemed to be manifesting.

The first result confirmed the dynamic component of homeodynamism. The immunological patients had a frequency profile very similar to the depressives—too much beta activity and not enough alpha (statistically significant at p < .05).[35] Two differences, however, stood out from the profile characteristic of depressives. These immunological patients also exhibited too much theta activity (p < .05), in some ways not altogether unlike the attention deficit population discussed earlier. As we shall see later in this section, there were other behavioral features which also resembled the ADHD population.

Furthermore, the patients also exhibited a lack of delta activity (p < .05) when compared to the normals. Normally, delta brainwaves prevail only during deep sleep. However, enough delta is present during the waking state to still measure and compare. This result was similar to the sleep studies (reported above) conducted on chronic fatigue and rheumatoid arthritis patients—the range of EEG activity was constricted due to a lack of delta activity during deep sleep.

The evoked potential tasks revealed that the healthy controls were able to manifest a larger electrical potential than the immune patients. On the flash visual evoked potential task (see Figure 1-1), the immunological patients had significantly lower amplitudes than the controls for the N75 and P100 components (p < .05). The auditory evoked potential tended to also favor the controls in amplitude for both the N100 and the P300, but was nonsignificant (see Figure 1-2). For both tasks, the distribution of electrical activity was much more focalized for the controls than the patients. These results also resembled previous research on depressives, who have evidenced reduced evoked potentials.

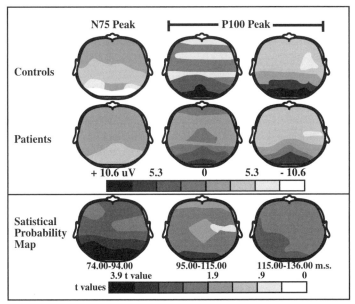

Figure 1-1. *Visual evoked potential differences between controls and patients.*

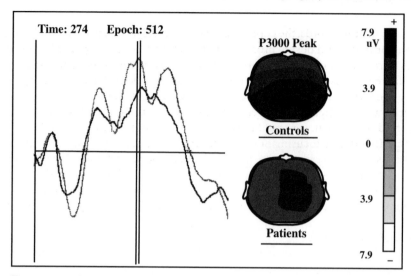

Figure 1-2. *P300 auditory evoked potential comparison between controls and patients.*

The contingent negative variation (CNV) was also examined in these patients. The (CNV) is the measure of the person's preparedness before responding to a stimulus. It is a slow, negative DC deflection in the EEG voltage prior to a task that, in this case, required the discrimination between high and low tones. This task has been found to distinguish between depressives and schizophrenics, two of the clinical groups reported above to exhibit, respectively, suppressed and enhanced immunity. Depressives have tended to elicit a larger than normal CNV whereas schizophrenics have yielded a lower than normal CNV. This seems to be because the higher anxiety levels of depressives makes them more hypervigilant toward outside stimuli. One might even hypothesize, based on our earlier discussion of the immunocompetence of schizophrenics over depressives, that immunological patients would have a larger CNV. This is precisely what was demonstrated by these patients. In temporal and parietal brain regions, the patients exhibited a significantly larger CNV than the healthy controls.

As a way of demonstrating the lack of mental shifting in the patients, means for the patients and controls were calculated on the number of seconds of synchronized (alpha or theta) brainwave activity during a sampling of 30 artifact-free seconds of EEG activity during eyes-open and eyes-closed conditions. Healthy subjects had a mean of 16 seconds of synchronized activity, or roughly half the time spent with eyes closed, whereas the patient mean was nearly half that of the controls (9 seconds). These differences were statistically significant.

The mean time spent in synchronized brainwave activity for the eyes-open condition was 6.91 seconds for the patients and 4 seconds for the controls. This difference was not statistically significant. Differences of synchronized brainwave activity between eyes-open and eyes-closed conditions were then calculated for each subject by subtracting the number of seconds of synchronized activity during eyes-open from that during the eyes-closed condition. Means for the groups were 2.09 for the patients and 12 for the controls, a highly significant finding.

In other words, the controls shifted back and forth between synchronized (alpha or theta) and desynchronized (beta) activity, depending on whether their eyes were open or closed. The patients' brainwaves, on the other hand, looked very similar regardless of eye condition. It were as if the patients were not resting when their eyes were closed and yet were not fully awake when their eyes were open. Interviews with these patients enabled me to confirm these EEG results. Patients reported that they never could fully relax. Furthermore, they indicated that they had a difficult time focusing or concentrating. Some patients described their condition as a "zombie-like" state, like the walking dead. In homeodynamic terms, their central nervous system was in a continuous state of idling (never off, never in drive). This constancy was demonstrated both electroencephalographically and behaviorally. And, I was convinced this phenomenon was accounting for their illnesses.

Recharging the Battery
Not only were the patients nonshifting throughout the day, but all were reporting poor deep sleep. As you will recall, this pattern was discovered with fibromyalgia and rheumatoid arthritis patients. What I am convinced is happening is that these homeodynamic shifts of electrical-mental activity are recharging the human battery. The different brainwave frequencies allow the ionic gates within each cell (in the brain and body) to open and close. This osmosis of ions, such as potassium and sodium, gradually creates a level of polarization that gives the battery, or the bodymind, its charge. Others have compared the neuron to a battery cell because its inside voltage is lower than the outside voltage.[39] The lack of such a charge in the patients is evident in the decreased amplitudes of the evoked potentials.

The weakened charge characterizing these patients was also manifested in another intriguing way which was discovered almost serendipitously. One day, in a fibromyalgia support group meeting in which I was explaining the brainmapping results, one of the patients humorously remarked that maybe this "lack of electric charge" was what was causing her credit cards to demagnetize so rapidly. I think I was the only one who laughed, because each of the other patients had a similar, if not identical, story regarding "electric" phenomena. Most patients had encountered these same credit card problems. Some had had experience causing microcomputers to stop processing and require rebooting. Many received electrostatic shocks from others of an intensity and frequency which seemed much higher than normal. One patient indicated that she regularly set off the magnetic detector in her video rental store. The most bizarre story related three incidents in which the same patient had been struck by lightening.

Were these patients acting like neutral lightening rods due to their reduced ability to concentrate and focus electrical energy of their own? Or did they exhibit some unique electromagnetic field, like a magnet, which was responsible for both their weakened immunity as well as the disturbances they encountered with other electromagnetic devices? At this point, the puzzle was leading me toward some interesting research which was being conducted on healing and the electromagnetic fields in the body.

Direct Current (DC) and the Bodymind

The purpose of the changing brainwaves is to recharge our living battery, of which each cell in our body is analogous to one of the individual cells in an actual battery. The type of electrical current produced by a battery, as well as by our body, is direct current (DC). One researcher has investigated for many years the behavioral responses of applying DC to animals and humans.[29] Consistent with the battery model of healing, Becker has found that DC induces sleep, analgesia from pain, and tissue and bone growth in wounds and amputated limbs. In these same experiments, hypnosis and imagery were demonstrated to evoke DC shifts on the scalp. It is for these reasons that imagery and hypnosis perform a facilitative role in the healing process. These techniques will be considered in detail in Chapter 5.

This puzzle finally seems to come together in recent discoveries of where in the body this DC electrical charge originates. It was long thought simply to be a manifestation of the nervous system. After all, this DC voltage made up the baseline of the EEG. Also, it was measurable throughout the body. Yet the character of this current was different from the pulsed, all-or-nothing current displayed by the nervous system, which acts more like alternating current. This DC activity waxed and waned. As it turned out this DC current actually emanates not from the nervous system, but from cells derived from the immune system!

The glial cells, which incidentally make up over 80% of the brain, are immune cells which are related to macrophages. In the body they are called Schwann cells. When they wrap around neurons they are called myelin, or the white matter in the brain. Their job is to guide developing neurons to their proper places, repair damaged neurons, and regulate metabolic pathways of practically all ions and neurotransmitters. Finally, they produce their own electrical current which is a slowly waxing and waning DC voltage. Immunologist Candace Pert has dubbed macrophages and their close relatives, the glial cells, a "mobile synapse" which appears stationary in the brain, but then moves around when activated to carry out duties of the immune system.[36] These glial cells found in the brain and spinal cord, along with their peripheral equivalents, the Schwann cells, form a complex analog (DC) electrical circuit capable of communicating information much more accurately and with greater ease of integration than in the digital (AC) nervous system.

Of great interest to the present discussion are experiments which have demonstrated that "healers," when projecting their healing energy onto patients, also elicit huge voltage changes in their body potentials.[37] Healers have also been found to exhibit extremely large amplitudes of all frequencies when meditating and focusing healing energies onto patients.[38] The immune system and nervous system work together through the glial-neuronal network to build these large electrical potentials capable of tissue reparation and restoration.

Therefore, homeodynamic shifts include both EEG frequency shifts as well as DC shifts, the latter of which may be the immune system's own communications with the rest of the bodymind. If we allow it to communicate fully, through its entire range of brainwave activity, then we heal more quickly and manage disease more effectively. It is not unusual that the immune system would seem to be in the driver's seat in this model. After all, the immune system is phylogenetically much older than the nervous system, and probably arose just after complex sugars began wrapping themselves around each other to make DNA.

This electrical field, composed of both the digital (AC) nervous system and the analog (DC) glial system, is both our mind and our body, simultaneously. A physical shift cannot occur without a mental shift, and vice versa. And, because all electromagnetic currents in the cosmos exert an influence on each other, our bodymind is connected to all the other bodyminds and interplanetary events in the cosmos. What would be described as the Bodymind, then, would be the force guiding our spiritual connections and our silent influences upon each other. In essence then, our thoughts are like silent drums beating out a pulse that our bodies and other bodyminds can march to if we listen carefully. However, all of our sense systems are based on movement and differentiation. We must move our eyes to focus, our ears to localize sound, and our fingers to touch. To listen to the cosmic drumming, we only need to create a homeodynamic shift to hear.

Shifting and Other Health Benefits

As I began to explore body systems outside of immunology I became fascinated as I learned that they too relied on a homeodynamic mechanism of shifting for optimum health. We will look at the musculoskeletal, cardiovascular, and psychological systems for further evidence of homeodynamism.

Muscle Health

Any muscle which stays contracted too long develops pain and inflammation. My electromyographic examinations of patients with "overuse syndromes" has revealed a close relationship between pain and over-activity of the musculoskeletal system. These pain syndromes include both tension and migraine headaches, and the "overuse" syndromes, such as carpal tunnel and thoracic outlet disorders. In all of these examples, muscular activity is exerted for a prolonged time without rest followed by a recovery period in which muscle relaxation is not reached. Instead, a new, higher baseline of muscular activity is set, initiating poor oxygenation and nutrition of the muscles, poor drainage of toxic substances (lactic acid) out of the muscles, and the buildup of so-called pain hormones (Substance P) and immune-based inflammatory chemicals (prostaglandins).

Any muscle which is devoid of contractions develops weakness and eventually atrophy. Underuse is certainly as critical as overuse. Pain often relates to this underuse as well. With my spinal pain patients, it is very common for chronic pain to occur not in muscles which are overly tense, but in the matched muscles on the opposite side of the body which have become weak. For example, whiplash injuries may cause a spinal muscle on the right side of the neck to reset to a higher baseline of activity, such as 10 uv (microvolts), whereas its counterpart on the left side of the neck is resting at 4 uv. However, the pain may be felt by the patient on the left side, due to the eventual weakness in the left spinal muscle. The left muscle can become weak because the patient learns to rely on the right muscle for neck support, since it is stronger.

Hence, optimum muscle health relies on a continuous, homeodynamic rhythm which oscillates between exertion within normal muscle load-limits and relaxation back to baseline levels.

Heart Health

A cardiovascular system which remains at capacity (high blood pressure, high heart rate, etc.) for too long is dangerous. The heart and the blood vessels are also muscle (smooth muscle) and require relaxation. Otherwise we put ourselves at risk for anginal pain, hypertension, and myocardial infarction.

A cardiovascular system which remains at rest is also dangerous. We've come to hear so much regarding Type A behavior and heart disease that it probably seems healthier to rest the vascular system than to exert it. Nevertheless, those who stretch the vascular system to its normal limits through exercise have over ten times better odds of not succumbing to a heart attack when walking up a flight of stairs as those who have not exercised.

Researchers have now determined in fact that a human with a more variable and chaotic heartbeat is much less likely to die of sudden heart failure than an individual with a less complex heartrate.[35] Furthermore, individuals who disclose more feelings and achieve more emotional closure in psychotherapy have been found to display a more variable and chaotic heartrate than those who exhibit more emotional repression.

My patients with coronary heart disease who are learning to manage their disease through biofeedback exemplify this lack of variability in another way. Respiratory sinus arrhythmia (RSA) is the medical name for the continuous phenomenon of heart rate acceleration and deceleration mediated by the inhalation and exhalation cycle, respectively. People with coronary heart disease, however, exhibit little RSA activity. The heart keeps beating at the same pace regardless of the phase of the breathing cycle, exhibiting more independence from the lungs. As the biophysicist Fred Alan Wolf has pointed out, organs which act independently from one another are not in resonance and therefore cause more energy expenditure by the bodymind. "Health," he states, "involves correlation or resonance among all cells in the body."[39]

Psychological Health

Homeodynamic shifting has been found by researchers to be the normal state of affairs for mental activity. Researchers William Dement and Nathaniel Kleitman were the first to discover the basic-rest-activity-cycle or BRAC.[40] This cycle consists of a ninety-minute cycle of rest and activity which helps explain human limits of constant performance or attentional demands. Concurrent with this data is the ninety-minute free-running shift in brain activity from one hemisphere to the other, and in most autonomic, motor, sensory-perceptual, and cognitive responses.[41] Little is known about the purpose of such a rhythm, although overriding the limits imposed by the BRAC often leads to psychophysiological stress and illness.

Dynamism of emotional states has for the most part escaped documentation, although with dynamism having been demonstrated within the autonomic nervous system, one could certainly speculate on a similar situation existing with mood. In other words, because we understand our emotions on the most basic level as deriving from body signs such as muscle tension, heartrate, stomach tightness, and tears, it would not be surprising to detect such emotional rhythms.

The apparent need for emotional rhythms was suggested by some research I had been conducting on music. For years I had been demonstrating a technique in music therapy called the "iso-moodic principle."[42] This procedure showed that people were more affected by a piece of music if the music first matched their mood. For example, the best way to bring a sad person out of their depression was to first play sad music, then gradually change the music to happier, more upbeat music. Such music is also called entrainment music.

My interest was in determining a corollary of the iso-moodic principle, which, succinctly stated, went as follows: Do people prefer music which matched their mood? My data on over 500 subjects indicated that people prefer music which almost, but not exactly, matched their mood.[43] Specifically, 85% of the respondents liked best the music (controlled for genre and style) which was slightly different from their mood. These data also indicated that the affective domain is a rather dynamic one, with periodic emotional shifts needed to perhaps provide the information and/or energy to self-regulate and survive. The healing effects of tapping into these emotional rhythms will be further demonstrated in Chapter 4.

Conclusion

The conclusions we have reached in this chapter are as follows. First, a case was developed for the dependence of health (in particular, to threats of immunological disease) upon mental shifting. This mental shifting is characterized by EEG frequency shifts. Inductively, we saw that high-shifting individuals such as those with multiple personality disorder, seizure disorder, or schizophrenia have exceptional immune systems as evidenced through decreased incidence of cancer and/or amazing feats of physical healing.

Second, we found that "low-shifters" such as those with depression, attention deficit disorder, and chronic fatigue syndrome have compromised immune systems. Next, clinical evidence obtained from patients with immune disorders corroborated the inductive proof for the relationship between homeodynamic shifts and health. These immune patients demonstrated less EEG variability through a paucity of delta and alpha brainwave activity. Furthermore, these patients exhibited lower evoked potentials.

Finally, we showed how these brain wave shifts are responsible for gating the ionic pumps which essentially recharge the human battery, allowing us to think and (immunologically) defend ourselves.

References

1. Putnam, F.W. (1984). The psychophysiologic investigation of multiple personality disorder. *Psychiatric Clinics of North America, 7*(1), 31–39.

2. Braun, B.G. (1983). Psychophysiologic phenomena in multiple personality and hypnosis. *American Journal of Clinical Hypnosis, 26*(2), 124–137.

3. Achterberg, J. (1985). *Imagery in healing.* Boston: Shambhala.

4. Whitmont, E.C. (1993). *The alchemy of healing.* Berkeley: North Atlantic Books.

5. Whitton, J.L., Moldofsky, H., & Lue, F. (1978). EEG frequency patterns associated with hallucinations in schizophrenia and "creativity" in normals. *Biological Psychiatry, 13*(1), 123–133.

6. Maurer, K, & Dierks, T. (1991). *Atlas of brain mapping.* Berlin: Springer-Verlag.

7. Rider, M., Achterberg, J., Lawlis, G.F., Goven, A., Toledo, R., & Butler, J.R. (1990). Effect of immune system imagery on secretory IgA. *Biofeedback and Self-Regulation, 15*(4), 317–333.

8. Halberg, F., Engel, R., Halberg, E., & Passouant, P. (1952). Diurnal variations in amount of electroencephalographic paroxysmal discharge and diurnal eosinophil rhythm of epileptics on days with clinical seizures. *Federation Proceedings*, 11, 62.

9. Carter, J.L. (1991). Measurable changes in brain functioning related to psycho-physiological self-regulation training. Symposium presented at the 22nd Annual Meeting of the Association for Applied Psychophysiology and Biofeedback, March, Dallas, TX.

10. Funderburk, W.H. (1949). Electroencephalographic studies in chronic alcoholics. *Electroencephalography and Clinical Neurophysiology,1,* 369–370.

11. Sealy, R.C., Bernstein, B.E., & Magid, D.T. (1991). New developments in brainwave training. Workshop presented at the 13th Annual Meeting of the Pennsylvania Society of Behavioral Medicine and Biofeedback, November 8–9, Valley Forge.

12. Shekelle, R.B., Raynor, W.J., Ostfeld, A.M., Garron, D.C., Bieliauskas, L., Liu, S.C., Maliza, C., & Paul, O. (1981). Psychological depression and 17-year risk of death from cancer. *Psychosomatic Medicine, 43*, 117–125.

13. Achterberg, J., & Lawlis, G.F. (1979). A canonical analysis of blood chemistry variables related to psychological measures of cancer patients. *Multivariate Experimental Clinical Research, 4*(1–2), 1–10.

14. Bartrop, R.W., Luckhurst, E., Lazarus, L., Kiloh, L.G., & Penny, R. (1977). Depressed lymphocyte function after bereavement. *Lancet, 1*, 834–836.

15. Kronfol, Z., Silva, J., & Greden, J. (1983). Impaired lymphocyte function in depressive illness. *Life Sciences, 33*, 241–247.

16. Schleifer, S.J., Keller, S.E., Meyerson, A.T., Raskin, M.J., Davis, K.L., & Stein, M. (1984). Lymphocyte function in major depressive disorder. *Archives of General Psychiatry, 41*, 484–486.

17. Berrettini, W.H., Cappellari, C.B., Nurnberger, J.I., & Gershon, E.S. (1987). Betaadrenergic receptors on lymphoblasts: A study of manic depressive illness. *Neuropsychobiology, 17*,8–15.

18. Black, D.W., Winokur, G., & Nasrallah, A. (1987). Mortality in patients with primary unipolar depression, secondary unipolar depression, and bipolar affective disorder: A comparison with general population mortality. *International Journal of Psychiatric Medicine, 17*, 351–360.

19. Levy, E.M., Borrelli, D.J., Mirin, S.M., Salt, P., Knapp, P.H., Pierce, C., Fox, B.H., & Black, P.H. (1991). Biological measures and cellular immunological function in depressed psychiatric patients. *Psychiatry Research, 36*, 157–167.

20. Moldofsky, H., Scarisbrick, P., England, R., & Smythe, H. (1975). Musculoskeletal symptoms and non-REM sleep disturbance in patients with "fibrositis syndrome" and healthy subjects. *Psychosomatic Medicine*, 37(4), 341–351.

21. Moldofsky, H., & Scarisbrick, P. (1976). Induction of neurasthenic musculoskeletal pain syndrome by selective sleep stage deprivation. *Psychosomatic Medicine*, 38(1), 35–44.

22. Moldofsky, H., Lue, F.A., Eisen, J., Keystone, E., & Gorczynski, R.M. (1986). The relationship of interleukin-1 and immune functions to sleep in humans. *Psychosomatic Medicine*, 48(5), 309–318.

23. Lubar, J.F. (1989). Electroencephalographic biofeedback and neurological applications. In J.V. Basmajian (Ed.), *Biofeedback*, 67–90. Baltimore: Williams & Wilkins.

24. Barkley, R.A. (1990). *Attention deficit hyperactivity disorder*. New York: Guilford Press.

25. Ochs, L. (1992). EEG treatment of addictions. *Biofeedback*, 20(1), 1, 9–16.

26. Lipsitz, L.A., & Goldberger, A.L. (1992). Loss of "complexity" and aging. Potential applications of fractals and chaos theory to senescence. *Journal of the American Medical Association*, 267(13), 1806–1809.

27. Petitto, J.M., Folds, J.D., Ozer, H., & Evans, D.L. (1991). Altered natural killer cell diurnal variation in major depression. *Biological Psychiatry*, 29, 596.

28. Becker, R.O. (1990). *Cross currents*. Los Angeles: Jeremy Tarcher.

29. Becker, R.O. (1985). *The body electric*. New York: William Morrow.

30. Nordenstrom, B.E.W. (1983). *Biologically closed electric circuits*. Stockholm: Nordic Medical Publications.

31. Besedovsky, H.O., & Sorkin, E. (1981). Immunologic-neuroendocrine circuits: Physiological approaches. In R. Ader (Ed.), *Psychoneuroimmunology*, 545–574. New York: Academic Press.

32. Korneva, E.A. (1987). Electrophysiological analysis of brain reactions to antigen. *Annals of the New York Academy of Sciences*, 496, 318–337.

33. Korneva, E.A., Grigoriev, V.A., & Stoljarov, I.D. (1988). Brain reactions to antigen. *Journal of Neuroscience Research*, 19, 272–280.

34. Saphier, D., Abramsky, O., Mor, G., & Ovadia, H. (1987). A Neurophysiological correlate of an immune response. *Annals of the New York Academy of Sciences*, 496, 354–359.

35. Rider, M., & Miller, D. (1993). Electroencephalographic differences between those with and without chronic disorders involving the immune system. Unpublished manuscript.

36. Pert, C.B., Ruff, M.R., Weber, R.J., & Herkenham, M. (1985). Neuropeptides and their receptors: A psychosomatic network. *The Journal of Immunology*, 135(2), 820–826.

37. Tiller, W.A. (1993). What are subtle energies? *Journal of Scientific Exploration*, 7(3), 293–304.

38. Fahrion, S.L., Wirkus, M., & Pooley, P. (1992). EEG amplitude, brain mapping, & Synchrony in & between a bioenergy practitioner & client during healing. *Subtle Energies*, 3(1), 19–52.

39. Wolf, F.A. (1986). *The body quantum*. New York: Macmillan.

40. Dement, W., & Kleitman, N. (1957). Cyclic variations in EEG during sleep and their relation to eye movements, body motility, and dreaming. *Electroencephalography and Clinical Neurophysiology*, 9, 673–690.

41. Rossi, E. (1982). Hypnosis and ultradian rhythms: A new state(s) theory of hypnosis. *American Journal of Clinical Hypnosis*, 25(1), 21–32.

42. Altschuler, I. (1948). A psychiatrist's experience with music as a therapeutic agent. In D. Schullian (Ed.), *Music and medicine*, 266–281.

43. Rider, M. (1987). Treating chronic disease and pain with music-mediated imagery. *Arts in Psychotherapy*, 14(2), 113–120.

CHAPTER TWO

Homeodynamics and the Resonant Bodymind

When I first conceived the term homeodynamism, I was intending to shed light on a concept complementary to homeostasis. The first publication of homeodynamic theory, in fact, dealt only with the importance of dynamic mental shifting in the healing process.[1] However, the more I compared the nervous and immune systems, the more I noticed similarities, not differences. Interestingly, the Greek word for "similar" is "homeo." Somehow, I had unconsciously chosen a prefix for "dynamic" which was to aptly describe a second mechanism within psychoneuroimmunology. This mechanism involving the identical nature of the nervous and immune systems would ultimately lead to one single entity called the bodymind.

In this chapter I will demonstrate the many unexplored similarities between the nervous and immune systems, which will all point to the conclusion that total communication between the two is inevitable. As discussed earlier, the immune system will be spotlighted as the behavioral representative for the body due to its phylogenetic age and its etiologic importance to perhaps all chronic diseases. At the end of this chapter I will reveal as yet undiscovered properties of non-resonance in the brain when the immune system goes awry.

Immunity is the species identification of self. In lower matter, fusion occurs regulary among widely varying cell types, so the immune system is unnecessary. However, as the ego grows phylogenetically, so does the autonomy of the individual to remain distinct from nonself. Not too many years ago, scientists held onto common-sensical beliefs when they postulated that the nervous system and the immune system were rather independent. After all, one was composed of seemingly stationary networks of electrically charged neurons based on distributions of chlorine, potassium, and sodium, while the other was segregated in the vasculature and connective tissue, composed of highly mobile cells which attacked and digested foreign invaders when they came into contact.

Nevertheless, the immune and nervous systems have much more in common than was previously thought. An obvious example is that as one climbs up the phylogenetic ladder through the vertebrates, both the nervous and immune systems become more complex. Furthermore, just as "ontogeny recapitulates phylogeny," the immune and nervous systems have a similarly correlated development in the life of a human being. The immune system is normally weakest at the beginning and ending of the human life-span, times when the nervous system is either underdeveloped or degenerating. As in Chapter 1, these similarities between the immune and nervous systems will be revealed like puzzle pieces. Once assembled, the puzzle will emerge into a fascinating picture of total integration and communication between these systems.

Structural Similarities Between the Nervous and Immune Systems

In this first section, attention will be given to structural similarities between mind and body, or more specifically, the nervous and immune systems. As this organizational puzzle unfolds, we will find that our minds and bodies are like the left and right hand of a Bach fugue, repeating and incorporating each other in a total dialogue. From their shared physical environments, to their electrochemical vocabularies, to their capacity for memory, the nervous and immune systems are in many ways inseparable.

Physical Environments Common to the Immune and Nervous Systems

The links between personality and immune diseases such as cancer have been discussed in many cultures for thousands of years (see Chapter 7). However, the initial evidence for talk between the immune and nervous systems came through research prompted by Dr. Hans Selye on the disease-causing nature of stress hormones.[2] As this research was advanced through the 1970's, an indirect loop between mind and body was established. Hormones secreted by the adrenal gland through prolonged exposure to stress were found to be toxic to the immune system. This adrenal cascade is initiated by mental activity, such as anxiety, depression, and feelings of helplessness and hopelessness. This stress causes the hypothalamus to produce corticotrophin releasing factor (CRF), which in turn stimulates the pituitary to release adrenocorticotrophic hormone (ACTH). The ACTH activates the adrenal gland which then produces a variety of hormones, such as cortisol and corticosteroids. These hormones are the ones which, over the long haul, become suppressive to the immune system. As one has probably guessed by now, this mechanism takes considerable time, and could not possibly account for any immediate healing processes.

In the 1980's evidence came for direct connections between the immune and nervous systems.[3] In contrast to the slower endocrine mechanisms described above, direct neural links were discovered between the autonomic nervous system and all of the major immune organs—the thymus, spleen, lymph nodes, and even the bone marrow. These nervous/immune system connections are extremely comprehensive. Both branches of the autonomic nervous system, the sympathetic ("fight or flight") and parasympathetic ("relaxation") trunks innervate immune tissues.[4] This means that both stress and eustress have direct involvements in the immune response.

Furthermore, the nerve endings in immune tissue are both afferent and efferent. This provides two-way communication to the brain. Foreign invaders can thus be detected immediately through the sensory branches and acted upon immediately through the motor branches.[5]

The immune organs themselves are not the only environments which are intimately shared by both the nervous and immune systems. In the brain exists perhaps the most extensive and complicated integration of these two systems. Over 80% of the brain is composed not of neurons, but of cells of immune derivation, called microglia, or glia. Their role has been somewhat obscure, but research continues to implicate them in some of the most fascinating bodymind phenomena.

This intimate relationship begins the moment life is conceived. One type of white blood cell, the monocyte, or mononuclear phagocyte (meaning "cell-eater with one nucleus"), moves freely between brain and body during fetal development. Its purpose is to feed the growing neurons in the brain with nutrients and guide their growth. Upon maturation, these monocytes become fixed in the brain as microglia and astrocytes, making up the bulk of the brain. Pert has described the immune system's macrophage population as a "mobile synapse" which transmits information from one area of the body to another.[6]

Glial cells are derived from macrophages, serve an intimate connection with the nervous system, and share many common properties with the nervous system. First, glial cells provide structural support for nerves. Second, they help repair nerves when damaged. Third, glia are responsible for the grouping of nerves into the patterns which have become a hallmark of neurology. Glia also help gate ions and neurotransmitters at the nerve synapse. They also form the myelin (or white matter) around nerves, which expedites and economizes nerve conduction.

In fact, in recent research efforts, it has become a formidable task to find any activities which exclude any of the components of nervous and immune systems, or mind and body. One can safely say, now more than ever, that the same parts of the brain and body are used to process thoughts, emotions, and immune responses. The nervous and immune systems are indeed ubiquitously at the same identical places throughout the body. Now that this puzzle piece is in place, let's determine what might be occurring at these sites within the body.

Chemical Messengers Common to the Nervous and Immune Systems

Pert and her colleagues revolutionized our understanding of these systems with the discovery of endorphins.[7] These neurotransmitters were found to play important roles in pleasure and pain. They have also been found to play a modulatory role in immune functioning. Recently they have been implicated to play an important role in addiction.

What Pert also discovered was that these endorphins were concentrated in areas of the nervous system which also subserved both emotional and sensory functions. Even more important, Pert and others learned that immune cells not only had receptors for endorphins and other neurotransmitters, but also produced them as well. Some of these commonly shared neuropeptides include interferons, interleukins, endorphins, glucocorticoids, corticosteroids, the classical neurotransmitters (norepinephrine, serotonin, and dopamine), and melatonin. In other words, these different systems that scientists had heretofore thought were quite distinguishable from one another were inseparable and basically spoke the same language. Pert has gone so far as to suggest that our emotions, senses, immune, and nervous systems are conceptually the same thing.[6] They may indeed be like different sides of the elephant to the blind men, one and the same.

This new puzzle piece demonstrating resonance in communication among mind, body, and emotions suggests one major concept. The body is in the mind and the mind is in the body. Our sensations, thoughts, and emotions are affected by what is happening to the body. I think this can be demonstrated in patients who will become cranky or sad sometimes just before they realize they are getting an infection, and then experience euphoria when the immune system has completed its mission. Also, many individuals who receive immuno-infusions for immune deficiencies feel this same euphoria following their treatments. Furthermore, the mind exerts its influence in remote parts of the body, as demonstrated by such phenomena as hypnotic control of bleeding. Many masseuses attest to the sudden recall of memories related to a specific muscle following massage of that muscle. In other words, the bodymind is one.

Common Memory

Our next puzzle piece takes us to the information storehouses for the nervous and immune systems. Learning for both systems is accomplished through the manufacture of messenger RNA (mRNA). The immune system memorizes the protein makeup of foreign antigens when it comes into contact with them. It then produces mRNA so the production of antibodies and complement can foster resistance to bolster the attack. Messenger RNA is composed of combinations of four nucleotides. The different combinations of nucleotides determines which of the twenty amino acids is produced. The amino acids in turn join in different combinations which become proteins. Antibodies and complement are just such proteins of the immune system, composed of long chains of amino acids.

The news which shocked the scientific community in the early 1990's was that neurons in the brain also secreted mRNA for complement proteins of the immune system.[8] In other words, the nervous system was acting like the immune system. Their role in doing so is still unclear. Preliminary evidence suggests that this action is involved in creating the plaques and consequent brain damage associated with Alzheimer's disease. The fascinating notion, however, is that both nervous and immune systems mimic each other.

Another feature of the memory system of both the nervous and immune systems is that learning is facilitated with multiple trials. Learning in the brain is accompanied by decreases in the brain's energy consumption.[9] After learning to perform a task, smarter individuals will exhibit larger decreases in overall brain metabolism than less smart people. Smart brains evidently learn which circuits not to use on subsequent trials.

Learning in the immune system is also accompanied by faster, more efficient immune responses upon subsequent antigenic stimulation. For example, the first bout with a particular virus causes a delayed immune reaction while the immune system is memorizing the antigen and producing the cells for the counterattack. On subsequent encounters with the same antigen, however, the antibody is already "on file" so that a quicker, more efficient resistance can be mounted.

Thus the body, like the nervous system, utilizes less energy upon repeated antigen stimulation.

Because both the nervous and immune systems utilize the same mRNA memory mechanism, it is very likely that each system is privy to learning in the other system, and, in fact, may have something to do with modulation of each other's memory mechanisms. Afterall, they both utilize the same neuro-immunomodulators.

In a demonstration of the memory cross-talk between the nervous and immune systems, one group of researchers recently administered a foreign antigen to rats while measuring their ability to learn to avoid electric shock.[10] The exciting results indicated that the rats failed to learn while their immune system was mounting an attack. This meant that the neurons and immune systems shared the same lines of communication and memory, which competed when they became overloaded. This is analogous to radio "cross-talk" when too many transmitters are competing for the same airwaves. In other words, learning and memory formation in one system does affect the other system.

This intriguing finding means that the bodymind responds as one. Our ability to learn is affected by our physical health. Learning which produces implicit psychological reinforcement and the internal neurochemical rewards that go along with it is going to boost the immune system. This very likely explains why the elderly who remain mentally active in their old age stay healthier than their less active peers. This also stresses the importance of creating optimal learning situations in our school systems, which make learning exciting. In so doing we might also reduce overall health expenditures.

Common Electrical Properties

At the core of memory formation is the mRNA production discussed in the last section. What seems to determine whether the mRNA production takes place is the electrical properties surrounding the genetic environment. These electrical properties are measured in individual brain structures and on the surface of the scalp and skin as direct current (DC) potentials. These DC potentials slowly wax and wane from negative to positive, but at frequencies much slower than the EEG frequencies. These potentials take several seconds to accomplish a shift, for example, from positivity to negativity. The contingent negative variation (CNV), discussed in Chapter 1 is an example of these slow DC potentials. The slow negative shift has been found to reflect an increased excitability of the underlying nervous system.[11]

Many exciting new discoveries are beginning to tie these slow potentials to learning within both the nervous and immune systems. Recent experiments have demonstrated that learning, for example on tasks of semantic meaning, was faster when presented to subjects during a negative DC shift as opposed to a positive shift.[12] On the other hand, Becker has demonstrated that positive DC shifts, measured on the scalp, were associated with both sleep and pain anesthesia.[13] On the frontier of this research into the relationship between DC potentials and learning in the nervous system is evidence that these potentials can be learned through biofeedback. This work has the exciting potential of teaching better learning skills, pain control, and a wide variety of additional adaptive behaviors.[12]

In the last section, the formation of mRNA was discussed as an identical mechanism of memory and learning in both the nervous and immune systems. What facilitate, this memory engram formation within the immune system are the same DC shifts enhancing learning in the nervous system. Studies have now confirmed that immune responses stimulated by the administration of foreign antigens initiated changes in the DC potentials of different brain structures.[14] These DC shifts occurred in primarily positive directions, suggesting a similarity between the immune response and sleep (or slow-wave activity). Other studies have documented changes in the action potentials of groups of neurons following antigen stimulation.[15] These changes were recorded in terms of frequency shifts in the firing rates of multiple units of neurons in the brain. The conclusion of these two groups of studies is that the immune system activates electrical alterations in the brain. These studies were confirmed by my own which demonstrated changes in the relative power of different frequency bands as well as in the evoked potentials of patients with immunological disease.[16]

These studies were like clues pointing in the direction of an even bigger puzzle piece regarding the identical natures of the immune and nervous systems. This puzzle piece came with the discovery that the immunologically-derived glial cells actually generate their own electric current! They are not excitable like neurons, but carry a DC current which slowly waxes and wanes. This electrical current of the glia is involved in opening and closing the ion channels of individual neurons, thus exerting another major influence over the nervous system in addition to the neurotransmitters they also produce. However, this electrical modulatory system of the glial cells in the brain and their relatives, the Schwann cells in the body, has the potential of producing a much faster and more accurate means of conveying information than through the neuroendocrine mechanisms.[13]

Another major implication for the neuroglia is that their DC current is the baseline for the EEG. Apparently then the EEG is an electrical representation not only of thought, but also of immune behavior as well.

It is as if the nervous and immune systems are each appliances plugged into the same power source, the bodymind. This power source activates and rests each of these appliances utilizing the same energy source of electricity. We have seen that modulation of these electric potentials affects learning in both the nervous and immune systems. Furthermore, our bodymind may reside in the glia which has qualities of both the immune and nervous systems. Like the quantum duality of light, it is both particle and wave at the same time.

Functional Similarities Between the Nervous and Immune Systems

The structural similarities between the immune system and nervous system were plentiful enough to really begin to consider body and mind one. Yet even more exciting were the discoveries about the similarities in which these two systems functioned. In terms of overall purpose, the similarities began to emerge immediately. One of the first commonalities jumped right out of the opening pages of one of the major immunology textbooks. "The immune system is the fourth type of defensive reaction next to fighting, fleeing, and disguising oneself to avoid threats to one's existence."[17] When one considers that fighting, fleeing, and disguising oneself are all functions of the nervous system, the immune system finds itself in the familiar pattern we have been considering throughout this book.

In that the immune system is phylogenetically older than the nervous system, one wonders if perhaps the immune system didn't perhaps have something to do with the evolution of the nervous system. It certainly does ontogenetically, in the developing fetus. More about this in the next section.

Other immunologists have made references to the immune system as a "mobile sense system," because of its reliance on signal detection, primarily through chemical means like smell or taste.[7] But if the other sense systems reside in the nervous system, isn't it time to rethink the relationship between the immune and nervous systems?

Our journey in this section will take us to some lesser-considered resonant properties of body and mind, culminating in one of the most unusual features about nervous-immune communication yet discovered.

Classical and Operant Conditioning

In this section we shall see that the immune and nervous systems learn through the same mechanisms. One of the most important puzzle pieces to come forth in the bodymind arena was the research conducted by Robert Ader in the 1970's and 1980's.[18] This research was seminal in developing the field called psychoneuroimmunology, as well as the first text by the same name. His now notable studies demonstrated that the immune system, like the nervous system, could be classically conditioned. Classical conditioning involves the pairing of an inert stimulus (doesn't produce a response) called the conditioned stimulus, with an unconditioned stimulus which always produces a response.

Utilizing experimental paradigms similar to those of Pavlov, Ader and his colleagues showed that the immune system could be suppressed by an inert saccharin solution alone, after first pairing it with the immunosuppressive substance cyclophosphamide. This meant that the immune system functioned in an identical way to the nervous system. This is not so surprising considering that the immune and nervous systems share the same structural basis for learning, through mRNA. Any stimulus therefore, even psychological, could suppress one's immunity if previously conditioned with illness in some way. This research has led to some innovative uses of modulating the immune system in cases of skin grafts and allergies. Because cyclophosphamide is a dangerous drug, these medical conditions potentially can be improved with less danger to the patients.

This revolutionary research opened the way for the testing of conditioning techniques to increase immune functioning. Success in this area was demonstrated in studies in which a drug designed to boost natural killer cell activity was paired with camphor.[19] After conditioning the camphor alone was able to boost immune system activity and shrink tumor growths.

Both the nervous system and the immune system have availed themselves to operant conditioning, or the change in some behavior contingent upon some desirable effect, such as reinforcement. Biofeedback represents a form of operant learning by the nervous system to attenuate some physiological response, such as muscle tension, through the reinforcement provided by audio-visual signals. Thus a patient can learn to control tension headaches by eliminating an audio tone which turns on if the electromyographic (EMG) signal is above a predetermined threshold.

The immune system has also been found to be operantly conditioned, although with less precision. This is because no immediate on-going feedback of the immune system is currently available. Researchers however have determined that one of the best behavioral criteria of improved immunity is not a physiological signal, but literally the perceived vividness and effectiveness of one's mental imagery of his/her immune system.[20] This exciting research found that the progress or remission of cancer in a group of stage IV cancer patients could be predicted with less than a 5% margin of error based simply on the mental imagery spontaneously produced by these patients when asked to close their eyes and visualize their immune systems battling their cancer! In fact, one of the main purposes of this book is to demonstrate the mechanisms by which mental imagery can produce accurate feedback and control of the immune system. More explicit discussions of the mechanisms involved in imagery-based assessment and modulation of the immune system can be found in Chapters 5 and 7. These mechanisms are not the result of placebo responses, which affect only about two-thirds of the population. Furthermore, these mechanisms are not the result of relaxation, the effects of which are slower than the more profound phenomena we are considering. Nevertheless other forms of operant conditioning of the immune system have been demonstrated with techniques which do activate certain homeodynamic mechanisms. These include music[21], humor[22], relaxation[23], positive affirmations[24], biofeedback[25], and self-disclosure of traumatic events.[26]

Learning Rhythms

The immune and nervous systems also share identical learning rhythms. For years I conducted research on cognitive development in children based on the Piagetian model. The main Piagetian concept is that cognitive development occurs in unique stages until full mental maturation in adolescence. One of the key features of this model is that development from one stage to another depends on a seesaw rhythm between two types of behavior—assimilation and accommodation. According to Piaget, a balance of these two learning styles facilitates the most efficient cognitive development. To exemplify each cognitive behavior, imitation would be representative of accommodation because one's internal cognitive structures are modified to fit the material being copied. In music, sight-reading and playing by ear are both accommodative behaviors. On the other hand, free-play would constitute an example of assimilation, because one is rearranging tools from the outside environment to fit certain internal cognitive schemata. Again from music, improvisation would be an assimilative behavior.

The point here is that the nervous system develops connections based on an ever-shifting balance between accommodative and assimilative behaviors. Hardly any evidence, however, can be found for developmental stages of the immune system, let alone a learning rhythm involving assimilation and accommodation. But in one area of immunity, this learning rhythm can be found in any immunology textbook. This has to do with antibody production.

The immune system learns through accommodation (imitation) in the following way. There are two branches of the immune system—adaptive and innate immunity. Within the adaptive branch, B lymphocytes carry on their surface a single type of antibody. These antibodies act as receptors. Foreign organisms also bear receptors on their surfaces, so that eventually, a B-cell with a matching receptor will attach to the antigenic (foreign) receptor. Once the key opens the lock, the B-cell begins to clone, or imitate, itself, creating millions of antibodies. A cascade of additional immune responses begins at this point, enabling the body to eradicate the foreign invaders.

The immune system also engages in assimilation or free-play. When not involved in an active immune response, the genes coding for antibody within an individual engage in a type of improvisational free-play which increases the diversity of response. In this case nature devised a rather fluid genetic system so that the inherited gene fragments would reassemble upon each lymphocyte division. Since lymphocytes are the most rapidly proliferating cells in the body, our ability to fight a wide variety of new invaders grows every minute.

Therefore the immune system functions similarly to the nervous system in regard to this learning rhythm of assimilation and accommodation. While specific stages of development within the immune system have not been identified, it perhaps is only a matter of time before this growth order is established. Pert argues that the wisdom of the immune system is in the receptors, very little of which is known. One of the things that receptors learn to do, according to Pert, is shape-shift, in order to fit a variety of molecules.[27] The wonderment of this aspect comes from what binds their shape in the first place—electrical and physical forces. The electrical energy which derives from both nervous and immunological processes, and hence the bodymind, very likely influences the wisdom of the receptors. If this wisdom follows the same stages of development as occurs in cognition, then we may be able to predict information about the immune system heretofore unknown.

Rhythmic Entrainment

As I continued my search for associations between the nervous and immune systems, I became fascinated one day when reading about a seven-day cycle discovered in the immune system's attack on malaria.[17] My first thoughts were that the seven day calendar played a role, such as in the "blue Monday" syndrome. But as I read on, I quickly found out that these rhythms were discerned in animals,who are not subject to the seven-day work/rest cycle like the rest of us. As it turns out, our seven-day week probably derives from circaseptan (about seven-day) physiological rhythms!

Thus far major components of our nervous, endocrine, and immune systems have evidenced circadian (about a day), circaseptan, and circannual rhythms. No doubt there are also shorter and longer rhythms associated with certain behaviors than these mentioned. The BRAC rhythm of cerbral hemispheric activation mentioned earlier is an ultradian rhythm of about 90 minutes. On the other hand, the influenza virus modulates itself against the most recent defense of antibodies so that a new virulent strain is produced about every ten years.[17]

But what are the meanings of these rhythmic fluctuations occurring in our bodies? The answer seems to be twofold. First, information can be transmitted by variations in any oscillating signal. When these variations are frequency-based (as opposed to amplitude), the information can be transmitted more efficiently. Secondly, energy can be saved and even created through an oscillating system. We have seen in Chapter 1 how the body replenishes its energy storehouses through brainwave shifts to lower frequencies during rest and sleep. We will now consider in this section the energy-saving mechanisms of oscillating systems as displayed in rhythmic entrainment.

Rhythmic entrainment is the amazing capacity one oscillator has of influencing the frequency of another oscillator with a similar frequency. Our daily sleep-wake cycle is actually about 26 hours long, as determined when subjects live in environments in which they are deprived of typical "day" and "night" cues. However, our solar cycle of 24 hours is close to our 26-hour sleep-wake cycle, and so we are easily entrained into the solar rhythm. In so doing, we allow ourselves to decrease the amount of energy we would normally need to sustain our cycle. Since we need to communicate with others, we would have to spend extra energy attempting to stay in synch with each other, making sure we were awake at the same times, etc.. The sun serves as a universal pacemaker (or "zeitgeber" in German, for "time-locker") so we can spend a little less energy worrying about whether we should be awake or asleep.

Our nervous system has neurons which fire at different rates depending on their location in the body and the urgency of the communicated message. Research has demonstrated that the administration of external electrical pulses is able to entrain neurons into firing at rates equal to those being stimulated, as long as the electrical stimulation rates are similar to the initial frequencies of the neurons. The light/dark cycle is also able to entrain neurons in the brain into not only firing at different rates, but also initiating the release of hormones, such as melatonin from the pineal gland.

These same entrainment mechanisms are also found in the immune system. In particular, they occur in autoimmune disease. Autoimmunity is the destruction of tissue by one's own immune system due to invaders initially making their way undetected into these tissues and organs. Entrainment turns out to be the camouflage. Viruses and other antigens mimic amino acid sequences natural to the organism in order to pass the immune system undetected. The complete copies of these amino acid sequences don't have to be made by these invaders because just getting part of the correct sequence allows for entrainment with regard to perception of the whole. It is as if one needs to enter only one syllable of a much longer password to gain access to the system.

Harmonic Organization

The discoveries of vibrational and entrainment mechanisms within the nervous and immune systems led to the recovery of the most exciting puzzle piece regarding homeo-resonant properties of the bodymind. This breakthrough was the understanding that mind, brain, and body are harmonically organized. Harmonic refers to a mathematical arrangement in which energy patterns exist in nodes corresponding to whole number multiples of a fundamental frequency, such as found in musical overtones and in the quantum physics of the atom. Furthermore, this harmonic organization enables instantaneous communication among these components. As we will see in Chapter 7, treating patients' symptoms as metaphors in their everyday life is one of the most fascinating and useful extensions of these homeo-resonant mechanisms.

Two of the most prolific and highly understood methods of communication among humans is through speech and the arts. No civilization has ever been found that didn't utilize these forms of communication. The physical basis of these forms of communication lies in the fact that they are really nothing more than organized patterns of vibration, whether colors on a canvas, words from a speech, or chords from a symphony.

Every cell in the human body talks through the oscillations by which it polarizes and repolarizes. Every molecule of hormone or neurotransmitter secreted by some organ or gland in the body speaks as well. The common element here is the fact that the vibrational patterns common to all life are but different voices, not speaking different languages, but merely operating at different frequencies that simply require tuning into by shifting to the different stations, as on a radio receiver. This is the essence of homeodynamic theory, that every atom, molecule, and cell in our body speaks the same language (homeo), and we just need to shift (dynamic) to the different mental frequencies to perceive this elegant symphony.

Harmonics of Mental Activity

My first glimpse of the harmonic organization of the bodymind came serendipitously many years ago while conducting some pilot research on synesthesia. Synesthesia is the ability to perceive untypical sensory information about a stimulus. The mechanisms are unclear but synesthesia appears to involve some sort of sensory crossover within the brain. For example, if a musical tone is played, a color is perhaps seen in addition to the tone being heard. Our own laboratory research indicated that there was no particular consistency among different synesthetics or controls for their specific tone/color associations. Yet a fascinating pattern did emerge from the data. Each individual's color associations with the tones of the scale were arranged in a harmonic way. Colors similar to each other (according to their wavelength, e.g., blue and green) were seen when evoked by tones which were harmonically related to each other, not because of the closeness of their frequencies. For example, some synesthetics have reported seeing the color blue to C and blue-green to its harmonic relative, G, while C# evoked reddish-brown. Harmonically-related pitches have frequencies which are integral multiples of each other (found by dividing or multiplying by the integers 2, 3, 4 and so on), and share common pitches in their respective harmonic series. In music, the "key signatures" of harmonically-related keys have nearly the same number of sharps or flats. (The keys of C and G major are related keys because they share four of their first twelve harmonics and have only one scale note different between them.)

As I consulted other sources about synesthesia, I discovered that this same harmonic pattern existed, but had not been reported in any of the literature. To me, this was an astounding piece of information about how the brain worked. To have similar images (colors) driven by harmonically-related stimuli (musical tones) implies that mental activity is harmonically-organized.

As I was to later find out, this was a major stepping stone to unraveling the language of the brain. The body, including the nervous, muscular, endocrine, and immune systems, is also harmonically organized. And, as we shall see in Chapter 7, this harmonic organization allows for a very important means of communication.

Harmonics of Physiological Activity

In Chapter 1 we looked at the oscillatory behavior of many components of our physiology, including the nervous, cardiovascular, endocrine, and immune systems. In fact, scientists in the field of chronobiology are beginning to find multiple-frequency oscillations in each of these systems. It turns out that these multiple rhythms within any one system are integral multiples of each other, making any one rhythm the harmonic of another.

The reason for the harmonic organization is that 1) it enables fine-tuning of transmitted information, 2) it reduces the background noise much the same way that frequency modulation (FM) accomplishes this in radio transmission, and 3) it more efficiently removes metabolites from tissues.[28]

Our Musical Muscles

Within the nervous system, harmonic behavior has been documented with several different measures. The musculoskeletal system has been observed in our lab to exhibit harmonics. When recording the electromyograph (EMG) from the skin surface, an oscilloscope will demonstrate the overtones within a frequency band from about 0–2000 Hz. The purpose of this harmonic organization within the somatic nervous system is still not understood. Very likely, pain mechanisms might be more associated with certain harmonic patterns than with others. Particular harmonic patterns appear to have unique gating properties on the ionic movement to and from each cell. The end result would be the modulation of neurotransmitter receptors within each synapse and the consequent conduction of the action potential. Further research will perhaps determine the messages communicated by these harmonic patterns.

Harmonics in Our Heads

The harmonic organization of the central nervous system was pointed out by Barbara Brown over twenty years ago.[29] This behavior was observed in the electrical activity of the brain, or the electroencephalogram (EEG). The EEG is organized according to the harmonic series (like auditory tones) where the frequency bands are integral multiples of each other. In our own lab, we have observed that in cycles-per-second (Hz), alpha is twice theta, and beta is twice alpha. If, for example, theta is 5 Hz, then alpha is 10 Hz and beta is 20 Hz. Delta may very well represent the first peak, or fundamental frequency. In the awake subject, delta would be a combination of true delta and movement artifact. Only artifact-free segments of EEG were evaluated in our studies, although it may have been impossible to exclude all such movements. However, since pure delta waves only occur during deep sleep, their harmonic relationship to the other frequency bands remains uncertain at this time.

In Figure 2-1 is displayed the brain map of a medically healthy subject at the predominant alpha frequency of 11 Hz. To the left of this brain map is the spectral analysis at several electrode sites showing the strength of the various specific frequencies. As can be seen, the first peak after delta is the theta frequency, the second, alpha, and the third, beta. These peaks were found to exhibit the frequencie of 5, 11, and 22 Hz, each very close harmonic doubles of the previous frequency.

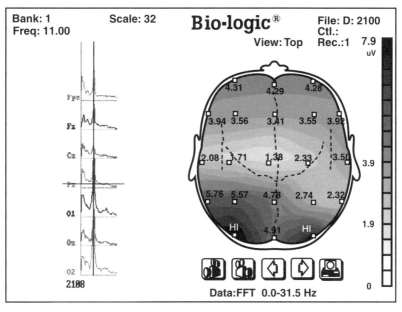

Figure 2-1. *Spectral analysis and alpha brain map of healthy control during eyes closed condition.*

The Harmonics of Health

To date, little is known about the harmonic organization of the immune system. Circadian (daily), circaseptan (weekly), and circannual (yearly) rhythms have been found in the immune system. Furthermore, these rhythms are in harmonic relationship with each other. But until now these facts have not helped us understand bodymind communication. We probably would have missed it in our own studies had we not been primed by some cosmic antigen which sensitized our focus in a particular direction.

My first excitement came when a group of European and Russian studies came to my attention in the early 1990's. These studies appeared to be the first showing the electrical activity of the brain following administration of an antigen designed to evoke an immune response. Animals were utilized in these studies so that microelectrodes could be implanted and precise recordings made.

The first finding supported the dynamic component of homeodynamic theory. Shifts in the DC (direct current) potentials of different brain structures occurred, usually in a positive direction.[14] My mind began to race toward some futuristic electroencephalographic measure of immune functioning based on evoked potential tasks. I felt that we were on the brink of revolutionizing the field of pyschoneuroimmunology by developing an immune evoked potential task (IEP) very similar to the visual or auditory evoked potentials.

The second finding was the one that alerted me to possible harmonic organization of the immune system. These researchers had also noted frequency changes in the firing of multiunit groups of neurons following antigen administration. As I poured over the results of these articles, I began to notice a pattern in these rate changes. One group of researchers reported hypothalamic neuronal firing rates following stimulation by various antigens. In each of these cases, the firing rates exhibited a very near doubling.[30]

Perhaps the real proof came in a study reported by a second group in which firing rates of hypothalamic neurons were found to decrease by a factor of two on the third day following antigenic stimulation.[15] By the fifth day, the firing rate peaked, evidencing a doubling of the initial rate (and quadrupling the lowest firing rate). These data were astounding in light of the double/quadruple relationships found in the frequency bands of the normal human EEG. In other words, a harmonic relationship seemed to exist in the communication between the nervous and immune systems.

Abruptly I wondered if the primary purpose of the human EEG frequency bands wasn't somehow involved with the immune system! Delta waves are critical for the production of many immune chemicals. In our EEG study of immune disorders, alpha was lacking in the patient group, suggesting a role for this brain wave in proper immune functioning. Theta waves have been identified by at least one neuroscientist as being critical to all survival behaviors, of which the immune system is perhaps the most important. In our study the patients exhibited an apparent overabundance of theta. Finally, beta waves were found to be the real immunological nemesis to our patients. So it appears that each frequency band does have some special relationship to immune functioning.

Then one day I was spreading brain maps across the floor using a primitive but valuable procedure called "eye-balling the data" to determine if there were any other possible conclusions generated by our study that could have been missed by the statistical analyses. Glancing away from the colored portion of the brain maps for a moment, I began to focus on the spectral analyses, showing the electrical power associated with every .5 increment from 0–30 Hz. Having previously studied spectral analyses of musical instruments, or acoustics, I began to notice that the patients exhibited much more complex patterns than the healthy controls. In other words, the patients seemed to have many more overtones, with multiple thetas, alphas, and/or betas. Sometimes these multiple overtones occurred within the same brain region and other times they were noted between front and rear regions.

For example, Figure 2-2 displays the brain map of a cancer patient. The spectral analysis shows approximate harmonic multiples of 5, 10, and 20 Hz for a directed imagery task. However, this patient also has a second harmonic pattern consisting of 8 and 15 Hz. After all this time supposing that all EEG's were har-

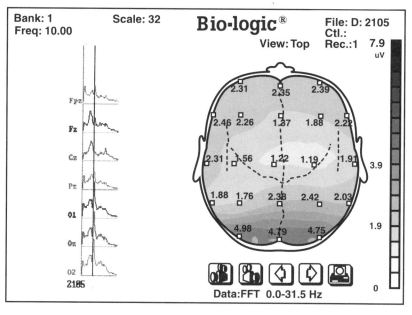

Figure 2-2.
Spectral analysis and alpha brain map of cancer patient during eyes closed condition.

monically organized, it dawned on me that this may only have been the case for healthy individuals.

As it turns out, this feature was found in every one of the over twenty brain maps conducted in those patients who were immunologically compromised. Only one of seven healthy controls so far brain mapped has exhibited this non-harmonic EEG pattern. In Figure 2-3 is displayed the brain map of an autoimmune patient with rheumatoid arthritis. Notice the two sets of harmonic frequencies in this pattern as well (5, 10.5, and 18 forming one quasi-harmonic set with an additional 15 Hz wave). If one made an analogy of the EEG to a radio, it is as if this patient has two radio frequencies tuned in at the same time on her receiver. This phenomenon would make communication more difficult than in the "single-station" analogy found in healthy controls.

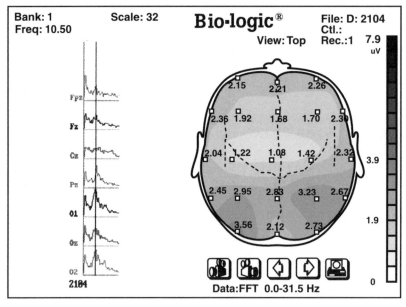

Figure 2-3. *Spectral analysis and alpha brain map of rheumatoid arthritis patient during eyes closed condition.*

This feature again illustrates Fred Wolf's indirect speculation on this harmonic organization when he stated that "illness and negative thinking create molecular islands of separation within our cells... healing energy counters this separation tendency by fostering correlations between molecules: one molecule heals another."[31] We now can see in the non-harmonic EEGs of immunological patients the presence of many more different vibrational frequencies or energies. Harmonic brains are in fact a perfect example of correlated neurons.

We are all musical instruments...our acoustic spectrum in this case is the waveform of the EEG. And, if we play out of beat with the cosmic drummer (nonharmonically), we steer further from health. The fact that harmonic organization is more prevalent in health than in disease has important things to say about the communication between the nervous and immune systems, and mind and body. As we shall see in Chapter 7, we receive salient messages from the immune system every day. Furthermore, we can send messages back to the immune system which increases the harmonic organization of the brain.

Our Harmonic Genes

Harmonics are determined by how many times something repeats. Harmonics can also exist in space as well as in time. Spatial harmonics yield visual patterns that can be translated into waves. This is the inverse process to that of creating a spectral analysis of harmonics from the EEG or a musical instrument. Paintings by the Swiss artist Paul Klee have repetitions of lines and spaces which art critics usually refer to as "rhythmic."

Each chromosomal gene is like a Paul Klee painting in that it forms a discrete spatial pattern composed of nucleotide bases instead of brush strokes. These same nucleotide bases form the DNA and RNA molecules. By arranging themselves in particular patterns, these nucleotides form specific amino acids, the building blocks of life. In music the progression of groups of chords is called the harmonic rhythm. Thus, each of the 20 different amino acids has a specific harmonic rhythm.

To demonstrate the close connection between the harmonic rhythms of music and our genes, geneticist Susumu Ohno has composed "DNA music." By assigning two musical notes each to one of the four nucleotides, melodies were created. Rhythms were based on the distances between the nucleotide bases. When played, this DNA music sounds hauntingly familiar to melodies that we have all heard before.[32]

But there is a coda to this musical analogy that continues the connections between non-harmonic patterns and disease, just as we discovered in the EEG's of our immunological patients. Certain diseases such as cancer and Huntington's chorea have recently been found to exhibit deviations in the DNA harmonic rhythms found on the genes.[33-34] Specifically, it was determined that individuals with these illnesses produced irregularities in the number of times that certain nucleotide sequences were repeated.

In music there are melodic and harmonic patterns that are more universally appealing than others. The so-called Lipps-Meyer Law finds that melodies which end harmonically are preferred by a proportion of 77 to 23.[35] For example, given the two possible ending notes of a melody, C and G, a greater sense of finality would be achieved if the order were G to C instead of C to G. This is because if C is the final note (and tonal center), its predecessor, G, is a harmonic neighbor. Ending on G however precedes it with a nonharmonic neighbor, C (C is not in the harmonic series of G; G, however, is the second overtone of C). Likewise DNA patterns which deviate outside the "harmonic" molds understood by our body mind create proteins which become harmful to us. Thus, even at the genetic level, our DNA must march to the cosmic drummer or our survival is at stake.

Wearing Your Health on Your Sleeve

In a symphony orchestra the conductor ensures that everyone is playing together in a harmonious fashion. In the immune system, the conductor is a molecule inside of macrophages called the major histocompatibility complex (MHC). When foreign viruses or parasites are ingested inside macrophages, these MHC molecules bring the ingested particles back to the cell surface and present pieces of it to other immune cells (T-cells) who can recognize it as foreign. Thus begins the cascade of immune reactions. What the MHC is presenting to the cell surface is a protein pattern of amino acids that is recognizable. What makes it recognizable is its harmonic relationship to the receptors on the T-cells. (Quantum factors determine the receptor mechanics, and, as we will see in the next section, harmonic organization of the atom is what gives quantum its name). Interestingly, immunologically-compromised individuals have a deficient conductor that doesn't time the cascade of immune reactions in an orderly manner. And if musical instruments in the symphony enter at the wrong times, then unusual harmonic patterns will sound which will evoke a different set of responses in the audience.

Patterns of amino acids make up all the proteins which constitute organic matter. Amino acid patterns which are similar, or harmonic, are called homologies. Certain life forms have evolved ways of communicating information about their immune system to each other through these homologies. Mice have been found to associate odors with specific homologies of the MHC.[36] These animals prefer to mate with other mice whose MHC patterns are most complementary to theirs. This insures that the offspring will have the largest diversity of immune defenses to afford the greatest protection. These animals' MHC is detected through smell. Therefore, information about their immunological system is conveyed through their nervous system. In a sense, the nervous system recapitulates the immune system.

Humans also seem to wear their health on their sleeves. The first way is through the thought patterns that are generated by the EEG. We have seen above how these patterns, when harmonic, are associated with greater health. Continuing with the musical analogies, the human voice may also do for us what smell affords the mouse. When spectrally analyzed the same way amino acids and brainwaves are, the voice has been found to exhibit about four different patterns that are associated with health, mental illness, and physical illness.[37] These patterns are no doubt recognized by us, particularly when we are trained to listen for it—for example the soft, weak voice of some patients I have seen with irritable bowel syndrome vs. The harsh, rapid voice of the hypertensive patient. Our voices then are like the immune system's MHC in that it is involved in bringing to the surface important features of what is happening on the inside.

Homeopathy: Harmonics of Disease and Treatment

The medical practice of homeopathy sheds further light on the harmonic organization of the immune system. This therapy is based on observations that water treated with molecular compounds which mimic the symptoms, and diluted in strength, will stimulate the immune system against the particular infection. The remarkable phenomenon is that homeopathy works in an inverse dose-dependent manner. That is, weaker dilutions of the compound activate the immune system to a stronger degree; so much so that the final homeopathic remedies actually contain no molecules of the compound. However, the water, after having been vigorously shaken after each dilution, becomes activated with the same energy as the electromagnetic configuration of the polymer which originally inhabited the water. Thus homeopathy can be viewed as utilizing harmonics of the remedy. Because the immune system is more strongly activated to each successive dilution, or harmonic, indicates that the immune system is also harmonically organized.

Hering's Law in homeopathy is a further demonstration of the harmonic organization of disease and immunity. This law states that pathological energy disturbances affect different organs based on the energy center (or harmonic) which is accentuated. Depending on the reversible time gradient which one view's a particular set of illnesses, separate and unconnected disturbances in the body are found to be connected to the same energy source, just as harmonics are different notes connected to the same fundamental frequency.[38] According to this law, diseases proceed in time from the body's periphery to the more vital organs deeper inside the body. This space- time relationship of disease suggests that at the initial stages of disease, low amplitude, high frequency harmonics prevail which would cause irritations at the level of the skin. As the condition becomes more chronic, or more energy becomes devoted to the pathological process, a higher amplitude, lower frequency harmonic (closer to the fundamental) begins to affect deeper, more vital organs. For example, in one reported case, successful topical treatment of eczema was found to be followed by an aggravation of a pre-existing condition of bronchial asthma. Upon homeopathic treatment, the asthma disappeared whereupon the eczema reappeared.[38] Thus both diseases were harmonically related to each other.

The Quantum Analogy

Although homeodynamic mechanisms as described here appear to explain adequately, albeit simplistically, a wide range of PNI and mind-body phenomena, a model easily springs to mind which neatly integrates all of these processes. As early as 1918, Bertrand Russell proposed an analogy between mentation and atomic events.[39] Russell related the neural processing of imagination to the electron sharing that occurs in the chemical bonds between hybrid atoms. This analogy led to the supposition that mental objects were linked by the sharing of neurons rather than electrons. This meant that a given neuron could take part in several "graphs" of different mental objects, while conserving its own unique properties which existed before the formation of the mental object. More recently, similar thoughts and images have been found to utilize some of the same subsets of neurons.

But the quantum analogy fits even more snugly given the properties of homeodynamism. The quantum world encounters dynamic shifts in the way of electron, or quantum, "leaps," and it also has harmonic organization. The orbits of the electron around the atomic nucleus, called valence shells or electron clouds, are arranged according to the natural harmonic series, just as we find in the case of the EEG and in acoustics. Electrons do their shifting from one valence level to another. For example, shifting from an inner level to an outer level requires energy (catabolic). Furthermore, shifting from an outer to an inner level gives off energy in the form of light (anabolic).

In homeodynamic terms, the bodymind downshift is represented in at least three ways. First, a mental shift is registered in the patient. The patient usually reports a more positive mental image or attitude suggestive of healing occurring inside the body.

Second, these mental shifts are accompanied by changes in the EEG. There is generally a lowering of the frequencies, usually showing a predominance of alpha activity. Just as in the electron, increased downshifting to alpha through relaxation and/or delta through deep sleep is always reported by patients as energy-producing. Also, mental images which patients report as more health-effective register a more harmonic EEG spectrum.

Finally, these mind and brain shifts are always associated with indices of physical improvement, reported by both patients and health professionals.

Even though the quantum model is only intended as an analogy to some more complicated healing process within the body, of relative interest is the unusually high incidence of patients who shift from concrete, anatomical imagery to light in their healing imagery. Together with the other two prolific imagery classes, animals and fluid movement, light seems to be the most commonly utilized. All three categories involve "movement" or "activity," hinting of the necessary dynamism proposed here. Achterberg and Lawlis also found that active images were strongly and positively correlated with cancer improvement.

When I first proposed this quantum analogy, I was not thinking that electromagnetic light was actually emitted somewhere in the body. However, some exciting new evidence suggests that this may very well be the case. Some of the immune cells called neutrophils have been found to "light up" following the ingestion of foreign microorganisms. This process, called "chemiluminescence," lasts for about fifteen minutes after the neutrophil has completed its meal.[17] Although too weak to be seen by the naked eye, wouldn't it be interesting if "seeing the light," associated with insight and reverie, wasn't a side effect of heightened immune functioning. I have had many patients remark on what an emotional high they were on after successfully overcoming an infection or virus. Even when I played skeptic and suggested that it may have been a relative feeling compared to how poorly they felt several days ago, many have said that they felt better than they had in months.

One final parallel can be drawn from this discussion of light and electromagnetic energy. Sunlight has been found to induce mRNA shifts on genes coding for vision.[40] Secondly, mental imagery involving visualization activates the same brain regions (in the visual and association cortex) as if actual photoreception had occurred. Furthermore, relaxation involving mental visualization has been found to activate cellular DNA repair.[41]

Because the immune system is the most sensitive tissue in the body to electromagnetic radiation, then it seems highly plausible to conclude that mental imagery and other homeodynamic healing techniques can stimulate an ample amount of electromagnetic energy to affect specific DNA and mRNA mechanisms involving immune responses. Pert has also demonstrated that the receptor shapes on immuno-modulators are quantum-like in that they take on different shapes to fit different immune cells depending on the electromagnetic properties of the cellular microenvironment.[27] Our thoughts, images, and feelings, therefore, have the power to produce electromagnetic perturbations which can 1) repair DNA mutations which could increase the risk for cancer, 2) signal DNA and mRNA to assist in the production of appropriate MHC and antibody proteins, and 3) alter receptor shapes on immuno-modulators which govern other immune responses.

My colleagues and I have concluded that electromagnetic forces are definitely involved to some degree in healing mechanisms.[13,16,27] Whether healing is taking place within one's body or transpersonally, as from a healer to a patient, strong electrical potentials have been registered during these phenomena. In other transpersonal experiments of so-called anomalous propagation such as telepathy, however, a non-local phenomena has been observed that messages mentally sent to "receivers" halfway around the globe sometimes arrived as much as three days before they were sent![42] Some have speculated that the forces responsible for these non-local phenomena would have to be either extremely slow electromagnetic forces or else another kind of force.

Subtler than the electromagnetic force, yet powerful enough to trigger a nuclear bomb is the "weak quantum force." The weak force is the fourth known in the universe, next to gravity, electromagnetism, and the strong quantum force (responsible for nuclear fusion, or the binding together of the atomic nucleus). The weak force governs nuclear fission, or the energy release following radioactive decay. It has also been targeted as the agent governing the remarkable behavior of DNA to coil only in a "left-handed" direction.[43]

Combine this knowledge of weak force quantum mechanics operating in the regenerative mechanisms of DNA and mRNA, with the results of experiments which have demonstrated that mental imagery influences the direction of radioactive decay[44], and you have some indirect evidence for the weak force governing bodymind phenomena. Furthermore, the weak force is the only one of the four forces which interacts with all of the known subatomic particles!

The electromagnetic force then may govern overt behavioral changes involving relaxation, pain relief, and so on. Activation of the weak force may require a deeper, spiritual revelation, of the type experienced by my "woman in the red dress." However the results of its influences might trigger quantum changes on the inside, with concomitant shifts in organ physiology, electromagnetic potentials, immune functioning, and mental imagery. The light at the end of the tunnel may very well be our own internal nuclear blasts occurring subatomically within every atom of our body, manifesting new creative potentials to be used for healing and empowerment.

Conclusion

In this chapter we explored the similar and sometimes identical natures of both the nervous and immune systems. These commonalities were found in the physical environments shared by the two systems, the identical messengers and rhythms employed in their two-way communication, their identical memory and learning systems, their complementary but interactive electrical systems, and their harmonic organization. All of these mutual properties add up to equal what we will refer to as the totally integrated and inseparable bodymind.

Furthermore, the bodymind operates via electromagnetic and (undoubtedly) weak quantum forces. These forces yield phenomena which are not restricted to individual bodymind shifts such as mental images and tissue repair, but also are highly implicated in transpersonal phenomena, again involving communication and healing.

References

1. Rider, M. (1992). Mental shifts and resonance: Necessities for healing? Foundations for a homeodynamic theory of psychoneuroimmunology. *Revision, 14*(3), 149–157.

2. Selye, H. (1956). *The stress of life.* New York: McGraw-Hill.

3. Felton, D.L., Felton, S.Y., Carlson, S.L., Olschowka, J.A., & Livnat, S. (1985). Noradrenergic and peptidergic innervation of lymphoid tissue. *Journal of Immunology, 135*(2), 755–763.

4. Rinner, I., & Schauenstein, K. (1991). The parasympathetic nervous system takes part in the immunoneuroendocrine dialogue. *Journal of Neuroimmunology, 34*, 165–172.

5. Jessel, T.M. (1985). Cellular interactions at the central and peripheral terminals of primary sensory neurons. *Journal of Immunology, 135*(2), 746–749.

6. Pert, C.B., Ruff, M.R., Weber, R.J., & Herkenham, M. (1985). Neuropeptides and their receptors: A psychosomatic network. *Journal of Immunology, 135*(2), 820–826.

7. Blalock, J.E., Harbour-McMenamin, D., & Smith, E.M. (1985). Peptide hormones shared by the neuroendocrine and immunologic systems. *Journal of Immunology, 135*(2), 858–861.

8. Pasinetti, G.M., Johnson, S.A., Rozovsky, I., Lampert-Etchells, M., Morgan, D.G., Gordon, M.N., Willoughby, D., & Finch, C.E. (1992). Complement C1qB and C4 mRNAs responses to lesioning in rat brain. *Experimental Neurology, 118*(2), 117–125.

9. Haier, R.J. (1992). Regional glucose metabolic changes after learning a complex visuospatial motor task: A PET study. *Brain Research, 570*, 134–143.

10. Shtark, M.B., Gainutdinov, Kh.L., Khichenko, V.I., Shevchuk, E.V., & Starostina, M.V. (1987). Biological effects of anti-brain antibodies. *Annals of the New York Academy of Sciences, 496*, 405–415.

11. Stamm, J.S., Whipple, S.C., & Born, J. (1987). Effects of spontaneous cortical slow potentials on semantic information processing. *International Journal of Psychophysiology, 5*, 11–18.

12. Rockstroh, B., Birbaumer, N., Elbert, T., & Lutzenberger, W. (1984). Operant control of EEG and event-related and slow brain potentials. *Biofeedback and Self-Regulation, 9*(2), 139–159.

13. Becker, R.O. (1985). *The body electric.* New York: William Morrow.

14. Korneva, E.A., Grigoriev, V.A., & Stoljarov, I.D. (1988). Brain reactions to antigen. *Journal of Neuroscience Research, 19*, 272–280.

15. Saphier, D., Abramsky, O., Mor, G., & Ovadia, H. (1987). A Neurophysiological correlate of an immune response. *Annals of the New York Academy of Sciences, 496*, 354–359.

16. Rider M., & Miller, D. (1993). Electroencephalographic differences between those with and without chronic disorders involving the immune system. Unpublished manuscript.

17. Klein, J. (1982). *Immunology.* New York: John Wiley & Sons.

18. Ader, R. (Ed.), *Psychoneuroimmunology*, 545–574. New York: Academic Press.

19. Ghanta, V.K., Hiramoto, R.N., Solvason, H.B., & Spector, N.H. (1985). Neural and environmental influences on neoplasia and conditioning of NK activity. *Journal of Immunology, 135*(2), 848–852.

20. Achterberg, J., & Lawlis, G.F. (1979). A canonical analysis of blood chemistry variables related to psychological measures of cancer patients. *Multivariate Experimental Clinical Research, 4*(1–2), 1–10.

21. Rider, M., Achterberg, J., Lawlis, G.F., Goven, A., Toledo, R., & Butler, J.R. (1990). Effect of immune system imagery on secretory IgA. *Biofeedback and Self-Regulation, 15*(4), 317–333.

22. Dillon, K.M., Minchoff, B., & Baker, K.H. (1985–86). Positive emotional states and enhancement of the immune system. *International Journal of Psychiatry and Medicine, 15*, 13–17.

23. Kiecolt-Glaser, J.K., Glaser, R., Williger, D., Stout, J., Messick, G., Sheppard, S., Ricker, D., Romisher, S.C., Briner, W., Bonnell, G., & Donnerberg, R. (1985). Psychosocial enhancement of immuno- competence in a geriatric population. *Health Psychology, 4*, 25–41

24. Bradley, L.A., Turner, R.A., Young, L.D., Agudelo, C.A., Anderson, K.O., & McDaniel, L.K. (1985). Effects of cognitive-behavioral therapy on pain behavior of rheumatoid arthritis (RA) patients. *Scandinavian Journal of Behavior Therapy, 14*(2), 51–64.

25. Peavey, B.S., Lawlis, G.F., & Goven, A. (1985). Biofeedback-assisted relaxation: Effects on phagocytic capacity. *Biofeedback and Self- Regulation, 10*, 33–47.

26. Pennebaker, J.W., Kiecolt-Glaser, J.K., & Glaser, R. (1988). Disclosure of traumas and immune function: Health implications for psychotherapy. *Journal of Consulting and Clinical Psychology, 56*, 239–245.

27. Pert, C.B. (1986). The wisdom of the receptors. *Advances, 3*(3), 8–16.

28. Carnes, M., Goodman, B.M., & Lent, S.J. (1991). High resolution spectral analysis of plasma adrenocorticotropin reveals a multi- factorial frequency structure. *Endocrinology, 128*(2), 902–910.

29. Brown, B. (1974). *New mind, new body.* New York: Harper & Row.

30. Besedovsky, H.O., & Sorkin, E. (1981). Immunologic-neuroendocrine circuits: Physiological approaches. In R. Ader (Ed.), *Psychoneuroimmunology*, 545–574. New York: Academic Press.

31. Wolf, F.A. (1986). *The body quantum.* New York: Macmillan.

32. Ohno, S., & Ohno, M. (1986). The all pervasive principle of repetitious recurrence governs not only coding sequence construction but also human endeavor in musical composition. *Immunogenetics, 24*, 71–78.

33. Krontiris, T.G., Devlin, B., Karp, D.D., Robert, N.J., & Risch, N. (1993). An association between the risk of cancer and mutations in the HRAS1 minisatellite locus. *New England Journal of Medicine, 329*(8), 517–523.

34. Orr, H.T., Chung, M.Y., Banfi, S., Kwiatkowski, T.J., Servadio, A., Beaudet, A.L., McCall, A.E., Duvick, L.A., Ranum, L.P., & Zoghbi, H.Y. (1993). Expansion of an unstable trinucleotide CAG repeat in spinocerebellar ataxia type 1. *Nature Genetics, 4*(3), 221–226.

35. Lundin, R.W. (1967). *An objective psychology of music.* New York: Ronald Press.

36. Beauchamp, G.K., Yamazaki, K., Wysocki, C.J., Slotnick, B.M., Thomas, L., & Boyse, E.A. (1985). Chemosensory recognition of mouse major histocompatibility types by another species. *Proceedings of the National Academy of Sciences, 82*(12), 4186–4188.

37. Ostwald, P. (1963). *Soundmaking: The acoustic communication of emotion.* Springfield, IL: Charles Thomas.

38. Whitmont, E.C. (1993). *The alchemy of healing.* Berkeley: North Atlantic Books.

39. Changeaux, J.P. (1985). *Neuronal man.* New York: Oxford University Press.

40. McGinnis, J.F., Whelan, J.P., & Donoso, L.A. (1992). Transient, cyclic changes in mouse visual cell gene products during the light- dark cycle. *Journal of Neuroscience Research, 31,* 584–590.

41. Kiecolt-Glaser, J.K., Stephens, R.E., Lipetz, P.D., Speicher, C.E., & Glaser, R. (1985). Distress and DNA repair in human lymphocytes, *Journal of Behavioral Medicine, 8,* 311–320.

42. Jahn, R.G., & Dunne, B.J. (1987). *Margins of reality.* San Diego: Harcourt Brace & Co.

43. Cline, D.B. (1993). Weak no more. *The Sciences, 33*(6), 20–27.

44. Radin, D., & Nelson, R. (1989). Consciousness-related effects in random physical systems. *Foundations of Physics, 19,* 1499–1514.

II

HEALTH BENEFITS OF SHIFTING

INTRODUCTION

In this section, a wide range of alternative medicine techniques, which have been demonstrated to positively influence physical healing, will be shown to operate via homeodynamic mechanisms.

This section is divided into four chapters, based on an organization of behavior which I have found clinically useful. As I describe it to my patients, these four areas of clinical focus are called "body, heart, mind, and spirit." I have found this organization useful because it seems to be a hierarchical order which governs the longevity and depth of the healing and/or disease management. Treatments working on the "bodily" or physical level alter changes in the body for the shortest duration whereas those operating on the "spiritual" level have deeper and longer lasting effects. This hierarchy was developed to give patients a graduated repertoire of successful experiences starting from the physical and working up to the spiritual. Behaviors and/or treatments at the lower end of the hierarchy can more readily stabilize a patient in crisis and allow the patient to successively attend to treatments/behaviors at the higher end. Conversely, changes made at the higher levels have a trickle-down effect and often affect behaviors on the lower levels.

A critical point that needs to be underlined here is that these treatments and behaviors can traverse across the category divisions I have arbitrarily created. For example, music is a technique that can be employed not only for emotional release, but also makes use of the physical, mental, and spiritual levels.

The first chapter centers on treatments or behaviors which are physical in nature. These include sleep, breathing, exercise, nutrition, therapeutic touch, acupuncture, and electromagnetic treatments. The second chapter focuses on techniques which operate on more emotional levels and includes psychotherapeutic catharsis and the arts, with special emphasis upon music. The third chapter in this section includes mental techniques such as relaxation/biofeedback, cognitive therapy, hypnosis, and meditation/imagery. This section concludes with treatments operating on what I call the sociospiritual domain, or any environment which helps the patient feel connected and a part of some larger entity, group, or power. Sociospiritual techniques include various forms of social support and transpersonal experiences such as prayer and healing-at-a-distance.

Within each subsection, the pertinent scientific literature supporting the validity of each treatment technique will be first discussed and then presented in tabular form for those desiring a more brief and cursory outline. Readers familiar with this research may wish to start with the table and then move on to the next subsection which is the presentation of evidence for homeodynamic mechanisms within each treatment technique. The Homeodynamic Mechanism subsection is presented only once in both Chapters 5 and 6 at the end of each chapter.

CHAPTER THREE

Healing Therapies and Behaviors Operating on the Physical Level

SLEEP

Of all the behaviors included in the physical domain, sleep is perhaps the quintessential homeodynamic behavior because it is literally defined by its shift in brainwave activity. Furthermore, sleep involves a dramatic series of brainwave shifts unlike any such EEG activity observed during wakefulness. All of the four brainwave rhythms, beta, alpha, theta, and delta are cycled through during the various phases of sleep. Consequently, the Homeodynamic Mechanisms subsection will be included in the literature review covering its healing effects instead of at the end of this subsection.

Of the four brainwave rhythms, delta is the only one experienced in a pure form by healthy individuals during what is called deep, or slow-wave, sleep. Dream sleep, on the other hand, is characterized by fast beta activity and rapid eye movements (REM's). The average person shifts from slow-wave to REM sleep in ninety-minute cycles about four or five times a night. In healthy people, the slow-wave portions of each cycle are longer than the REM portions during the first two episodes, whereupon REM then increases and delta sleep declines.

Sleep quality and quantity are difficult behaviors to voluntarily control. We can make ourselves go to bed and awaken at specific times, and we can control the consistency of this behavior over a period of time. Yet, "getting a good night's sleep" is intimately connected to many other behaviors, some of which appear later in this chapter.

Some of what is known about the therapeutic benefits of sleep include the following. Deep sleep is critical to 1) the electrical recharging of the nervous system, 2) the functioning of the immune system, and 3) the prevention of depression. Dream sleep, on the other hand, is crucial for learning and the consolidation of memory. Finally, sleep onset inconsistency, such as is found in rotating shift-workers, is stressful. For an overview of the research on the health benefits of sleep, see Table 3-1.

TABLE 3-1.   *SLEEP AND PHYSICAL HEALING*

1st Author	Date	Results
Moldofsky	1975	Sleep EEGs of fibrositis patients yielded a lack of delta rhythms during stage 4 sleep; normals deprived of deep sleep exhibited fibrositis-like symptoms
Moldofsky	1976	Subjects deprived of deep sleep experienced more fibrositis-like symptoms (pain and muscle tenderness) as opposed to those deprived of REM sleep
Moldofsky	1980	Chlorpromazine improved deep sleep in fibrositis patients, thus reducing pain and mood disturbance
Moldofsky	1983	Rheumatoid arthritis patients exhibited a lack of delta rhythms during stage 4 sleep and increased pain following sleep
Moldofsky	1986	Serial blood sampling from normal subjects indicated that interleukins-1 and -2, and B-cell activity significantly increased during deep sleep; T-cell activity dependent on stage 2 sleep
Moldofsky	1988	EEG sleep anomaly of alpha-replaced deep sleep (alpha-delta sleep) identical in fibrositis and chronic fatigue syndrome patients
Palmblad	1979	Sleep deprivation of normal subjects decreased the in vitro DNA synthesis of lymphocytes after PHA stimulation
Vogel	1975	REM deprivation significantly relieved depression in hospitalized patients
Winson	1990	Theta brainwave rhythm important for survival behaviors and memory consolidation
Drucker-Colin	1976	DNA protein synthesis found to occur during REM sleep
Takahashi	1979	Growth hormone secreted during deep sleep

Slow-Wave Sleep and Recharging the Nervous System
      Strong connections between the slow-wave sleep cycle and the electrical potentialization of the nervous system have begun to be made. Moldofsky has referred to slow-wave sleep deprivation as similar to an "electric battery losing its charge."[1] It is not surprising that individuals who report problems during slow-wave sleep also experience a variety of symptoms characteristic of a depressed nervous system: fatigue, muscular weakness, and difficulty with concentration. Moldofsky has determined in a number of studies that arthritic-like pain can even be induced in normal subjects by depriving them of slow-wave sleep.

A fascinating finding that I have made further makes a link between slow-wave sleep and the electrical recharging of the body. Patients who have reported poor quality of deep sleep have also described experiencing electromagnetic anomalies (also described in Chapter 1) such as being sensitive to electrostatic shocks, demagnetizing credit cards, and causing electrostatically-induced computer shutdowns. These same patients also had significantly reduced amplitudes of brain electrical activity on some evoked potential tasks.

The implication that the body is a wet cell battery has some merit, for the solutions that the cells in our bodies are bathed in are called electrolytes. Electrolytes are ionic, or charged, molecules such as calcium, potassium, and sodium. "Pumps" constantly work to move these ions through the cell membranes to create the electrical differential that exists between the inner and outer cellular environment.

Becker has discovered that the body also operates on the basis of semiconduction as well as on the ionic conduction characteristic of individual cells.[2] The difference is that with semiconduction, unlike ionic conduction, only small currents can be carried. However, they can be conducted more accurately and over longer distances than through ionic conduction. Proteins serve as the semiconducting mobile phone lines for these smaller electrical charges. These are the substances which make up most of the bulk in the body, and thus are needed when healing is to occur. However, for protein synthesis to occur, amino acids (the building blocks for proteins) must enter the cell. It just so happens that the chemical transporting them into the cell, growth hormone, is secreted primarily during slow-wave sleep. And if amino acids can't get into the cell, a sufficient supply of ATP cannot be produced. ATP is the energy currency of the body. In addition to supplying the energy for muscular contraction, ATP drives the electrolyte pumps which give the ionic battery its charge. Thus we can see now how a deprivation of slow-wave sleep can easily lead to fatigue, muscle weakness, electrical imbalances, nervous system depression, and an inability to heal.

To continue the battery analogy, Becker has demonstrated that the human body has its positive terminals over the brain and spinal cord (the central nervous system), whereas the negative terminal is over the arms and legs (peripheral nervous system).[2] He has also shown that an organism's (direct) current shifts in a positive direction when it falls asleep, and back to negative when it awakens.

Slow-wave Sleep and Immunity

As mentioned earlier, at no time is the amplitude and frequency of electrical brainwave activity more variable than during sleep. The immune system is also most productive during the shifting sleep cycles. Most critical to our immune response however is slow-wave sleep.

Moldofsky and his colleagues have probably contributed the most to the study of the immune system during sleep. By simultaneously monitoring EEGs and immune functioning through indwelling venous catherization, these researchers determined that the immune system is remarkably periodic.[3] More importantly, this dynamism peaks for the most critical components of the immune system during slow-wave sleep. For example, the alleged initiators of all immune activity, called the interleukins, are practically nonexistent until slow-wave sleep is entered. The antibody response of the humoral component of our immune system is also most active during slow-wave, or delta, sleep. Unlike the humoral immune system, cell-mediated immunity, especially involving T-cells and natural killer cells, has an oppositional rhythm with its peak during wakefulness. Thus slow-wave sleep creates just the right electrophysiological environment for the production of secretory substances such as antibody and immunomodulators. These secretory substances then play a major role in activating the cellular immune system.

Natural killer cell (NKC) activity was demonstrated only during the daytime. Nevertheless, sleep deprivation has been found to diminish cellular immunity (T cell and NKC), suggesting that the decrement of interleukin during slow-wave sleep is the most important step in the immune response.[4-5]

The symphony of periodic rhythms accomplished by the immune system suggests the image of a merry-go-round, with each component of the immune response represented by one of the horses. At any one point in time, one horse is always rising and another falling. Slow-wave sleep may be the mechanism which drives the electrical circuitry so that the merry-go-round continues to operate.

Moldofsky confirmed the clinical importance of slow-wave sleep deprivation in demonstrating the absence of delta EEG activity in patients with fibrositis and rheumatoid arthritis.[6-10] Rheumatoid arthritis is an autoimmune disorder and fibrositis has been associated with increased numbers of infections. He further demonstrated that the immune-mediated, pain-inducing inflammatory reactions common to both diseases could be reproduced in normal, healthy subjects by selective slow-wave sleep deprivation.[11]

Slow-wave Sleep and Depression

Another chemical produced during slow-wave sleep is serotonin. Serotonin is one of the key neurotransmitters involved in psychiatric depression. It is not surprising then that one of the characteristics of depression is a lack of deep sleep. One study has even found that depriving a group of hospitalized depressives of dream sleep, and thus indirectly promoting an increase in slow-wave sleep, led to such a significant amelioration of the depression that half the patients were released from the hospital without using medication or shock treatments.[12]

Dream Sleep and Learning

Dream sleep is a period of vivid imagery production. Some view dreams as a by-product of neuronal activity which have no importance.[13] The hypothesis also exists that dreams and imagery can trigger behaviors which might be crucial to survival, including learning, memory consolidation, and immune enhancement.

Learning appears to be enhanced by these shifting sleep cycles. Experiments have determined that more material is retained if learning trials are followed by a period of sleep rather than a period of wakefulness. Attempts have been made to account for these results based on retroactive interference by material encountered during the period of wakefulness following learning.[14] It has now been demonstrated that learning and memory consolidation are due to an active process of RNA synthesis during sleep which is mediated by a shifting of brainwaves.[15] Protein synthesis has been documented to occur during REM, or dream sleep, when the brainwaves are shifting between low and high frequencies.[16]

Breathing

Like sleep, breathing is another basic vegetative function of life which initiates homeodynamic healing mechanisms. Breathing as a therapy has been an integral component of ancient meditation strategies such as yoga and transcendental meditation as well as modern pain-relief techniques including Lamaze childbirth preparation. For an overview of the research on the health benefits of breathing training, see Table 3-2.

TABLE 3-2. *BREATHING AND PHYSICAL HEALING*

1st Author	Date	Results
Fried	1987	Diaphragmatic breathing reduced hyperventilation syndrome and autonomic arousal
Jain	1993	Yoga breathing exercises led to increased pulmonary functions and exercise tolerance in asthma patients
Telles	1993	Yoga breathing training increased fine-motor coordination over control group
Joshi	1992	Balanced right and left nostril breathing (pranayama) in normals lowered respiratory rate and increased forced vital capacity, forced expiratory volume, and peak expiratory flow rate
Wood	1993	Pranayama breathing program more effective than visualization and relaxation in increasing mental and physical energy in normals
Shields	1992	Lymphocyte circulation directly related to depth of pulmonary volume

Very few studies have focused exclusively on the healthy effects of breathing. However, practically all relaxation techniques either employ breathing directly or elicit a slower, deeper respiration pattern indirectly as a by-product of autonomic low-arousal. Yoga is such a technique involving special breathing and stretching exercises. Yoga has been shown to increase pulmonary functions and exercise tolerance in patients with chronic bronchial asthma.[17] One-year follow-up found that these patients still had reductions in both symptoms and drug requirements. In another study, ten days of similar yoga breathing techniques increased fine-motor performance and concentration in children.[18]

Another yoga breathing technique is called pranayama. This technique involves the alternation of nostrils using one's hand as a clamp to the side of the nose. In a study of normal subjects, six weeks of yoga rhythmic breathing techniques have been found to stimulate increased pulmonary functions in the form of lowered respiratory rate, increases in forced vital capacity, forced expiratory volume, and peak expiratory flow rate.[19] In a comparison study of pranayama breathing techniques to both visualization and relaxation, the breathing techniques increased perceptions of physical and mental energy as well as feelings of alertness and enthusiasm over the other two techniques.[20]

One researcher/clinician, Robert Fried, has found deep breathing to be successful in eliminating the hyperventilation syndrome.[21] This syndrome, characterized by rapid, shallow breathing and a decreased CO_2 concentration, tends to simulate the fight or flight response by constricting blood vessels, increasing anxiety, and decreasing the amount of oxygen to the brain and other organs. As many psychosomatic disorders such as migraine headaches and Raynaud's syndrome involve increased autonomic arousal, deep breathing helps in the management of these problems.

Fried also discovered a relationship between the respiratory sinus arrhythmia (RSA) and hyperventilation, primarily, that it was absent during this condition. The RSA is the normal acceleration and deceleration of the heartrate coinciding with inhalation and exhalation, respectively. He found deep breathing was able to not only reduce the hyperventilation, but also to induce the RSA to reappear. I have found that deep breathing training has been a crucial element in the treatment of both essential and preeclamptic (pregnancy-induced) hypertension. Maintaining an RSA variability between minimum and maximum heartrates of about 8–10 beats-per-minute has been found in my clinical practice to lower blood pressures within a single session about 10–15 mm systolic and 5–10 mm diastolic. Patients have been able to reduce or terminate medication usage, or in the case of preeclamptic women, to carry their babies to full term.

Little research has been documented on the beneficial effects of deep breathing on immunological disorders. I have found in my own practice that patients with immunological problems of the gut, including Crohn's disease, chronic ulcerative colitis, and irritable bowel syndrome all exhibit hyperventilatory breathing. Very likely the presence of gastrointestinal pain may inhibit abdominal breathing in much the same way that lower back pain does, consequently leading to shallow, chest- centered, hyperventilatory breathing. These patients all respond positively to the initiation of deep breathing.

One study has described the intimate relationship between deep breathing and the immune system. Lymph glands are responsible for filtering lymph coming from regional cells. Lymph is produced in these cells as a by-product of the oxidation of food. This lymph forms the interstitial fluid between cells as well as the blood plasma. Lymph is also rich in immune products, such as immunoglobulins and lymphocytes (hence the name).

Researchers have concluded that the immunity afforded by these immune products is proportional to the volume of lymph transported from the lymphatics to the bloodstream. Hence, the lymphatic system is the primary transport for our immune system from one body region to another. Where deep breathing fits into this immune transport system as a key player is that the lymph joins the blood supply proportionately to the depth of the respiration.[22] The deeper the breath that's taken, the more available the immune system is to be transported where it is needed.

As Fried has pointed out, hyperventilation causes the ph of the blood to become more alkaline whereas deep breathing initiates more acidic conditions. Alkaline conditions are optimal for some phases of the immune response, such as the ability of cationic proteins in neutrophils to kill bacteria.[23] However, lysosomal enzymes (also within neutrophils) operate more effectively in killing other types of bacteria under acidic conditions. It thus appears that neither a constant alkaline nor acidic ph of the blood would confer the greatest resistance to bacteria. Instead, conditions which shift back and forth between the two ph levels would offer the greatest immunity. According to this homeodynamic model, periods of hyperventilation might be somewhat desirable as long as they are interspersed with periods of deep breathing. The important health benefit appears to be in the periodic shifting from one state to another.

Another mechanism involved in the breathing/immunity connection is stress and anxiety. Hyperventilatory breathing is highly associated with anxiety and panic states.[21] In my own work I have discovered that patients with panic attacks practically always exhibit shallow, rapid breathing at rates between 20–30 breaths/minute. Furthermore, these same patients evidence other signs of autonomic stress, such as vasoconstriction (cold hands), sweating, and high muscle tension levels. Stress is another factor which has proved to have differential effects upon the immune system. Acute stress has been found to increase certain parameters of the immune system.[24] On the other hand, chronic stress generally has been shown to be immunosuppressive, due to the buildup of circulating adrenal corticosteroids.

Homeodynamic Mechanisms of Breathing

It appears that homeodynamic shifts in breathing rate between slow and fast may elicit the most adaptive and healthy environmental conditions for an optimum functioning immune system. Whether these changes accomplish their benefit via changes in the blood, such as ph and carbon dioxide levels, or through changes in the electrical recharging of the nervous system through brain wave shifts is unclear. Nevertheless, changes in breathing rates definitely cause EEG frequency shifts as well. For documentation of these breathing-mediated shifts, see Table 3-3.

TABLE 3-3.   *HOMEODYNAMIC MECHANISMS OF BREATHING*

1st Author	Date	Results
Fried	1987	Deep breathing increased alpha and decreased theta
Satyanarayana	1992	Deep breathing increased alpha and decreased beta
Sun	1994	Deep breathing increased alpha activity and frontal-occipital coherence
Telles	1993	Deep breathing increased auditory-evoked potentials
Lorig	1988	Inhalation/exhalation cycle induced beta/theta cycle
Svebak	1985	Relationship discovered between serious-mindednessand hyperventilation; and between play and non-hyperventilation
Shannahoff-Khalsa,	1989	Right/left breathing activates hemispheric and autonomic shifts

Several studies have determined that during deep breathing, increases in alpha activity occur followed by decreases in theta and beta.[21, 25] In another study, increases were not only found in the alpha band, but increased coherence at specific brain wave frequencies between frontal and occipital areas were also evident following various types of Qigong breathing exercises.[26] Apparently breathing techniques initiate homeodynamic mechanisms in the truest sense through the elicitation of 1) mental/brain-electrical shifts, and 2) physiological resonance.

As found in the validation studies of homeodynamic theory, brain electrical amplitudes seem to be also affected by breathing techniques. Evoked potential research has demonstrated that deep breathing elicits increases in components of the auditory-evoked potential.[27] Our homeodynamic studies indicated that the visual-evoked potential was significantly higher in healthy as opposed to immunologically-compromised individuals. In other words, the nervous system appears to be recharged electrically through the periodic practice of deep, relaxed breathing.

Breathing offers a richly complex behavioral phenomenon that on many levels appears to stimulate the kind of electrical brain wave variability that homeodynamics suggest is needed for health. When respiration is slow enough, i.e., non-hyperventilatory, brain waves have been found to vary between inspiration and expiration. Theta activity has been found to increase during exhalation with beta increasing during inhalation.[28] This behavior may reflect the tendency of the heart to relax during exhalation (called the respiratory sinus arhythmia). These researchers also discovered that nasal breathing elicited greater spatial differences in beta activity between the posterior and anterior brain than mouth breathing.

This difference between posterior and anterior brain electrical activity has been implicated in research on the differentiation between individuals who are serious-minded (telic) as opposed to those who are playful (paratelic). Greater electrical activity was discovered posteriorly in the playful subjects.[29] These paratelic individuals also exhibited greater aversiveness to hyperventilation breathing, suggesting that they have a built-in feedback system (supposedly via norepinephrine pathways) which is more sensitive to stress-producing conditions. This also suggests a relationship between hyperventilation and serious-mindedness as well as a deep breathing-mediated health benefit to playfulness. The ability to shift into playfulness was described in Chapter 2 as an integral cycle in the learning rhythms of assimilation and accommodation.

Therefore, breathing alternation from hyperventilatory to diaphragmatic may selectively activate the motor (anterior) and sensory (posterior) areas of the brain. While this rhythm was earlier suggested to activate different ph-mediated components of the immune system, it may also be crucial to the sensory and motor functions of the immune system in detecting and responding to pathogens. As we will see in Chapter 7, autoimmune patients often are telic individuals, whose anterior (motor) brain activation may very well drive their overactive motor component of their immune system.

Optimal immune functioning may also depend on a rhythm of cerebral hemispheric alternation initiated by another breathing technique. As advanced yoga meditators have known for years, each nostril tends to dominate in an ongoing ultradian rhythm which takes from two to four hours.[30] An important feature of this rhythm is that it is correlated with the cerebral ultradian rhythm associated with hemispheric dominance. Breathing through one nostril has the effect of activating the opposite side of the cerebral cortex. In fact, nasal opening and closing (congestion) is a function of the same lateralized sympathetic and parasympathetic activity which Kleitman labeled the Basic Rest Activity Cycle (BRAC).[31] This homeodynamic shift in autonomic activity serves to exercise the neural connections within each half of the body as well as the brain.

Yogic medicine researcher, David Shannahoff-Khalsa, has also demonstrated that nasal dominance is not only an indicator of which side of the brain/body the autonomic nervous system is activated, but perhaps more importantly, that forced nasal breathing through the congested nostril can shift both autonomic and cerebral hemispheric lateral dominance.[30] Breathing into the left nostril, for example, stimulates more creative, right-brained thinking while right nostril breathing is more conducive to verbal discourse. Right nostril breathing apparently also stimulates appetite and digestion.

Appreciating the gender differences of his research offers some explanations to the need for alternation of energies in a sexually satisfying relationship. Quoting Shannahoff-Khalsa, "sexual intercourse is most satisfying for both partners when the man is dominant in the right nostril and the woman in the left." Perhaps the concept of homeodynamics can also be applied to health within human relationships. Shifts in energies (sexual, emotional, cognitive, etc.) can be found when such polarities exist as feminine/masculine and right-brain/left-brain, to mention a few. The notion of "opposites attracting" suggests that with polarities among personality styles, that psycho-spiritual energy may be able to be created which can propel a healthy relationship through time. Conversely, if energies (or personality traits) completely match such that polarities don't exist, can the necessary rhythms be created to energize and sustain a relationship?

His research into nostril breathing suggests the potential for treaments of immune disorders. As was discussed earlier in this section, deep sleep is deprived among several types of immune disorders including rheumatoid arthritis, fybromyalgia, and as I have discovered, cancer. However, deep sleep may be facilitated according to Shannahoff-Khalsa through forced breathing into the left nostril. Persons with a paucity of slow-wave activity might thus be able to recharge the nervous and immune systems through these selective breathing techniques.

Shannahoff-Khalsa also has found a high prevalence of nostril shifting in multiple personalities.[30] This conclusion corroborates the previously reported incidences of physical healing demonstrated by MPDs as being due to the prolific alterations of nervous system activity. He goes on to report that schizophrenic-like psychoses, which we discussed in Section I as being immune-enhanced, are primarily left hemispheric dysfunctions. Depression and other emotional disorders, on the other hand, are right hemispheric dysfunctions. As we found in Section I, the affective disorders evidence suppressed immunity. The implication is that forced nostril breathing may provide for the exercising of hemispheric deficits and consequent immunological boosting. These hypotheses remain to be tested.

Exercise

Since the advent of physical education programs during the Kennedy years, physical activity and exercise have long been considered to be important health maintenance behaviors. The mechanisms involved in the health benefits of exercise are somewhat controversial, and are probably multifactorial. For an overview of the research on the health benefits of exercise, see Table 3-4.

TABLE 3-4.   *EXERCISE AND PHYSICAL HEALING*

1st Author	Date	Results
LeBow	1989	Obesity associated with cardiovascular disease and cancer
Sandvik	1993	Total work done on bicycle ergometer predicted mortality by all causes; high fitness associated with 54% lower mortality rate than low fitness
Paffenberger	1993	Beginning moderately vigorous exercise associatedwith a 23% lower mortality rate than not doing so

(continued)

TABLE 3-4. *EXERCISE AND PHYSICAL HEALING (continuation)*

1st Author	Date	Results
Blumenthal	1990	Aerobic exercise increased oxygen consumption, and decreased cardiovascular and sympathoadrenal responses of mental stress over strength training
Brown	1988	Exercise acted as buffer against negative effects of stress upon health
Simpson	1990	10 weeks of exercise training in mice enhanced splenic natural killer cell cytolytic activity against tumor targets
MacNeil	1993	9 weeks of chronic exercise in mice enhanced natural killer cell cytotoxic mechanisms
Coleman	1993	8 weeks of exercise in mice increased Con-A mitogen responses over controls
Esterling	1992	Aerobic exercise and cognitive behavioral stress management equally were effective in increasing immune responses as measured by reduced antibodytiters to EBV-VCA and HHV-6
Fiatarone	in press	Vigorous exercise increased natural killer cell activity in young and elderly subjects
Tvede	1993	Natural killer cell and lymphokine-activated killer cell activity increased following a single bout of exercise
Bernstein	1994	Four hours of exercise weekly during childbearing years reduced incidence of breast cancer by 58%
Nieman	1993	12 weeks of moderate exercise effective in reducing upper respiratory tract infections over calisthenic group in elderly women
Ortega	1993	Conditioned sportswomen evidenced higher phagocytic activity than matched group of sedentary women

In one study of nearly 2,000 men, greater physical fitness, as determined by total work performed on a bicycle ergometer, was found to be a significant predictor of mortality from all causes.[32] Physical fitness was a slightly better predictor of death by cardiovascular disease than other causes.

In terms of cardiovascular disease, one of the primary determinants of pathology is obesity and high levels of serum cholesterol, specifically the LDL's or low density lipoproteins.[33] Obesity puts added pressure on the heart muscle to work harder. High LDL levels increase the amount of plaque-forming cholesterol which decrease vascular flexibility and occlude arterial pathways. Physical activity serves as a major deterrent to these risk factors through the speeding of basal metabolism rates, the consequent burning of fat, and the lowering of extra weight. The initiation of moderately vigorous sports activity and the consequent maintenance of lean body bass have been found to lower mortality risk by as much as 25%.[34]

Physical activity also can be healthy through the exercising of the cardiopulmonary system, especially in the case of aerobic exercise. In one study, 12 weeks of aerobic exercise (three times weekly) was compared with a Nautilus training program over the same amount of time.[35] Results indicated that oxygen consumption increased significantly in the aerobic group over the weight training group. Aerobic training also evidenced significantly greater decreases in heart rate, diastolic blood pressure, and epinephrine secretion, as well as showing faster recovery than the strength group. The aerobic group was found to exhibit lower cardiovascular reactivity to mental stress following training.

Mechanisms other than obesity and the sheer exercising of the cardiopulmonary system may be involved in the health link between exercise and health. Constant exercising of the cardiovascular or musculoskeletal systems can actually lead to dangerous levels of activity, as witnessed by the number of individuals who, although being in excellent physical shape, succumb following running and bicycling marathons. Research on the immune system offers some clues about these alternate theories.

First of all, obesity is associated with immune suppression and infectious disease to almost the same degree as cardiovascular disease.[36] Many cancers, especially those related to the sex organs and gut, have a higher incidence due to obesity.[33] Conversely, exercise has been found to be a significant buffer against the negative effects of stress. Studies show that increasing levels of physical activity are associated with less physical illness.[37]

These results are somewhat contradictory with the known research demonstrating that the stress of athletic training temporarily depresses cellular immunity and augments infection rates in athletes.[38] One of the immediate effects of exercise upon the immune system is leucocytosis, or the destruction of white blood cells.[39] This effect is proportional to the intensity and duration of the physical activity. However, leucocytosis has been found to be lesser in trained athletes than in unconditioned subjects. Hence, regular exercise offers a protective mechanism against the destruction of too many cells within the immune system.

Short-term Exercise

Even though the numbers of white blood cells are temporarily depleted by vigorous exercise, the qualitative functioning of the immune system is improved through regular physical activity. In one study using mice, investigators found that although intense exercise was stressful to the immune system, regular exercise training (on a treadmill) actually enhanced the activity of splenic natural killer cells against tumor targets.[40] Other animal studies have determined that eight weeks or more of exercise, whether forced or voluntary, led to greater cytoxicity against tumor cells[41] and increased lymphocyte proliferation[42] when compared to inactive controls.

In a study of gay men awaiting HIV status notification, aerobic exercise was found to be as instrumental as cognitive stress management in enhancing humoral immunity.[43] Antibody titers to Epstein-Barr virus and human herpesvirus type-6 decreased significantly over those of control group patients following only five weeks of intervention.

Other studies of the effect of bouts of vigorous exercise on natural killer cell activity have also confirmed these results for human subjects.[44] These researchers also implicated endorphins as a causative link in boosting NKC activity.

Studies of different intensities of exercise have determined that light and moderate levels of exertion enhance both cellular and humoral immune responsivity during the physical activity.[45] Heavy exertion leads to decrements in immune functioning. These declines in immunity have been documented to normalize after about 120 minutes.[46]

Long-term Exercise

While the effects of immediate exercise on health remains somewhat phasic depending on the intensity of the exercise and at what time during or after measurements are taken, there are no doubts about the health benefits of long-term physical conditioning.

In a recently reported study in the Journal of the National Cancer Institute, it was found that women who had exercised four hours per week during their childbearing years ran a 58% lower risk of breast cancer.[47] Even one to three hours per week of physical exercise reduced the risk of breast cancer by 30%.

Another study found long-term but not short-term effects of exercise on immune functioning.[48] A group of elderly women participated in a 12-week program of either walking (with cardiorespiratory increase) or a calisthenics control group (no cardiorespiratory increase). When compared with an age-matched group of women in good physical condition, the latter group experienced superior cellular immune functioning (NKC and T cells) and a significantly lower incidence of upper respiratory tract infection when compared to either the walking or control groups. Nevertheless, the walking group did evidence lower incidence of respiratory illness and higher oxygen capacity than the control group.

One final study sought to contrast immune functioning in athletes vs. inactive individuals as a measure of long-term physical conditioning. In comparing phagocytic functioning in neutrophils between sedentary women and sportswomen, three immune functions—chemotaxis, ingestion, and killing abilities—were each found to be significantly higher in the athletes.[49]

Homeodynamic Mechanisms of Exercise

If exercise has immediate stressful effects upon the immune system, then could another mechanism account for the benefits shown following a longer regimen of physical activity? The answer may lie in the finding that exercise acts through homeodynamic mechanisms by creating brain wave changes, which have the longer-term effect of recharging the nervous and immune systems. Documentation for these homeodynamic effects of exercise can be found in Table 3-5.

TABLE 3-5. *HOMEODYNAMIC MECHANISMS OF EXERCISE*

1st Author	Date	Results
Beyer	1976	EEG frequency shifts were induced by exercise
Walsh	1984	Following exercise, slow-wave sleep increased and REM sleep declined
Torsvall	1984	Following exercise, slow-wave sleep increased and REM sleep declined
Dustman	1990	Physically active individuals evidenced higher visual-evoked potentials

Several studies have been conducted on the effects of exercise upon the nervous system, although none actually while the exercise was occurring. Nevertheless, frequency shifts have been observed immediately following exercise,[50] and shifts in both the power and frequency spectra have been noted during nocturnal sleep due to exercise. The most prominent finding of the sleep studies following exercise is that slow-wave sleep (SWS) increased and REM sleep decreased.[51-52] SWS, or delta, was described earlier to be the restorative stage of sleep. Because exercise induces more delta wave activity, this accounts for the enhancements found in the immune system, as delta sleep is the prolific period of activity for immunity. The nervous system has also been found to be honed due to exercise. Higher visual-evoked potentials and shorter latencies have been demonstrated in more physically active individuals.[53]

In conclusion, exercise is one behavior which stimulates a homeodynamic shift in an indirect way. First, exercise induces a relatively intense stressful experience on the body, which then gives way to relaxation and restoration. Finally, the immune system, which experiences an initial but transient suppression following exercise, rebounds to an even higher level of functioning, especially during the restorative phases conferred by the increased delta wave activity.

Therapeutic Touch

There are several varieties of energy field modulation for the purpose of healing using the hands. Some of the ones which are currently being clinically applied are therapeutic touch (both noncontact and contact) and biocircuits. Each of these techniques has similarities to the others and operate via subtle energy pathways. These subtle energy pathways, while not detectable by conventional measurement devices, are beginning to be demonstrated in the scientific literature. For an overview of research on therapeutic touch and physical healing, see Table 3-6.

Table 3-6. *THERAPEUTIC TOUCH AND PHYSICAL HEALING*

1st Author	Date	Results
Krieger	1979	Red and white blood cell counts changed through non-contact therapeutic touch
Wirth	1990	Noncontact therapeutic touch increased wound healing in humans in a double-blind study
Schwartz	1990	Water treated with noncontact therapeutic touch was significantly altered as measured by spectrophotometry
Isaacs	1991	Copper biocircuits transmitting subjects own energies increased muscular, vascular, and mental relaxation in a double-blind study
Field	1986	Tactile stimulation of premature infants led to higher weight gains and decreased hospitalizations
McKorkle	1974	Touch was found to significantly reduce cardiovascular reactivity on a coronary care unit

Therapeutic touch has been utilized in one form or another for centuries. Current literature on application and research has been promoted during the last 50 years.[54-55] It involves the modulation of weakened or disturbed energy in a healee through the energies transmitted by the healer. The hands of the healer are the tuning forks which redirect the disturbed energy in the healee. Biocircuits is an application of therapeutic touch in which the proposed directional pathways of energy are aligned without the use of a healer. Instead copper connectors are used to establish the desired links.

In one controlled study of non-contact therapeutic touch, identical wounds were incised on subjects' shoulders and then they were exposed to daily five-minute regimens of either non-contact therapeutic touch by a hidden practitioner or a sham treatment condition.[56] Results indicated that significant acceleration of wound healing occurred in the treatment group as compared to the control group. Furthermore, by the sixteenth day following incision, 13 of 23 of the treated wounds had completely healed whereas none of the 21 sham treated wounds had done so.

In a second experimentally controlled study, the infrared spectra of water samples was measured through spectrophotometry following either treatment by non-contact therapeutic touch practitioners or no contact.[57] The treated water samples were found to exhibit significantly more spectral variability following treatment as compared to the controls. This experiment was also carried out using blind and randomization procedures. The differences were not explainable due to differences in temperature, barometric pressure, or sampling order.

Other studies which have been reported include Kreiger's own work in demonstrating hemoglobin and immunological differences in subjects before and after non-contact therapeutic touch.[54] Clinical examples reported by Krieger include the eradication of pain due to arthritis, headaches, and cancer, as well as the modulation of severe fever.

Biocircuit research has allowed the person to act as both healer and healee. Using copper plates with wires attached, energies can be redirected to one's body with the hands. Results of a double-blind study of biocircuits demonstrated that subjects experienced increased levels of EMG muscle relaxation, higher skin temperatures, and felt more relaxed when the biocircuits were connected.[58]

Research on touch has demonstrated that premature infants who received tactile stimulation for only ten days were significantly healthier than their untouched counterparts.[59] Such indices included greater weight gains, higher alertness and activity levels, and an average cost savings of $3,000 per infant. Michael Lerner and Rachel Naomi Remen have reported another unpublished study in which premature infants exhibited an increased survival rate when they were held and stroked. Stimulated by this study and the exciting results of Krieger's work, they began to implement touch and massage into the regimen of the Commonweal Cancer Help Program in northern California. According to them, "touch is intimately connected with the stimulation of the will to live."[60]

Touch has also been found to convey caring attitudes by health practitioners. Significant changes in cardiovascular activity as measured by EKG were elicited by nurses when they touched their patients while talking to them as opposed to verbalization alone.[61]

Homeodynamic Mechanisms

What are the healing mechanisms responsible for the positive effects shown through these therapies? Can these mechanisms even be known without being able to measure the subtle energies purportedly responsible for them? Fortunately some studies have been conducted utilizing measurable components of the nervous system following non-contact therapeutic touch. For an overview of this documentation, see Table 3-7.

TABLE 3-7. *HOMEODYNAMIC MECHANISMS OF THERAPEUTIC TOUCH*

1st Author	Date	Results
Krieger	1979	Noncontact therapeutic touch produced alpha EEG activity in a healee
Fahrion	1992	Noncontact therapeutic touch produced theta shifts in a healee
Brown	1977–78	Noncontact therapeutic touch produced beta shifts in healers
Green	1991	Noncontact therapeutic touch accompanied by unusually high electrostatic surges in a healer
Isaacs	1991	Biocircuits induced synchronous theta activity

In a study of one healer, alpha brain wave activity was present during the baseline before non-contact therapeutic touch.[54] Immediately after commencing treatment, the healer's EEG evidenced an unusual phenomenon—the presence of synchronized beta activity. With non-contact therapeutic touch, the three patients were found to exhibit a predominance of large amplitude alpha waves characteristic of relaxation. The healer's EEG, however, contained greater shifts than did those of the patients.

These results matched an EEG study of non-contact therapeutic touch in which the healer experienced brainwave shifts into synchronous beta while the healee exhibited theta wave amplitude surges.[62] Another EEG study of non-contact therapeutic touch practitioners demonstrated similar findings. Five healers were found to exhibit increases in beta activity during therapeutic touch conditions.[63] This differentiated their brainwave states of lower frequency activity (alpha and theta) found during conditions of relaxed meditation.

Electrostatic surges of dramatic proportion have been detected in non-contact therapeutic touch practitioners.[64] Measured by an electrometer floated above the practitioners' heads, these near-200 volt surges were interesting in that they were usually positive during meditational states but negative when focused on patients. If these surges are measuring some potential related to EEG, they were nearly a million times stronger than typical brainwave amplitudes. There could be some relationship between these electrostatic surges in healing practitioners and the electrostatic phenomena we witnessed in our own EEG study of patients with immunological syndromes reported in Chapter 2. Possibly due to a dirth of their own electric potentials, these patients were attracting electrostatic energy from other sources, such as people, lighting, and electromagnetic sensing devices.

That people can affect themselves with their own healing energies has been demonstrated with biocircuit research. One study measured EEG in subjects exposed to real or sham biocircuit procedures. Results of this study indicated that homeodynamic shifts into slower and more synchronous theta EEG activity resulted following one session.[64]

These shifts into synchronous brainwave activity (whether higher frequencies in healer or lower ones in patients) constitute homeodynamic shifts of the kind postulate to be healing to the bodymind. There is a dynamic shift in brain wave frequency which serves to alter neuronal gating potentials and thus recharge the nervous system and other systems within the body.

The synchronous activity signifies that resonance is occurring which allows all systems in the bodymind to communicate efficiently and completely. This is very likely the source of the symbols, images, and mandalas that appear after training in such techniques as non-contact therapeutic touch, Reiki, and other forms of meditation. Krieger discusses the evolution of geometric mandalas intuited by healers from their clinical practice.[53] As Reike therapists develop in their progression into "master" status, symbols take on a very important dimension to their healing work. Sensations which one picks up via touch-oriented therapies from energy fields of their patients may have the potential of becoming translated into these symbols and mandalas as a manifestation of the resonant, homeodynamic bodymind.

Acupuncture

Acupuncture and acupressure are ancient Chinese healing techniques employing the use of needles or tactile pressure along specific pathways in the body called meridians. According to this healing philosophy, energy called Qi (chi) runs along 12 meridians which run lengthwise up and down the body. The meridians link particular organs into groups, and thus account for connections between parts of the body not normally correlated in Western medicine. For example, the knee and stomach share the stomach meridian.

The energy system Qi has not been found to follow Western anatomical pathways of bones, muscles, vasculature, or lymphatics. Nevertheless, this system has now been validated in research employing radioisotopes injected into classical acupuncture points.[65] When traced using a gamma-camera, these isotopes followed the traditional meridians.

In other contemporary biophysical studies of acupuncture points and meridians, electrical measurements have yielded some fascinating results which bear strongly on the bioelectrical hypotheses suggested in this book. In these experiments it has been determined that the electrical resistance between two acupuncture points is about 100 times less than the resistance between non-acupuncture points covering the same skin distance.[66] Hence the electrical current (amperage) is much higher between acupuncture points than non-acupuncture points. Relative to other discussions in this section, sleep, hypnosis, and emotional excitation have each been found to elicit profound changes in the electrical fields around acupuncture points. For an overview of the research on the beneficial effects of acupuncture on physical health, see Table 3-8.

TABLE 3-8.   *ACUPUNCTURE AND PHYSICAL HEALTH*

1st Author	Date	Results
Liu	1993	Clinical symptoms and cellular/humoral components of the immune system improved in rheumatoid arthritis patients following acupuncture
Xiao	1992	Clinical symptoms improved and IL-2 increased in rheumatoid arthritis patients following acupuncture
Still	1985	Acupuncture in parasitically-invaded dogs led to increased immune responsiveness
Requena	1986	Acupuncture was found to reduce hypertension in dogs through reduction of angiotensin II
Millstein	1994	Review of study in which acupuncture led to greater reduction in cocaine abuse
Lin	1993	Acupuncture effective in treating diarrhea and in improving cellular and humoral immunity in children

(continued)

TABLE 3-8. *ACUPUNCTURE AND PHYSICAL HEALTH (continuation)*

1st Author	Date	Results
de Aloysio	1992	Acupressure yielded 60% improvement in morning sickness symptoms in pregnant women whereas placebo acupressure resulted in only 30% amelioration
Gieron	1993	Acupressure decreased postoperative nausea 53% whereas placebo acupressure resulted in only 23% decline
Kuzmina	1987	Laser acupuncture decreased radiation edemas and improved immune functioning in breast cancer patients
Yuan	1992	Laser acupuncture of lymphatic areas in rats found to enhance cellular and humoral immune system
Saletu	1975	Experimental pain was more effectively decreased in normal subjects by electroacupuncture, hypnosis and drugs than acupuncture alone; acupuncture at specific loci more effective than at nonspecific loci
Glavinskaia	1989	Electroacupuncture with scleroderma patients resulted in both clinical and immunological improvement in 83% of patients

Regarding the value of acupuncture, positive results have been found for certain clinical areas. Immune enhancement has been demonstrated in a number of studies following acupuncture. One study demonstrated both positive clinical effects and an enhancement of immune factors in rheumatoid arthritis patients.[67] Changes in both humoral and cellular components of the immune system were noted following acupuncture. Another study of rheumatoid arthritis determined that pretreatment levels of interleukin-2 (IL-2) were significantly lower in patients than in controls.[68] Following treatment, the IL-2 levels increased significantly in the patients.

Unlike many behavioral techniques, acupuncture is amenable to eliminating the effects of placebo by utilizing animal models. For example, parasitic invasion in dogs has been found to be effectively treated by acupuncture. In a study in which dogs were experimentally exposed to a harmless parasite, 20 minutes of acupuncture led to significantly improved immunological behavior as measured by blood serum protein sedimentation, serum globulin levels, and albumin levels.[69] In another study using dogs, acupuncture has been shown to be useful in decreasing high blood pressure through the reduction of angiotensin II.[70]

In a review of several projects sponsored by the National Institute on Drug Abuse, acupuncture has shown promise in the treatment of drug addictions.[71] Two studies revealed significant reductions in cocaine metabolite levels in addition to lower reported use after several weeks of acupuncture treatment. The suggested mechanism in this treatment has been hypothesized to be the endogenous opioid system. This system, which affects endorphin levels and pain sensitivity,has also been implicated in Peniston's studies of addiction treatment utilizing biofeedback-mediated brain wave shifts (see Chapter 5).

Modulation of the meridian system through several different procedures has been demonstrated with gastrointestinal problems. Acupuncture has been shown to have a superior edge in easing childhood diarrhea over the use of drugs.[72] The application of pressure over acupoints, known as acupressure, has also been demonstrated in this area. Morning sickness has been effectively reduced by as much as 60% with this procedure.[73] A similar level of nausea reduction (53%) has been obtained in treating postoperative nausea and chemotherapy-induced nausea with acupressure.[74] Placebo acupressure in these two studies yielded no better than a 30% amelioration of pain.

Studies have begun to show that electrical or laser stimulation of acupoints has even better clinical and experimental effects than acupuncture needling alone. Laser acupuncture has been found to add significantly to the recovery of lymphocyte counts and blastogenesis in breast cancer patients receiving radiation therapy.[75] Secondary radiation edemas were found to heal faster in the laser acupuncture group also. In another study, utilizing rats as subjects, electron microscopy was used to note structural changes in lymphocytes following treatment by laser acupuncture.[76] Significant structural changes were noted in B-cells, T-cells, and macrophages after the treatment.

Electroacupuncture, or the administration of electrical currents into acupuncture needles, has been found to be similarly quite useful. While acupuncture has yielded positive results in reducing pain, several studies have demonstrated the superiority of electroacupuncture over traditional acupuncture in the treatment of pain.[77] The validity of acupuncture sites was upheld in this study as these treatments were compared at both specific and nonspecific loci. Specific acupuncture loci were more effective for both electroacupuncture and acupuncture than nonspecific loci. Electroacupuncture was also as effective as hypnosis and morphine, although less effective than ketamine in reducing pain.

In turning to skin diseases, effective treatment rates for patients with local scleroderma have been found to be as high as 83% with electroacupuncture.[78] Immunological changes following treatment included increased T-cell counts and reduced circulating immune complexes.

Homeodynamic Mechanisms

There was some initial difficulty in identifying acupuncture as a homeodynamic healing technique. Chinese medicine includes the concept of balance between diametrically opposed forms of energy called yin and yang. Yin embodies passivity, coldness, darkness, and wetness whereas yang represents activity, heat, light, and dryness. Like the Western medical concept of homeostasis, health in the Chinese system is reflected by a balance of yin and yang. However, Chinese medicine is unclear about the dynamic, temporal movement between these two states. Yet when polarities between two states are espoused, there is the strong likelihood that dynamic movement between the two is also essential for health, as in homeodynamism. Chinese physicians refer to diseases as having "blocked energy" in one or more meridians. Knowing that electrical energy is conducted more easily down these conduits than elsewhere in the body, one might form a hypothesis about the relationship between this blocked energy and the newly discovered lack of variability in the electrical brain wave activity found in patients with chronic disease. Perhaps homeodynamic brain wave shifting is intimately connected with the unblocking of meridians. Furthermore, a passive technique like acupuncture may stimulate an increase in brain wave activity. An overview of such research can be found in Table 3-9.

TABLE 3-9. *HOMEODYNAMIC MECHANISMS OF ACUPUNCTURE*

1st Author	Date	Results
Saletu	1975	Alpha and high beta EEG activity were increased following acupuncture
Kochetkov	1983	Synchronized alpha EEG shifts were induced by acupuncture
Koekina	1988	Hemispheric symmetry was increased following acupuncture

In analyzing the brain wave mechanisms by which acupuncture and meridian manipulation medicine achieve their health benefits, a picture begins to emerge suggesting the presence of homeodynamic mechanisms indeed. In one of the studies with normal subjects, EEG shifts to alpha and extremely high beta activity were elicited by acupuncture.[79] The application of electricity through the needles significantly increased the alpha activity even further. This study was also important in comparing acupuncture with hypnosis. Acupuncture was found to elicit a more stimulatory effect than hypnosis as brainwave shifts to theta and delta were noted during hypnosis.

In another study of acupuncture-treated depressives, EEG shifts involving highly synchronous, slower frequency activity were concurrently demonstrated along with emotional and sleep-related improvement.[80] This homeodynamic synchronization was also observed in another study of depressives. In this study, one course of acupuncture enhanced hemispheric symmetry and decreased the amount of somatic complaints in the patients.[81]

In conclusion, the brain wave activity during acupuncture involves dynamic shifts of frequency, directionally depending on the baseline state of the subject or patient. If highly aroused, a shift would likely occur to lower frequencies. If in a low state of arousal, perhaps increases in brain wave frequencies would result. In either state a shift occurs, which in homeodynamic terms stimulates the productivity of the immune system (receptor molecules, antibodies, and lymphocytes). This shift leads to enhanced resonance in brain wave activity which stimulates both a more efficient and a more communicative bodymind system.

Electric Therapies

Probably no healing technique is more controversial than the many and varied uses of electricity. Undoubtedly the widest range of images are elicited from those associated with birth, as in Mary Shelley's Frankenstein, to death by electrocution. Even electromagnetic pollution has become a recently validated concept. For an overview of the research on the beneficial effects of electric therapies on physical health, see Table 3-10.

TABLE 3-10.   *ELECTRIC THERAPIES AND PHYSICAL HEALING*

1st Author	Date	Results
Schaerf	1989	Electroconvulsive therapy was successful in treating depression in HIV-positive individuals
Heiberg	1993	Account of woman whose breast cancer remissed following lightening strike
Everson	1966	Accounts of spontaneous remissions from cancer following ECT treatments
Fischler	1992	ECT elicited increases in both lymphocyte activation and in natural killer cell activity in depressives
Wood	1993	Electric footshock in rats was found to increase cellular and humoral immunity
Albrecht	1985	Long-term depressives with higher blastogenesis rate than normals experienced reduction into normal range following several ECT treatments
Nordenstrom	1983	Application of electric currents into tumors induced remission of cancer in terminal patients and increased three-year survival rate
Becker	1985	Electric currents applied externally through electric stimulation or internally through amputation/ regeneration led to remission in mice tumors, elimination of infections, and faster healing in bone fractures
Devi	1993	Electrical stimulation of hippocampus enhanced phagocytic activity and decreased immunosuppressive hormones
Ratzlaff	1992	Peripheral denervation-induced immune suppression was restored with electrical stimulation of nerve
Han	1991	Transcutaneous Electrical Nerve Stimulation (TENS) reduced pain in humans

(continued)

TABLE 3-10. *ELECTRIC THERAPIES AND PHYSICAL HEALING (continuation)*

1st Author	Date	Results
Shealy	1989	Reduction of depression and anxiety as well as restoration of blood hormone levels was accomplished through Transcranial Electric Therapy (TET)
Krupitsky	1991	TET reduced affective disturbances in alcoholics and increased monoamine and GABA levels
Patterson	1992	Withdrawal symptoms and relapse rates were reduced in various addictions through TET
Subrahmanyam	1993	Rheumatoid arthritis symptoms were reduced through pulsed magnetic fields
Hongshi	1990	Electroacupuncture was found more effective in reducing pain symptoms than acupuncture; music-electro-acupuncture however was more beneficial than either
Saletu	1975	Electroacupuncture was found more effective in reducing pain symptoms than acupuncture; equivalent to hypnosis and drug therapy

Electroconvulsive Shock Therapy

One of the first uses of electricity in healing was electroconvulsive shock therapy (ECT). The primary goal of ECT has been for the remediation of symptoms associated with psychiatric illnesses such as depression and schizophrenia. As stated in Chapter 1, physical symptomatology has been found to be greater in depressives than in schizophrenics. According to homeodynamic theory, this difference is due to the reduced EEG frequency variability in the depressives and the seizure-like theta spikes found in the schizophrenics. Because ECT produces a seizure, one might also hypothesize that depressives would fare better than schizophrenics following ECT treatment.

This is indeed what has been found in the literature. Those with affective disorder were found to exhibit higher reductions in mental/emotional symptoms than schizophrenics following ECT.[82] Presumably the seizure produced by the ECT facilitated a regulation of immunological and neuroendocrine factors which consequently affected the symptomatology of depression. The schizophrenics already had more variable brain electrical activity before the ECT and didn't evidence as much improvement. Psychotic depression in AIDS and HIV-positive patients has also been found to be successfully treated with ECT. Unfortunately, however, immunological measures were not assessed and no determination was made regarding the beneficial effects, if any, of ECT on the progression of AIDS.[83]

Very little data exists on the effects of ECT on physical healing. However, as early as 1776 medical journals had described the case of a woman with breast cancer who was hit in the shoulder by lightening. All evidence of her tumor subsequently disappeared.[84]

In their description of 176 case reports of spontaneous regression of cancer, Everson and Cole found that remission had occurred in some cases following ECT treatments.[85] One of the reasons for this may reside in the documented boost in both natural killer cell activity and numbers of lymphocytes expressing T-cell and interleukin antigens following ECT.[86] These cells have been targeted as the principle players in the immunological defense against cancer.

ECT has also been found to regulate cellular immune activity in a group of hospitalized depressed patients who had been depressed for nearly 1 1/2 years on the average.[87] Unlike most studies which had shown a suppression of lymphocyte blastogenesis following short-term depression, these patients interestingly manifested abnormally high pretreatment blastogenesis rates compared to healthy controls. Yet the ECT treatment seemed to provide a homeodynamic jolt to the system which shifted the immune response in the direction of normalcy.

In an animal study employing experimental shock, more support was provided for the notion that short-term electrical shock treatments induce homeodynamic shifts which help regulate the immune system. Brief stress administered to rats through the delivery of electric footshock has been found to enhance immune system activity as determined by increased splenocyte proliferation and IgG levels.[88]

Electrical Stimulation

Electrical stimulation is proposed to activate health through the stimulation of homeodynamic shifts in the nervous system. In these cases, the electrical stimulation can be very weak as compared to those of ECT. Nevertheless, weak electrical stimulation has been documented to manifest changes in cell membrane surfaces[89] and in the activation of receptors on the surfaces of cells such as lymphocytes.[90]

One of the most exciting uses of electrical stimulation of the immune system has been the revolutionary work of Bjorn Nordenstrom.[91] He developed a theory that the body is a system of biologically-closed electric circuits, amenable to influence of externally-applied electric currents. His technique of inserting electrodes into cancer tumors has established radically superior three-year survival rates for liver and lung cancers when compared to the same rates of conventionally-treated patients as reported in the United States.[92] These techniques are currently being tested with extremely favorable results against breast and lung cancer.

Becker has proposed and tested some very interesting hypotheses about the effects of electrical stimulation and cancer. Of critical importance is early medical research which has documented that cancer tends to grow in parts of the body least innervated by the nervous system.[93] This demonstrates that cancer may be a disease, not of the immune system, but of a body which has lost its electrical communication system. Pathologist Gerald Dermer corroborates this view in describing the post-mortem battlefield from cancer invasion as showing no evidence of immunological counterattack.[94]

The evidence is mounting that cancer is just normal tissue which has dedifferentiated to more primitive, embryonic cells which then commenced on a rampant path of faster growth and metabolism. Unfortunately, the mature environment surrounding the tumor has lost the means of controlling the cancer's growth. Becker experimentally verified that electrical stimulation introduced either externally (through pulsed currents) or internally via the nervous system following amputation and consequent regeneration, induced further dedifferentiation in tumor cells.[93] In one study, 60% remission was observed in mice with fast-growing skin tumors following electrical stimulation whereas all control animals died.

Becker has also been one of the primary discoverers of the resident electrical potentials in the body and the use of electric currents to facilitate bone healing.[93] His research demonstrated that bone was a semiconductor material which utilized electrical energy from light to grow. With non-healing bone fractures, he demonstrated that negative direct currents could be used to stimulate more rapid healing. Becker also found that by reversing the polarity of negative currents, thus making them positive, that he could retard cell growth. This technique became useful when applied to bacterial infections. In fact, aluminum foil, an emitter of positive ions, had been used in medicine to cure bacterial infections before antibiotics were invented. He subsequently documented the use of positive electrical stimulation through silver ions to control runaway malignant fibrosarcoma mitosis.

Electrical stimulation of the immune system has been found to be successful with a number of other different types of application. Direct stimulation of brain structures has been found to cause shifts in immune activity. Stimulation of the hippocampus, for example, has yielded increased phagocytic activity in neutrophils and decreases in the plasma concentrations of the immunosuppressive hormone, corticosterone.[95] This data implicates the potential health benefits of learning and memory consolidation, as these are primary functions of the hippocampus.

Applications of direct currents to peripheral nerves has demonstrated that inflammatory responses mediated by the immune system are subject to nerve innervation throughout the nervous system. When nerves were denervated in mice, IgE inflammatory responses were found to be significantly reduced following exposure to an antibody which the animals were previously sensitized.[96] Hence electrical stimulation of the nerve below the point of denervation restored the immune response.

The application of electrical stimulation has now begun to be utilized with many other diagnostic categories with positive results. Transcutaneous Electrical Nerve Stimulation (TENS) has been shown to modulate pain impulses through the interference provided by the electrical current along larger, faster sensory fibers.[97]

Transcranial Electric Therapy (TET), a variation of TENS applied to the head, has been utilized successfully now with anxious and depressive patients. One study found that clinical success of the treatment of affective disorders with TET was correlated with increased serotonin and norepinephrine levels, and normalized serotonin/beta-endorphin and norepinephrine/cholinesterase ratios.[98] Other studies have demonstrated successful TET treatment of alcoholism and addiction,[99] while one of these studies also demonstrated concurrent increases in blood monoamine and GABA levels following TET treatment.[100]

Pulsed magnetic fields have been found effective in the amelioration of the inflammatory response in rheumatoid arthritis.[101] Even acupuncture appears to work better when electrical currents are applied through the needles.[77]

Homeodynamic Mechanisms

Many of these studies have also begun to show that a common homeodynamic mechanism exists in the application of electrical stimulation. This is not surprising in light of the fact that one of our critical measurements of homeodynamic changes has been electrical brain wave activity. For an overview of research documenting the homeodynamic mechanisms of electric therapies, see Table 3-11.

TABLE 3-11. *HOMEODYNAMIC MECHANISMS OF ELECTRIC THERAPIES*

1st Author	Date	Results
Becker	1985	Sleep was produced in subjects with positive DC currents
Nordenstrom	1983	Body's electric field alternates between positive and negative during natural healing
Krupitsky	1991	Synchronized alpha EEG increased following TET
Saletu	1975	Electro-acupuncture induced more synchronized slow wave EEG activity than acupuncture alone
Kerr	1993	Magnetic fields increased seizure activity in epileptics

Increases of synchronized, slow-wave shifts in brain wave activity have been observed following stimulation by electricity or magnetic fields. Becker's work led to the realization that the positive electric stimulation which had stopped the spread of bacterial infections also elicited anesthesia and sleep in humans and animals.[93] EEG recordings during his experiments revealed the presence of large delta waves following positive D.C. stimulation. This finding corroborates research reported in the Sleep subsection of this chapter showing a relationship between delta sleep and immune enhancement.

Nordenstrom's work demonstrated that tissue injuries were followed by a repair mechanism that consisted of alternations in electric charge back and forth between positive and negative.[91] This evidence suggests that nature's own healing mechanisms operate via shifts in electrical polarity, which Becker has shown are associated with different mental states.[93] All of these techniques then are merely influencing different levels of a grander homeodynamic life-sustaining mechanism.

In TET treatment studies of addiction, synchronized alpha EEG activity was entered more rapidly in treatment subjects than in controls.[100] In acupuncture studies, needling tended to elicit shifts into faster rather than slower EEG activity. However, when electric currents were applied through the needles, increases in alpha emerged.[79] New evidence has been found for the induction of epileptic seizures with weak magnetic fields.[102] Very possibly this may explain the positive effect of magnetic fields on rheumatoid arthritis which were previously discussed. Epileptic activity in general, and as found in schizophrenic patients and through ECT has become associated in the homeodynamic theoretical model with immune enhancement.

Therefore, mechanisms involved with electrical treatments appear to be homeodynamic in that brainwave shifts are generally found to exhibit synchronized activity, usually alpha.

Nutrition and Pharmacotherapy:
The Next Homeodynamic Frontier?

This last behavior/technique is somewhat speculative due to a lack of synthesis between the disciplines of nutrition and psychology, or even nutrition and medicine for that matter. Therefore, this area will be treated somewhat differently than the previous behaviors and presented as a single section to try to create the most integrated case for inclusion as a homeodynamic treatment.

At least two factors seem to camouflage the existence of eating behaviors as homeodynamic treatments. First, substances can be ingested which seemingly may not cause a homeodynamic shift, yet are beneficial to the system. Water may be one of these. If we indeed fit the "wet battery" analogy of Moldofsky's and Becker's, then the rehydration of our bodily fluids and electrolytes through the ingestion of water allows for the neurophysiological experience of the homeodynamic shift. The homeodynamic shift could not exist without the electrophysiological properties conferred by the electrolytes supplied by water. We certainly understand the mental effects of severe dehydration caused by hangovers, jet lag, and acute diarrhea.

Second, there are substances which have been demonstrated to cause definite CNS shifts, yet which cause considerable risk for harm. One might suggest that some abusable or harmful substances don't cause homeodynamic shifts because brain electrical activity may decrease in coherence, or resonance, even though a shift occurs nonetheless. The field of clinical ecology has confirmed that the ingestion of toxic or allergic substances such as lead, pesticides, insecticides, and even sensitive foods often produce both damping of the central nervous system and deficiencies in the immune system.[105-106] Measures of CNS functioning following exposure to these substances have included lower scores on intelligence and neuropsychological tests.[107], which although not accompanied by EEG's in these studies, have in past research demonstrated a strong correlation with diminished electrical brain wave activity.[108] Immunological activity has been characterized by decreased lymphocyte blastogenesis, decreased circulating levels of complement and T-cells (particularly T8 suppressor cells), and lower IgG but higher IgE antibody levels.[109]

In a previously healthy patient of mine with synthetic adjuvant syndrome caused by the leakage of silicone from breast implants, a number of immunological abnormalities developed, including chronic recurrent infections, allergic reactions, inflammatory pain conditions, and slow-healing wounds. Neurological testing confirmed decreased variability in her EEG with increased latencies on evoked-potential tests. Problems with short-term memory and confusion had also developed.

In the following discussion, an overview of potential homeodynamic treatments provided by drugs, nutritional supplements, and homeopathic remedies will be covered. The information is still incomplete on either a verifiable mental or neurophysiological homeodynamic shift. What is known about the homeodynamic mechanisms of each of the individual therapeutic approaches will appear within the descriptions, rather than appearing at the end, as in the previous sections.

Drugs

Certain psychedelic substances have been found to be therapeutic. However, because of the disregard for the profound nature of the potential mystical experience, people sometimes end up taking "bad trips." Some cultural groups utilize psychedelics or other elixirs in spiritual ceremonies, which, when conducted with preparation and respect lead to transformative events.[103] Very likely some of these substances may be homeodynamic and through some dramatic electrochemical, resonant shifts evoke powerful changes. LSD has been tested with some merit as a treatment for alcoholism.[104] Under optimal clinical conditions, with counseling available, insights and increased affective responses of a beneficial therapeutic nature were found to occur.

Other drugs have been demonstrated to yield therapeutic results as well as concomitant homeodynamic shifts. Haloperidol treatment of schizophrenia has been found to increase synchronized brainwave activity, indicating an increase in electrical resonance.[110] Antidepressants have been noted to induce a shift from diffuse beta activity in depressives to increased alpha production. Furthermore, evoked potentials increased in amplitude, demonstrating both a shift in frequency as well as increased resonance.

As an antibiotic, penicillin has infection fighting properties. Yet it has also been found to trigger brainwave frequency shifts and increased amplitudes of evoked potentials.[110] This also suggests homeodynamic mechanisms.

Attention deficit-hyperactivity disorder is a syndrome that has been found to be treated with various stimulants, such as methylphenidate (ritalin). Following drug treatment, EEG topographic frequency shifts have been found from a primary frequency of theta brainwave activity to that of alpha and beta dominance.[111] The increases in synchronous brainwave activity as well as in the evoked potential amplitudes again suggest homeodynamic mechanisms.

Nutrition

Although many diets have been proposed for health maintenance, the "balanced" diet remains the optimal choice among nutritional experts. Although different experts differ as to what it is that is being balanced, the concept infers an even more basic quality of dynamics in which different foods are chosen for one's menu. According to Western nutritional standards, balance is sought between the four main food groups—vegetables, fruits, meats, and carbohydrates. The balance reflects the body's need for different vitamins and neurotransmitters, which each endure a separate dynamic ultradian rhythm. Some nutritional experts have begun to identify at which times of day certain food groups should be eaten to coincide with nature's natural, dynamic neuroendocrine shifts.

For example, depressives have been found to exhibit lower than normal brain levels of serotonin, the neurotransmitter which antidepressants boost. This diagnostic group also has been shown to have more immunosuppression and higher rates of cancer. On the other hand, serotonin administered in chronic doses has an immunosuppressive effect.[112] In terms of its influence upon the central nervous system, serotonin has a sedative effect. Complex carbohydrates initiate their sedating effect through the production of serotonin. On the other hand, norepinephrine exerts a stimulatory effect upon both the central nervous and immune systems on a short-term basis. Long-term activation of this neurotransmitter system, however, as is associated with the fight-or-flight syndrome has a more suppressive effect upon health.

Hence the optimal state for health appears to be one in which there is a shift from one neurotransmitter system to another. This is accomplished nutritionally through shifts from carbohydrates to proteins and back again. Digestion of foods stimulates the production of opiate-like peptides and other hormones which modify CNS activity. These endorphins are, like the other neurotransmitters, both stimulatory in the short run and suppressive in the long run to the immune system and health in general. Therefore a wide range of homeodynamic CNS shifts appear to be activated from the ingestion of different food groups, and are consequently health-producing due to this dynamism.

The evidence for homeodynamic nutritional effects has been demonstrated in a few additional areas. Breast-fed infants have been found to exhibit superior immune resistance to infections. The reasoning could perhaps relate to the increased delta wave sleep which breast-feeding confers to infants.[113] In our own research, this brain wave was found to be especially important to normal immune functioning. Conversely, diets high in fat are perhaps endemically unhealthy due to the reduced EEG frequency and amplitude variability these foods have been found to cause.[114] Finally, deficiencies in iron, thiamin, and riboflavin have been found to reduce alpha wave EEG activity[115], another brain wave which has demonstrated its importance to the immune system.

Other substances such as vitamins and enzymes have been shown to be effective in stimulating immunity. Vitamins C, A, and E have been found to be powerful antioxidants and anticancer agents as well as having a stimulatory effect upon the immune system.[116] Many of these antioxidants are naturally endowed through fruits and vegetables. Although no direct neurophysiological data is available on homeodynamic shifts induced by these foods, many people report a stimulatory effect from them—even from vegetables, which don't contain the sugar found in fruits. It turns out that, due to the reduced bulk of fruits and vegetables, less oxygen is needed by the gut during their digestion,[117] which allows more oxygen to be sent to the brain. This increased oxygenation of the brain produces a stimulatory effect, which is probably evident through brain wave changes or potentials. Therefore the antioxidants very likely accomplish their healing goal through homeodynamic mechanisms.

One particular enzyme, pancreatin, has demonstrated anticancer success without an understanding of the exact mechanism.[118] The release of pancreatic enzymes occurs simultaneously with parasympathetic stimulation of the vagus nerve, and consequent relaxation.[119] In other words, the nutritional addition of pancreatic enzymes may stimulate parasympathetic relaxation with a shift to perhaps larger amplitude, synchronized brain wave activity. This, in turn, may stimulate either enhanced immune activity or better neuronal and cellular communication through homeo-resonance, resulting in reduced potential for tumor activity.

One final area of nutrition which has all the appearance of a homeodynamic mechanism is that of Ayervedic medicine. This herbal/nutritional approach considers not the balance of the four basic food groups, but rather the balance of three energetic qualities, or doshas, to be central to health and longevity.[120] These doshas—Pitta, Vata, and Kapha—are dynamically shifting in importance throughout the day. Disease presents itself when too much of one dosha has predominated, thus throwing the overall balance out of kilter. A nutritional diet is chosen in Ayervedic medicine based upon dynamics guided by our taste buds for six flavor qualities: bitter, sweet, sour, salty, pungent, and astringent. Thus nutritional dynamism is essential to Ayervedic medicine.

Homeopathy

The final area to be discussed under pharmacotherapy techniques is homeopathy. This treatment is completely counterintuitive to allopathic, or modern medicine. Its remedies invoke the same symptom as that which is being attempted to remediate, instead of being oppositional (allopathic) to the symptom. Another difference is that unlike modern allopathic drugs, homeopathic remedies are diluted in water and shaken vigorously until not a single molecule of the substance actually remains in the liquid. The remedy works because the water is potentized and stimulates the body's own defenses into fighting the cause of the symptoms rather than attempting to bring superficial relief.

Evidence of homeopathic treatment has come from double-blind studies demonstrating that hayfever symptoms were relieved through potentized solutions of pollens.[121] Another convincing study indicated that 82% of a group of rheumatoid arthritis patients experienced relief of symptoms while only 21% of those who had been given a placebo exhibited a similar degree of improvement.[122]

Immune mechanisms were affected in a study which underwent extensive replication at several universities. White blood cells called basophils were found to increase in number when exposed to microdoses of a homeopathic antigen.[123]

Evidence for homeodynamic mechanisms being involved in homeopathic treatments is scarce, although one physician has commented upon the ability of certain remedies such as Mugwort to help patients shift into alpha brainwave states.[124] More research is certainly needed in this area to confirm the homeodynamic mechanisms of homeopathy as well as in the drug and nutritional therapies. Nevertheless, the available evidence seems to give inductive proof that no treatment is therapeutic unless it involves homeodynamic mechanisms.

References

1. Moldofsky, H., Scarisbrick, P., Eng,and, R., & Smythe, H. (1975). Musculoskeletal symptoms and non-REM sleep disturbance in patients with "fibrositis syndrome" and healthy subjects. *Psychosomatic Medicine, 37*(4), 341–351.

2. Becker, R.O. (1985). *The body electric.* New York: William Morrow.

3. Moldofsky, H., Lue, F.A., Eisen, J., Keystone, E., & Gorczynski, R.M. (1986). The relationship of interleukin-1 and immune functions to sleep in humans. *Psychosomatic Medicine, 48*(5), 309–318.

4. Palmblad, J., Petrini, B., Wasserman, J., & Akerstedt, T. (1979). Lymphocyte and granulocyte reactions during sleep deprivation. *Psychosomatic Medicine, 41*(4), 273–278.

5. Irwin, M., Smith, T.L., & Gillin, J.C. (1992). Electroencephalographic sleep and natural killer activity in depressed patients and control subjects. *Psychosomatic Medicine, 54,* 10–21.

6. Moldofsky, H., & Lue, F.A. (1980). The relationship of alpha and delta EEG frequencies to pain and mood in "fibrositis" patients treated with chlorpromazine and L-tryptophan. *Electroencephalography and Clinical Neurophysiology, 50,* 71–80.

7. Moldofsky, H., Lue, F.A., & Smythe, H.A. (1983). Alpha EEG sleep and morning symptoms in rheumatoid arthritis. *The Journal of Rheumatology, 10*(3), 373–379.

8. Moldofsky, H., Tullis, C., Lue, F.A., Quance, G., & Davidson, J. (1984). Sleep-related myoclonus in rheumatic pain modulation disorder (fibrositissyndrome) and in excessive daytime somnolence. *Psychosomatic Medicine, 46*(2), 145–151.

9. Saskin, P., Moldofsky, H., & Lue, F.A. (1986). Sleep and posttraumatic rheumatic pain modulation disorder. *Psychosomatic Medicine, 48*(5), 319–323.

10. Moldofsky, H., Saskin, P., & Lue, F.A. (1988). Sleep and symptoms in fibrositis syndrome after a febrile illness. *The Journal of Rheumatology, 15*(11), 1701–1704.

11. Moldofsky, H., & Scarisbrick, P. (1976). Induction of neurasthenic musculoskeletal pain syndrome by selective sleep stage deprivation. *Psychosomatic Medicine, 38*(1), 35–44.

12. Vogel, G., Thurmond, A., Gibbons, D., Sloan, K., Boyd, M., & Walker, M. (1975). Sleep reduction effects on depressive syndromes. *Archives of General Psychiatry, 32,* 765–777.

13. Crick, F., & Mitchison, G. (1983). The function of dream sleep. *Nature, 304*(5922), 111–114.

14. Jenkins, J.G., & Dallenbach, K.M. (1924). Obliviscence during sleep and waking. *American Journal of Psychology, 35,* 605–612.

15. Winson, J. (1990). The meaning of dreams. *Scientific American,* November, 86–96.

16. Drucker-Colin, R.R., & Spanis, C.W. (1976). Is there a sleep transmitter? *Progress in Neurobiology, 6,* 1–22.

17. Jain, S.C., & Talukdar, B. (1993). Evaluation of yoga therapy programme for patients of bronchial asthma. *Singapore Medical Journal, 34*(4), 306–308.

18. Telles, S., Hanumanthaiah, B., Nagarathna, R., & Nagendra, H.R. (1993). Improvement in static motor performance following yogic training of school children. *Perceptual Motor Skills, 76*(3, Part 2), 1264–1266.

19. Joshi, L.N., Joshi, V.D., & Gokhale, L.V. (1992). Effect of short term "Pranayama" practice on breathing rate and ventilatory functions of lung. *Indian Journal of Physiology and Pharmacology, 36*(2), 105–108.

20. Wood, C. (1993). Mood change and perceptions of vitality: A comparison of the effects of relaxation, visualization and yoga. *Journal of Research in Social Medicine, 86*(5), 254–258.

21. Fried, R. (1987). *The hyperventilation syndrome.* Baltimore: The Johns Hopkins University Press.

22. Shields, J.W. (1992). Lymph, lymph glands, and homeostasis. *Lymphology, 25*(4), 147–153.

23. Roitt, I.M., Brostoff, J., & Male, D.K. (1985). *Immunology.* London: Gower Medical Publishing.

24. Monjan, A.A. (1981). Stress and immunologic competence: Studies in animals. In R. Ader (Ed.), *Psychoneuroimmunology.* New York: Academic Press.

25. Satyanarayana, M., Rajeswari, K.R., Rani, N.J., Krishna, C.S., & Rao, P.V. (1992). Effect of santhi kriya on certain psychophysiological parameters: a preliminary study. *Indian Journal of Physiology and Pharmacology, 36*(2), 88–92.

26. Sun, F., Wang, J., Liu, G., Jiao, X., Zhang, Z., Shi, Y., & Zhang, T. (1984). An analysis of EEG power spectrum and coherence during quiet state in Qigong. *Acta Psychologica Sinica, 16*(4), 422–427.

27. Telles, S., Joseph, C., Venkatesh, S., & Desiraju, T. (1993). Alterations of auditory middle latency evoked potentials during yogic consciously regulated breathing and attentive state of mind. *International Journal of Psychophysiology, 14*(3), 189–198.

28. Lorig, T.S., Schwartz, G.E., Herman, K.B., & Lane, R.D. (1988). Brain and odor: II. EEG activity during nose and mouth breathing. *Psychobiology, 16*(3), 285–287.

29. Svebak, S. (1985). Serious-mindedness and the effect of self- induced respiratory changes upon parietal EEG. *Biofeedback and Self-Regulation, 10*(1), 49–61.

30. Shannahoff-Khalsa, D.S. (1989). Rhythms of the mind and breath. *Advances, 6*(2), 51–55.

31. Kleitman, N. (1969). Basic rest-activity cycle in relation to sleep and wakefulness. In A. Kales (Ed.), *Sleep: physiology and pathology.* Philadelphia: Lippincott.

32. Sandvik, L., Erikssen, J., Thaulow, E., Erikssen, G., Mundal, R., & Rodahl, K. (1993). Physical fitness as a predictor of mortality among healthy, middle-aged Norwegian men. *New England Journal of Medicine, 328,* 533–537.

33. LeBow, M.D. (1989). *Adult obesity therapy.* New York: Pergamon Press.

34. Paffenberger, R.S., Hyde, R.T., Wikng, A.L., Lee, I.M., Jung, D.L., & Kampert, J.B. (1993). The association of changes in physical- activity level and other lifestyle characteristics with mortality among men. *New England Journal of Medicine, 328,* 538–545.

35. Blumenthal, J.A., Fredrikson, M., Kuhn, C.M., Ulmer, R.L., Walsh- Riddle, M., & Appelbaum, M.(1990). Aerobic exercise reduces levels of cardiovascular and sympathoadrenal responses to mental stress in subjects without prior evidence of myocardial ischemia. *American Journal of Cardiology, 65,* 93–98.

36. Palmblad, J. (1981). Stress and immunologic competence: Studies in man. In R. Ader (Ed.), *Psychoneuroimmunology.* New York: Academic Press.

37. Brown, J.D., & Siegel, J.M. (1988). Exercise as a buffer of life stress: A prospective study of adolescent health. *Health Psychology, 7,* 341–353.

38. Gray, A.B., Smart, Y.C., Telford, R.D., Weidemann, M.J., & Roberts, T.K. (1992). Anaerobic exercise causes transient changes in leukocyte subsets and IL-2R expression. *Medicine and Science in Sports and Exercise, 24*(12), 1332–1338.

39. McCarthy, D.A., Perry, J.D., Melsom, R.D., & Dale, M.M. (1987). Leukocytosis induced by exercise. *British Medical Journal, 295,* 636.

40. Simpson, J.R., & Hoffman-Goetz, L. (1990). Exercise stress and murine natural killer cell function. *Proceedings of the Society for Experimental Biology and Medicine, 195,* 129–135.

41. MacNeil, B., & Hoffman-Goetz, L. (1993). Chronic exercise enhances in vivo and in vitro cytotoxic mechanisms of natural immunity in mice. *Journal of Applied Physiology, 74*(1), 388–395.

42. Coleman, K.J., & Rager, D.R. (1993). Effects of voluntary exercise on immune function in rats. *Physiology and Behavior, 54*(4), 771–774.

43. Esterling, B.A., Antoni, M.H., Schneiderman, N., Carver, C.S., LaPerriere, A., Ironsan, G., Klimas, N.G., & Fletcher, M.A. (1992). Psychosocial modulation of antibody to Epstein-Barr viral capsid antigen and human herpesvirus type-6 in HIV-1-infected and at-risk gay men. *Psychosomatic Medicine, 54*, 354–371.

44. Fiatarone, M.A., Morley, J.E., Bloom, E.T., Benton, D., Solomon, G.F., & Makinodan, T. (1989). The effect of exercise on natural killer cell activity in young and old subjects. *Journal of Gerontology.*

45. Tvede, N., Kappel, M., Halkjaer-Kristensen, J., Galbo, H., & Pedersen, B.K. (1993). The effect of light, moderate and severe bicycle exercise on lymphocyte subsets, natural and lymphokine activated killer cells,lymphocyte proliferative response and interleukin 2 production. *International Journal of Sports Medicine, 14*(5), 275– 282.

46. Shinkai, S., Shore, S., Shek, P.N., & Shephard, R.J. (1992). Acute exercise and immune function: Relationship between lymphocyte activity and changes in subset counts. *International Journal of Sports Medicine, 13*(6), 452–461.

47. Bernstein, L. et al. (1994). *Journal of the National Cancer Institute,* September

48. Nieman, D.C., Henson, D.A., Gusewitch, G., Warren, B.J., Dotson, R.C., Butterworth, D.E., Nehlsen-Cannarella, S.L. (1993). Physical activity and immune function in elderly women. *Medicine and Science in Sports and Exercise, 25*(7), 823–831.

49. Ortega, E., Barriga, C., De la Fuente, M. (1993). Study of the phagocytic process in neutrophils from elite sportswomen. *European Journal of Applied Physiology, 66*(1), 37–42.

50. Beyer, L., Pickenhain, L., & Schuman, H. (1976). The application of EEG frequency analysis of the varying characteristics of psycho- physical competence. *Zeitschrift fur Psychologie, 184*(4), 562–569.

51. Walsh, B.T., Puig-Antich, J., Goetz, R., Gladis, M., Novacenko, H., & Glassman, A.H.(1984). Sleep and growth hormone secretion in women athletes. *Electroencephalography and Clinical Neurophysiology, 57*(6), 528–531.

52. Torsvall, L., Akerstedt, T., & Lindbeck, G. (1984). Effects on sleep stages and EEG power density of different degrees of exercise in fit subjects. *Electroencephalography and Clinical Neurophysiology, 57*(4), 347–353.

53. Dustman, R.E., Emmerson, R.Y., & Shearer, D.E. (1990). Aerobic fitness may contribute to CNS health: Electrophysiological, visual and neurocognitive evidence. *Journal of Neurologic Rehabilitation, 4*(4), 241–254.

54. Krieger, D. (1992). *The therapeutic touch.* New York: Simon & Schuster.

55. Eeman, L.E. (1987). *Cooperative healing.* Mokelumne Hill, CA: Health Research.

56. Wirth, D.P. (1990). The effect of non-contact therapeutic touch on the healing rate of full thickness dermal wounds. *Subtle Energies, 1*(1), 1–20.

57. Schwartz, S.A., De Mattei, R.J., Brame, E.G., & Spottiswoode, J.P. (1990). Infrared spectra alteration in water proximate to the palms of therapeutic practitioners. *Subtle Energies, 1*(1), 33–49.

58. Isaacs, J., & Patten, T. (1991). A double blind study of the "biocircuit," a putative subtle-energy-based relaxation device. *Subtle Energies, 2*(2), 1–28.

59. Field, T.M., Schanberg, S.M., Scafidi, F., Bauer, C.R., Vega-Lahr, N., Garcia, R., Nystrom, J., & Kuhn, C.M. (1986). Tactile/kinesthetic stimulation effects on preterm neonates. *Pediatrics, 77*(5), 654–658.

60. Lerner, M., & Remen, R.N. (1987). Tradecraft of the Commonweal cancer help program. *Advances, 4*(3), 11–26.

61. McKorkle, R. (1974). Effects of touch on seriously ill patients. *Nursing Research, 23*(2), 125–132.

62. Fahrion, S.L., Wirkus, M., & Pooley, P. (1992). EEG amplitude, brain mapping, & synchrony in & between a bioenergy practitioner & client during healing. *Subtle Energies, 3*(1), 19–52.

63. Brown, C.C. (1977–78). The EEG in meditation and therapeutic touch healing. *Journal of Altered States of Consciousness, 3*(2), 169–180.

64. Green, E.E., Parks, P.A., Guyer, P.M., Fahrion, S.L., & Coyne, L. (1991). Anomolous electrostatic phenomena in exceptional subjects. *Subtle Energies, 2*(3), 69–94.

65. de Vernejoul, P., Albarede, P., & Darras, J.C. (1985). Etude des meridiens d'acupuncture par les traceurs radioactifs. *Bulletin de l'Academie Nationale de Medecine, 169*(7), 1071–1075.

66. Tiller, W.A. (1982). Explanation of electrodermal diagnostic and treatment instruments: Part I. Electrical behavior of human skin. *Journal of Holistic Medicine, 4*(2), 105–127.

67. Liu, X., Sun, L., Xiao, J., Yin, S., Liu, C., Li, Q., Li, H., & Jin, B. (1993). Effect of acupuncturologic function in rheumatoid arthritis. *Journal of Traditional Chinese Medicine, 13*(3), 174–178.

68. Xiao, J., Liu, X., Sun, L., Ying, S., Zhang, Z., Li, Q., Li, H., Zhang, Z., Jin, B., & Wang, S. (1992). [Experimental study on the influence of acupuncture and moxibustion on interleukin-2 in patients with rheumatoid arthritis]. *Chen Tzu Yen Chiu, 17*(2), 126–128, 132.

69. Still, J., & Konrad, J. (1985). [The effect of acupuncture on hematologic and biochemical values in dogs with endoparasitic infections]. *Veteranarni Medicina (Praha), 30*(11), 687–698.

70. Zhu Jialong. (1980). Effects of acupuncture on plasma angiotensis II in the dog. First National Congress of Acupuncture and Moxibustion (1979). *Beijing: people's acupuncture.* Medical Publishing House.

71. Millstein, R.A. (1994). Acupuncture research sponsored by the National Institute on Drug Abuse (NIDA), NIH. *Alternative Medicine, 1*(3), 3.

72. Lin, Y., Zhou, Z., Shen, W., Shen, J., Hu, M., Zhang, F., Hu, P., Xu, M., Huang, S., & Zheng, Y. (1993). Clinical and experimental studies on shallow needling technique for treating childhood diarrhea. *Journal of Traditional Chinese Medicine, 13*(2), 107–114.

73. de Aloysio, D., & Penacchioni, P. (1992). Morning sickness control in early pregnancy by Neiguan point acupressure. *Obstetrics and Gynecology, 80*(5), 852–854.

74. Gieron, C., Wieland, B., von der Laage, D., & Tolksdorf, W. (1993). [Acupressure in the prevention of postoperative nausea and vomiting]. *Anaesthesist (Berlin), 42*(4), 221–226.

75. Kuzmina, E.G., & Degtiareva, A.A. (1987). [Restoration of immunologic indices following reflexotherapy in the combination treatment of radiation-induced edema of the upper limbs]. *Meditsinskaia Radiologiia (Moskva), 32*(7), 42–46.

76. Yuan, D., Fu, Z., & Li, S. (1992). [Effect of He-Ne laser acupuncture on lymph nodes in rats]. *Chen Tzu Yen Chiu, 17*(1), 54–58.

77. Shi-Jing, L., Hui-Ju, S., Guo, W., & Maranto, C.D. (1991). Music and medicine in China: The effects of music electro-acupuncture on cerebral hemiplegia. In C.D. Maranto (Ed.), *Applications of music in medicine,* 191–199. Washington, D.C.: The National Association for Music Therapy.

78. Glavinskaia, T.A., Rezaikina, A.V., & Smirnova, A.V. (1989). [The immune status of scleroderma patients undergoing electro- acupuncture].*Vestnik Dermatologii i Venerologii (Moskva), 4,* 44–47.

79. Saletu, B., Saletu, M., Brown, M., Stern, J., Sletten, I., & Ulett, G. (1975). Hypnoanalgesia and acupuncture analgesia: A neurophysiological reality. *Neuropsychobiology, 1,* 218–242.

80. Kochetkov, V.D., Mikhailova, A.A., & Dallakyan, I.G. (1983). Acupuncture of neurotic patients with depressive-hypochondriac manifestations. *Zhurnal Nevropatologii Psikhiatrii imeni S.S. Korsakova, 83*(12), 1853–1855.

81. Koekina, O.I., Gaidamakina, A.M., & Volkova, R.P. (1988). Possible correction of EEG interhemispheric asymmetry by reflex therapy of depressions with pain syndromes. *Zhurnal Nevropatologii i Psikhiatrii imeni S.S. Korsakova, 88*(10), 102–107.

82. Small, I.F., Milstein, V., Miller, M.J., Malloy, F.W., & Small, J.G. Electroconvulsive treatment—indications, benefits, and limitations. *American Journal of Psychotherapy, 40*(3), 343–355.

83. Schaerf, F.W., Miller, R.R., Lipsey, J.R., & McPherson, R.W. (1989). ECT for major depression in four patients infected with human immunodeficiency virus. *American Journal of Psychiatry, 146*(6), 782–784.

84. Heiberg, E. (1993). Biologically closed electric circuits and electrochemical treatment of cancer. *Bridges, 4*(4), 5–6.

85. Everson, T.C., & Cole, W.H. (1966). *The spontaneous regression of cancer.* Philadelphia: Saunders.

86. Fischler, B., Bocken, R., Schneider, I., de Waele, M., Thielemans, & Derde, M.P. (1992). Immune changes induced by electroconvulsive therapy (ECT). *Annals of the New York Academy of Sciences, 650*, 326–330.

87. Albrecht, J., Helderman, J.H., Schlesser, M.A., & Rush, A.J. (1985). A controlled study of cellular immune function in affective disorders before and during somatic therapy. *Psychiatry Research, 15*, 185–193.

88. Wood, P.G., Karol, M.H., Kusnecov, A.W., & Rabin, B.S. (1993). Enhancement of antigen-specific humoral and cell-mediated immunity by electric footshock stress in rats. *Brain, Behavior and Immunity, 7*(2), 121–134.

89. Lee, K.Y.C., Klingler, J.F., & McConnell, H.M. (1994). Electric field-induced concentration gradients in lipid monolayers. *Science, 263*(5147), 655–657.

90. Pert, C.B. (1986). The wisdom of the receptors. *Advances, 3*(3), 8–16.

91. Nordenstrom, B.E.W. (1983). *Biologically closed electric circuits.* Stockholm: Nordic Medical Publications.

92. Heiberg, E. (1993). Biologically closed electric circuits and electrochemical treatment of cancer. *Bridges, 4*(4), 5–6.

93. Becker, R.O. (1985). *The body electric.* New York: William Morrow.

94. Dermer, G.B. (1994). *The immortal cell.* Garden City Park, NY: Avery Publishing Group.

95. Devi, R.S., Namasivayam, A., & Prabhakaran, K. (1993). Modulation of nonspecific immunity by hippocampal stimulation. *Journal of Neuroimmunology, 42*(2), 193–197.

96. Ratzlaff, R.E., Cavanaugh, V.J., Miller, G.W., & Oakes, S.G. Evidence of a neurogenic component during IgE-mediated inflammation in mouse skin. *Journal of Neuroimmunology, 41*(1), 89–96.

97. Solomon, S., & Guglielmo, K.M. (1985). Treatment of headache by transcutaneous electrical stimulation. *Headache, 25*, 12–15.

98. Shealy, C.N., Cady, R.K., Wilkie, R.G., Cox, R., Liss, S., & Clossen, W. Depression: A diagnostic, neurochemical profile and therapy with cranial electrical stimulation (CES). *Paper presented at the Southern Medical Association*, November, 1988.

99. Patterson, M., Flood, N.V., & Patterson, L. (1992). Neuroelectric therapy(NET) in addiction detoxification. *Subtle Energies, 3*(3), 1–24.

100. Krupitsky, E.M., Burakov, A.M., Karandashova, G.F., Katsnelson, Ja. S., Lebedev, V.P., Grinenko, A.Ja., & Borodkin, Ju.S. (1991). The administration of transcranial electric treatment for affective disturbances therapy in alcoholic patients. *Drug and Alcohol Dependence, 27*, 1–6.

101. Subrahmanyam, S., & Sanker Narayan, P.V. (1993). Pulsed magnetic field therapy. *Bridges, 4*(4), 11–13.

102. Kerr, R.A. (1993). Magnetism triggers a brain response. *Science, 260* (June 11), 1590.

103. Campbell, J. (1988). *The power of myth.* New York: Doubleday.

104. Gaston, E.T., & Eagle, C.T. (1970). The function of music in LSD therapy for alcoholic patients. *Journal of Music Therapy, 7*(1), 3–19.

105. O'banion, D.R. (1981). *An ecological and nutritional approach to behavioral medicine.* Springfield, IL: Charles C. Thomas.

106. Bell, I.R. (1982). *Clinical ecology.* Bolinas, CA: Common Knowledge Press.

107. Rea, W.J., Butler, J.R., Laseter, J.L., & DeLeon, I.R. (1984). Pesticides and brain-function changes in a controlled environment. *Clinical Ecology, 2*(3), 145–150.

108. Staudenmayer, H., & Selner, J.C. (1990). Neuropsychophysiology during relaxation in generalized, universal "allergic" reactivity to the environment: A comparison study. *Journal of Psychosomatic Research, 34*(3), 259–270.

109. Rea, W.J., Johnson, A.R., Youdim, S., Fenyves, E.J., & Samadi, N. (1986). T- and B-lymphocyte parameters measured in chemically sensitive patients and controls. *Clinical Ecology, 4*(1), 11–14.

110. Maurer, K, & Dierks, T. (1991). *Atlas of brain mapping.* Berlin: Springer-Verlag.

111. Klorman, R., Salzman, L.F., Pass, H.L., Borgstedt, A.D., & Dainer, K. B. (1979). Effects of methylphenidate on hyperactive children's evoked responses during passive and active attention. *Psychophysiology, 16*, 23–29.

112. Hall, N.R., & Goldstein, A.L. (1981). Neurotransmitters and the immune system. In R. Ader (Ed.), *Psychoneuroimmunology.* New York: Academic Press.

113. Butte, N.F., Jensen, C.L., Moon, J.K., Glaze, D.G., & Frost, J.D. (1992). Sleep organization and energy expenditure of breast-fed and formula-fed infants. *Pediatric Research, 32*(5), 514–519.

114. Miles, J.M., Cattalini, M., Sharbrough, F.W., Wold, L.E., Wharen, R.E., Gerich, J.E., & Haymond, M.W. (1991). Metabolic and neurologic effects of an intravenous medium-chain triglyceride emulsion. *Journal of Parenteral and Enteral Nutrition, 15*(1), 37–41.

115. Tucker, D.M., Penland, J.G., Sandstead, H.H., Milne, D.B., Heck, D.G., & Klevay, L.M. (1990). Nutrition status and brain function in aging. *American Journal of Clinical Nutrition, 52*(1), 93–102.

116. Sharma, H. (1993). *Freedom from disease.* Toronto: Veda Publishing.

117. Institute for Natural Resources (1994). *Mood, mind, and appetite.* Workshop conducted in Dallas, TX, October 6.

118. Gonzalez, N.J. (1994). "Best cases" of an anzyme-based cancer therapy. *Alternative Medicine, 1*(6), 3.

119. Guyton, A.C. (1981). *Textbook of medical physiology.* Philadelphia: W.B. Saunders.

120. Chopra, D. (1991). *Perfect health.* New York: Harmony Books.

121. Reilly, D.T., Taylor, M.A., McSharry, C., & Aitchison, T. (1986). Is homeopathy a placebo response? Controlled trial of homeopathic potency with pollen in hayfever as model. *Lancet, October 18*, 881– 886.

122. Gibson, R.G., Gibson, S.L.M., & MacNeil, A.D. (1980). Homeopathic therapy in rheumatoid arthritis: Evaluation by double-blind clinicaltherapeutic trial. *British Journal of Clinical Pharmacology, 9*, 453– 459.

123. Davenas, E., Beauvais, F., Amara, J., Oberbaum, M., Robinzon, B., Miadonna, A., Tedeschi, A., Pomeranz, B., Fortner, P., & Belon, P. (1988). Nature, 333(6176):816–818.

124. Gerber, R. (1988). *Vibrational medicine.* Santa Fe, NM: Bear & Co.

CHAPTER FOUR

Health Benefits of Emotion Shifting

Psychotherapy, Catharsis and Emotional Expression

We saw in the last chapter that physical health and the healing potential were increased following the implementation of physical behaviors which served to increase the variability of central nervous system activity. These shifts in CNS activity provide for both a resonant electrical system able to communicate integrity to all parts of the body, and to provide a balanced supply of neurotransmitters and immunomodulators enabling optimum health. This chapter deals with the notion that techniques which stimulate a dynamic balance of all emotions will also promote healing processes.

Depression and chronic stress are two such disorders which are characterized by imbalances of emotionality, neurotransmitters and electrical brain wave activity. These disorders are also associated with more health problems. The research on stress has been somewhat confirmatory in its conclusions that it produces a reduced immunological response. Stressors such as marital disruption through death or divorce[1], bereavement[2], marital discord[3], caregiving[4], and test-taking[5] have each been found to induce significant depression of the immune system. Furthermore, the immune system doesn't seem to be selective; the stress induced by major life changes increases the probability of contracting everything from the common cold to cancer. Although life changes can be both negative or positive, those who experience more "bad" stress have been found to exhibit significantly less lymphocyte proliferation in response to a novel antigen than those experiencing "good" stress.[6]

In my clinical work I have discovered that there are really four basic feeling states, which occur in the following order, accompanying any major life change or loss: bad (fear), mad, sad, and glad. I utilize the rhyming scheme to assist patients' memory of them. "Bad" is used for "fear" because that emotion often has the somatic qualities of physical illness, as stated in the phrase, "I feel bad." Everyone has a different rhythm for proceeding through this progression of feelings. To block this dynamic flow, however, creates stress.

Emotional Repression

While the experiencing of negative emotions appears to be unhealthy, the consequences of repressing these emotions as opposed to expressing them can be disastrous. One study measured psychological attributes of women entering a hospital for breast lumps, but before knowledge of the pathology results.[7] They found that one factor distinguished the women who were subsequently diagnosed with malignant breast cancer—either extreme suppression or expression of anger. Another study demonstrated, this time in normal subjects, that again both extreme repressors or expressers of anger manifested significantly lower T-cell and delayed hypersensitivity skin testing.[8]

Other studies of cancer patients in contrast to other patients have confirmed that one of the primary personality features is repressive coping. For example, cancer patients have been found to exhibit less Type A behavior and aggression than benign controls.[9] In fact, researchers have coined the term Type C in referring to the repressive coping style of cancer patients as compared to that of cardiovascular patients.[10] Cancer patients have been discovered to verbally deny their emotional reactions to provocative slides, although physiological measurements indicated otherwise.[11]

Emotional Expression and Health

The picture that is emerging from this research is that no one emotion is desirable all the time. Otherwise, the other feelings become repressed. Therefore, a homeodynamic mechanism appears to be the healthiest. One reason for this may lie in the findings that positive emotions are processed more in the left cerebral hemisphere, whereas negative emotions reside more in the right side of the brain. The ultradian rhythms discussed earlier in which normal hemispheric shifts were found to occur every 90 minutes may play a role in helping us understand the adaptive necessity for emotional shifting. Several groups of researchers have documented the health benefits of emotional expression in a variety of ways. For an overview of research on the health benefits of emotion shifting, see Table 4-1.

TABLE 4-1.   *EMOTIONAL EXPRESSION AND PHYSICAL HEALTH*

1st Author	Date	Results
Knapp	1992	Reliving negative memories decreased lymphocyte blastogenesis more than positive memories
Cousins	1979	Personal account of a recovery from catastrophic illness using positive emotions and humor.
Berk	1989	Humor video was found to reduce stress hormones and increase lymphocyte proliferation in normal subjects
Dillon	1985–86	Humor video increased sIgA antibody production

(continued)

TABLE 4-1. *EMOTIONAL EXPRESSION AND PHYSICAL HEALTH (continuation)*

1st Author	Date	Results
Martin	1988	Hassles were negatively correlated with sIgA production, although less so in those using humor as a coping skill
Melnuchuk	1988	Positive emotions were associated with improved wound healing
Weinstock	1977	Review of case studies of cancer remission in which over 50% were due to psychotherapy or emotional catharsis
Ikemi	1975	Review of case studies of cancer remission in which all were preceded by cathartic expression of emotion and an altered outlook on life
Frey	1985	Emotional tears found to be qualitatively different from irritant tears; stress hormones were released in tears
Pennebaker	1988	Students who wrote about traumas had increased lymphocyte blastogenesis and decreased health center visits
Spiegel	1989	Group psychotherapy doubled survival time in breast cancer patients over controls
LeShan	1989	Psychotherapy was associated with increasing long-term remission in cancer patients from 0 to 50%
Rider	1987	Psychotherapy and imagery were more effective in decreasing pain and increasing disease management than imagery alone in rheumatoid arthritis and lupus patients
Groassarth	1984	Psychotherapy increased longevity of metastatic breast cancer patients
Solomon	1987	Increased survival of AIDS patients was related to positive attitudes and emotional resilience
Clynes	1977	General health and mood was increased in subjects practicing daily sentics cycles
Spingte	1988	ACTH and beta-endorphin levels decreased in subjects practicing sentics cycles

Short-term effects of negative emotions are a temporary suppression of the immune system. When married couples have been asked to discuss marital problems for brief time intervals, those whose interactions were marked by hostility experienced greater reductions in immune functioning in the following ways: decreased natural killer cell function, low blastogenic response to antigens, low proliferative response to a monoclonal antibody to the T3 receptor, larger increases in total and helper T lymphocytes, and higher Epstein-Barr virus titers.[12]

Healthy subjects have also been found to sustain more dramatic decreases in immune functioning when recalling and reliving negative as opposed to positive emotional experiences.[13] Both positive and negative memories stimulated decreases in blastogenesis to the antigens ConA and PHA, although moreso with negative recollections. Immune functioning was found to fully recover within an hour of the emotional recollections.

Even though positive emotions exerted a temporary suppression of immune system activity in the above study, other studies demonstrate that positive attitudes enhance health. One of the most effective short-term methods of producing positive emotions is through laughter. Norman Cousins outlined the uses he made of humor in recovering from a catastrophic illness in his book Anatomy of an Illness.[14] Since then, other reports have been published documenting the health benefits of laughter.

In a series of studies conducted at Loma Linda University Medical Center, viewing a one-hour video of the comedian Gallagher was found to lower the stress hormones cortisol and epinephrine in normal subjects.[15] Furthermore, the laughter boosted immune measures including increased lymphocyte proliferation and natural killer cell activity. Laughter generated from watching a humorous video has also been demonstrated to increase salivary IgA antibody production.[16] Those who used humor as a coping skill had the highest initial antibody secretion rates and changed the least following the video, suggesting both a preventive stress- buffering role for humor as well as a ceiling effect for the degree of immune enhancement. The stress-buffering role of humor has been subsequently confirmed through findings that subjects scoring low on a sense of humor scale revealed a stronger negative relationship between perceived "daily hassles" and antibody production than those with high humor scores.[17]

The role of natural opioids has been speculated upon in their role between positive emotions and health. Opioids produced through positive emotions such as laughter have been found to increase the rate of wound healing.[18] However, opioids have been found to exert both positive and negative effects on both immune activity and cancer growth.[19-20] The point may be that there is no linear, causal relationship between one single emotion, such as humor, and health. At times, laughter may be curative. But, at other times, if overused as a defense mechanism, laughter may cause psychogenic stress and immunosuppression. Therefore, a wide variety of emotions may provide the best balance for the optimum dose of chemicals associated with health.

The maintenance of positive attitudes through a chronic illness also seems to offer a certain amount of protection. However, this feat involves not so much a repression of negative emotions, which one undoubtedly feels through the course of catastrophic illness, but instead a successful grieving through the stages of loss that accompany any significant life change. This involves the feelings of denial, fear, anger, sadness, and finally acceptance. It is at the stage of acceptance that a person doesn't necessarily succumb to their illness, but rather learn what there is to learn from having a disease.

One of the most successful techniques to facilitate the normal movement of emotions in the grieving process is catharsis. This procedure has been researched in a variety of settings from psychotherapy to religious conversion. Case studies have been documented of a variety of spontaneous cancer remissions following intense emotional awakenings or transformations.[21-23]

Larry LeShan has written a major testimonial on the importance of psychotherapy and emotional expression to both long-term remission and/or increased longevity of cancer patients.[24] LeShan incorporated into his psychotherapy approach with cancer patients the additional components of physical and spiritual growth. He discovered that patients who used cancer as a turning point to make new discoveries about their lives and, to find meanings in their daily existence which spawned hope rather than despair, enabled half of his "terminal" patients to go into long-term remission. Although the physical and spiritual components of LeShan's approach are considered in other chapters in this book, of relevance to the present chapter is the emotional shift through catharsis and grieving which was required for his patients to remove the blocks to finding meaning and hope in their lives.

In one of the landmark studies of the effects of group psychotherapy on chronic disease, psychologist David Spiegel has demonstrated a doubling in the survival time of advanced breast cancer patients participating in the 16-week program.[25] While this form of support group will be covered in more detail in Chapter 6, one of the key components of Spiegel's approach involved the expression of emotions.

Psychotherapy in addition to standard medical treatment has been documented to increase longevity in metastatic breast cancer patients.[26] Even without psychotherapy, the maintenance of positive attitudes and adaptive coping through emotional resilience has been shown to be associated with longer life expectancy in AIDS patients.[27]

Researchers know now that emotional tears are qualitatively different from tears produced by irritants such as onions.[28] Furthermore, individuals with stress disorders tend to view crying more as a sign of weakness than healthy persons. The fact that stress hormones are present in tears suggests that crying reduces stress. Partial evidence for this comes from the findings that women cry five times more than men; furthermore they live about seven years longer than men. This suggests that emotional shifts extending through the full range from positive to negative may be the healthiest state of affairs for human beings.

One of the pivotal points behind psychotherapeutic release is a reduction in inhibition. Having studied the art of lie detection and determining that a significant amount of autonomic relaxation occurred following confession by criminals, psychologist James Pennebaker began to study the effect of writing about previously unreported traumas on clinical health and the immune system.[29] His research has documented that students who engaged in this technique for only five days experienced greater lymphocyte blastogenesis and less visits to the campus health center.[30] When applied to a group of laid-off white-collar workers, this self-disclosure technique led to significantly higher rates of reemployment than in the control groups.[31]

Emotional catharsis has been found to assist in removing impediments to effective mental imagery of one's active immune system and subsequent health. In a study of the effects of imagery alone and psychotherapy- mediated imagery on the disease management of rheumatoid arthritis and lupus patients, the psychotherapy group was found to exhibit superior control over their disease and pain.[32] Important imagery shifts were found to occur following emotional catharsis of repressed events. In this way, emotions served as a dynamic obstacle-remover to free the way to a normal functioning of the body. Emotional catharsis is somewhat akin to what I call an "Emoto-rooter."

Some evidence exists for the accrual of health benefits from a non-psychotherapeutic technique employing emotion-shifting. Researcher Manfred Clynes developed a technique for recording emotional "signatures" using a simple mechanical transducer activated by vertical and horizontal finger pressure.[33] He found that when subjects reenacted different emotions motorically through finger pressure, that each emotion had a specific wave form. Furthermore, these "sentic" signatures were consistent across cultures.

What was discovered serendipitously by Clynes was that when he had subjects practice a daily ritual of reenacting each of the emotional qualities through the finger movements, that their mood and general health seemed to improve. No placebo was involved because Clynes had no idea that this regimen would produce such benefits. However, a follow-up study demonstrated that ACTH and beta-endorphin levels decreased significantly following training in reproducing the sentic cylces.[34] It is as if the emotion centers, such as the limbic system, need to be exercised for optimal functioning just as other parts of our bodies need physical activity.

Homeodynamics of Emotional Expression

The postulated mechanisms for the health benefits of psychotherapy have included a purging of stressful hormones, such as cortisol and norepinephrine. Furthermore, expressing a dynamic range of feelings appears to confer the greatest health benefits. Therefore, emotional expression appears to have important criteria for consideration as a homeodynamic phenomenon. For an overview of research demonstrating that emotion shifting operates through homeodynamic mechanisms, see Table 4-2.

TABLE 4-2.   *HOMEODYNAMIC MECHANISMS OF EMOTION SHIFTING*

1st Author	Date	Results
Redington	1992	Psychotherapy was associated with a higher heartrate variability
Singer	1988	Sudden cardiac arrest was associated with low heartrate variability
Ori	1992	Diabetes was associated with low heart rate variability
Lovallo	1990	Lowered hormonal response was associated with low heart rate variability

(continued)

TABLE 4-2. *HOMEODYNAMIC MECHANISMS OF EMOTION SHIFTING*
(continuation)

1st Author	Date	Results
Temoshok	1991	Higher heart rate reactivity was associated with long-term survival rates in AIDS patients
McCraty	in press	The emotional state of sincere appreciation was associated with high variability and harmonic organization of heart rate
Morishige	1975	Initial emotional recall was associated with high frequency, desynchronized brainwave activity
Clynes	1977	Emotion shifting led to wide variations in base DC EEG, from synchronous 12 cpm activity to short burts
Sobotka	1992	Positive emotions activated the left hemisphere whereas negative feelings induced a shift to the right hemisphere
Karle	1980	Sleep EEG following short-term therapy produced shorter REM latencies and K-complexes
Hoffman	1983	Long-term primal therapy produced alpha EEG shifts from left to right hemisphere
Karle	1973	Three weeks of primal therapy produced EEG shifts from beta to more synchronized alpha activity
Buysse	1992	Psychotherapy produced increased delta wave sleep

Strong evidence exists for the alteration of physiological processes following the appropriate expression of repressed feelings as through psychotherapy. Recently, one set of homeodynamic shifts were reported to occur in the autonomic nervous system during psychotherapy. At those moments when psychotherapy patients were most congruent between their emotional and mental states (being genuine instead of defensive), the widest range of complexity and variation was occurring in their heart rates.[35] Much simpler changes in heart rate behavior took place when patients were less candid about their feelings or were engaged in less insight-oriented moments of their psychotherapy session. Low heart rate variability has been associated with a variety of medical conditions including sudden cardiac arrest[36], diabetes[37], and lowered hormonal response[38]

In another study of this type, heart rate variability was measured during different mental and emotional states.[39] The states of "sincere appreciation" and "frustration" exhibited the greatest heart rate variability. However, only sincere appreciation demonstrated a harmonic organization (with heart rate rhythm spectral peaks occurring at roughly 3.5, 7.7, and 15 bpm). In other words, the dynamic and harmonic activity of this mental state qualified it as a truly homeodynamic behavior. This state is also only reached in psychotherapy after having resolved other feelings in the grief process.

Something spectacular showed up in the data of a study of AIDS patients which also supports the homeodynamic role of emotions and the nervous system. Distress turned out to be effective in the early stages of the disease in boosting immune functioning.[40] In the later stages of the disease, however, a different set of phenomena became predictive of longer-term survival. A higher heart rate reactivity and a more balanced expression of a wider range of emotions were found to be the best predictors of survivability. Heart rate reactivity is defined as a wider variation of heart rate activity from baseline to arousal. Just as Pennebaker and others have documented with autonomic activity, I have also detected highly elevated heart rates in patients inhibiting intense emotions, only to be followed by significant decreases once the feelings were expressed. It is as if this balance of inhibition and emotional expression were exercising the nervous system activity.

Futher evidence that psychotherapeutic catharsis involve homeodynamic mechanisms is found in studies of central nervous system activity. These studies can be grouped into two phases of EEG shifts depending on the duration and intensity of therapy.

The first phase of nervous system activity relates to changes while the emotional experience is being recalled. During therapeutic reactivation of emotional dream content, experimenters have found initial EEG shifts of desynchronized beta activity, characteristic of anxiety or arousal.[41] The elicitation of anger in subjects has been observed to induce dramatic shifts in the base DC level of the EEG.[33] These electrical bursts however differed considerably from the synchronous, ultra-slow waxing and waning of the EEG (approximately 12 cycles-per- minute) discovered when these same subjects reproduced the emotion of "love." This same rhythm has also been detected from individuals who are in a process of shifting from the waking state to the hypnotic state, a state that we will see in the next chapter produces homeodynamic brainwave shifts.[42]

Brain laterality studies have indicated that positive emotions are processed more efficiently with the left cerebral hemisphere (in right handed subjects), whereas negative feelings are done so with the right.[43] The adaptive nature of this hemispheric specificity regarding emotional behavior is that the expression of different feelings allows for a dynamic shifting between the two halves of the brain. The ultradian 90-minute rhythm alternating from one hemisphere to the other is another biological example of this dynamic mechanism serving to maintain a wide range of adaptability, reduce overuse of certain neural circuits, and to constantly recharge the electrochemically polarized cellular environment within the body.

Sleep studies conducted after one or two therapy sessions are still consistent with this first phase. There appear to be changes in which the emotional content which has been repressed becomes activated during sleep. In the EEG, shifts following therapy first seem to be characterized by decreases in REM latency and the presence of K-complexes.[44-45] REM activity represents the processing of emotional content through dreams. The K-complexes are large voltage EEG shifts occurring during stage II sleep and signify additional cognitive arousal and activation.

The second phase represents a different set of EEG shifts which occur after more intense or more prolonged therapy. For example, one investigation discovered that 18 months of primal, abreactive psychotherapy yielded significant shifts in alpha activity from the left to the right hemisphere.[46] This meant that patients were more dominant in the left hemisphere after psychotherapy (all patients were right-handed). Since positive emotions are processed primarily in the left hemisphere, and vice versa with negative emotions, this study can be interpreted as a confirmation that psychotherapy produces healthy benefits through homeodynamic shifts in the nervous system.

Even three weeks of primal psychotherapy has been found to induce significant shifts in the overall frequency of the EEG.[47] Specific changes were noted from beta to alpha, with concommitant synchronization of the brain waves. In other words, catharsis produced a homeodynamic change in central nervous system activity.

Some studies have demonstrated that psychotherapy produces significantly increased delta wave sleep.[48-49] Delta wave sleep, or slow wave sleep, was shown to be correlated with longevity of wellness from depression. This finding is in agreement with the decreased delta activity found by us and other researchers in patients with chronic disease.

One study demonstrated that psychotherapy was equally effective when compared to biofeedback or autogenics in increasing sleep quality in chronic sleep insomniacs.[50] Although no EEG measures were assessed, sleep quality is often enhanced when delta sleep increases. Probable demonstration of neuropharmacological changes is further demonstrated by the fact that less insomnia medication was required by these patients following psychotherapy.

Intense emotion-based psychotherapy has also been found to significantly elevate remission rates in alcoholics.[51] The mechanism in this treatment appears to have been homeodynamic, as significant abatement of electrophysiological syndromes (as denoted in the EEG) occurred following psychotherapy.

Music

As we saw in Chapter 3, some of the homeodynamic techniques are behaviors which are also necessary for life, such as sleep, breathing, nutrition, and to an extent, exercise. Outside of these, probably no behavior comes close to the power and diversity of music in eliciting homeodynamic shifts. As compared to the other sensory modalities, hearing is the one behavior that the least amount of habituation and adaptation occurs by an organism.[52] In other words, no matter how often they are repeated, sounds create more profound psychophysiological shifts than most other stimuli.

It is a little unfair to sequester music into the chapter on the health benefits of emotion shifts when music acts in a powerful way on each of the other levels as well. For example, music is equally adept at stimulating physical responses as demonstrated through its prolific use with such activities as dance and aerobics. This so-called "thalamic" response has been felt by every human being as the uncontrollable desire to tap some part of his or her body when music suddenly becomes audible. Anthropologists have suggested that one of the possible origins of music is that it arose simultaneously with dance and rituals in primitive cultures.

Music also evokes an overwhelming aesthetic response, which involves higher cognitive functions. As such, music can symbolically represent scenes from nature and ideas. It can make complex puzzles out of a primal rhythm and it can beautify mathematics. Plausible origins of music in this mental domain involve the leisure time activity of imitating sounds in nature as well as the use of rhythms to communicate over large distances.

Music can also connect humans with their spiritual sides. Plato called music the "food of the soul." No culture has ever been discovered which has not used music somewhere in its religious rites and ceremonies, hence accounting for yet another potential origin of music.

And for all its diversity of uses, the emotional function may be the strongest. As the quote which has survived for hundreds of years goes, "music hath charms to soothe the savage breast."[53] Perhaps because only one other homeodynamic technique, psychotherapy, falls under the umbrella of emotion-based therapies, should music and the other arts be included in this section as well. Although each of the arts meets the homeodynamic criteria of facilitating physical healing through the induction of central nervous system shifts and resonance, music seems to have a much wider research base. This is perhaps due to the ease with which music can be integrated into the medical milieu despite conditions of pain, anesthesia, paralysis, etc. Art, drama, and dance therapy have been shown to have profound beneficial effects upon many psychiatric conditions. Furthermore, none of the arts is probably given its due recognition for curative powers other than to distract and relax during times of extreme stress, and since music is so readily available and demanding (as one cannot shut it out except to turn it off), people become affected by its many levels of influence by simply turning it on. Consequently, even though the only therapeutic art reported on here is music, this is by no means a rejection of the potential uses of the other arts in healing.

As regards the emotional impact of music, however, none touch the emotions like music. I am a great lover of each of the arts. Yet, I never cried in a museum until I saw Michelle Zacheim's Tent of Meeting[54], a multisensory dedication to the great religions of the world, which included a sound track by David Hykes' Harmonic Choir.[55] I have been deeply moved by the theater and ballet, although the tears fall far more frequently at the movies, where a sound track is playing. Even aside from personal anecdotes, studies have demonstrated that when music was paired with paintings of contrasting mood, the mood change was always in the direction of the music, not the painting.[56] In a survey of the greatest thrill-causing behaviors, music was the highest of all, including the other art forms and even sex.[57]

Music and Health

Twenty years ago, the Chicago Sun Times reported on a study of the life span of musicians.[58] According to the article, a physician named Dr. Donald Atlas at the University of California at San Diego determined that symphony orchestra conductors had an average life span which was five years longer than that of the average American male. In fact, not one of the conductors died before the age of 58. Atlas went on to describe the two largest factors of longevity as being job satisfaction and overall happiness.

Why should this occupational group be so content with their job and happy about life in general? One clue to this puzzle comes from the repertoire which conductors are exposed—classical music. I have no preference of my own for this type of music over any other genre. However, this finding may be particularly germane to an initial understanding of the homeodynamic mechanisms involved in musical behaviors. First, evidence presented in the section on emotion shifting demonstrated that one of the hallmarks of classical music—rhythmical inconsistency—has been found to yield a more intense expression of emotions than a regular beat, the latter of which serves more to vent or purge the feeling before it is completely sensed.[33] Classical music can in this regard be like a roller coaster as it waxes and wanes, builds, falls, races, stops, and then breathes before it continues on. Secondly, classical music has become the music of choice in Helen Bonny's Guided Imagery through Music (GIM) approach to the evocation of emotional imagery.[59] Again, other more rhythmic types of music were found to hinder the appropriate therapeutic buildup of emotions leading to catharsis and insight.

The curative values of music have been recognized more and more through the advent of the discipline of music therapy. An impressive body of literature has been written on the value of music to evoke positive responses in particularly-hard-to-reach individuals, such as terminally ill, developmentally disabled, and chronic psychiatric clients.[60-63] When verbal and other normal communication pathways have become dysfunctional for some reason, music offers one of the most powerful tools in reaching to the core of these individuals. Perhaps this is because, even in handicap, emotions are still present and need to be nourished. Music provides a tool for the homeodynamic exercising of the emotions. As music therapist and composer Paul Nordoff said in reference to this notion that "exceptional" individuals still have the same emotions as the "normal" population, "the music child within (the handicapped child) is not handicapped."[64]

The "Iso-Moodic" Principle and Entrainment

Throughout the primitive history of the shamanic use of music in medicine, music has served as a curative element through its emotionally purgative powers. Anthropologist Gilbert Rouget has found extensive use of music by many cultures to drive its members into frenzied exhaustion whereupon healing could more easily occur.[65] This use represents probably the earliest use of catharsis to establish cures from both physical and mental disease, whether in exorcising the patient of demon possession or repressed emotions. Music gains its power from its dynamic flow and its ambiguity. We can at one and the same time associate a musical passage with either an emotion or the symbolic representation of a diety. Rouget makes a particularly good case for the healing powers of shamanic music to establish "identification." Through the ability of music to identify, or resonate, with either the sick person's emotional state, or with the god(s) responsible for causing the affliction, the healing process was facilitated. This identification process is somewhat akin to what psychologists today call "empathy," or the ability to understand another's feelings. As we shall see later in this chapter, music has the ability to communicate this emotional empathy more than any other single behavior.

In the research of Clynes, reported earlier in this chapter, an extension was made of his sentic, or emotional, signatures to music. He found that when performers made the same finger movements to the music of various composers as his subjects had done in earlier research to different emotional states, that consistent sentic signatures were derived. Beethoven, for example, yielded a sentic cycle which resembled the emotion of sexual passion, whereas, Mozart's sentic signature looked more like that of joy. Thus, music is like a ground wire for the venting of repressed emotions.

Almost fifty years ago, psychiatrist Ira Altschuler made a brilliant application of this identification-empathy process.[66] He found that he could change moods in depressed or anxious patients most easily by playing music on his piano that first matched the mood of the patient. Later, he would alter the mood of the music to entrain the patient in the desired direction. Altschuler coined the phrase "iso-moodic" to describe this mood-changing principle.

The music therapist team Nordoff and Robbins made extensive use of this principle in their highly innovative improvisational music which was found to bring about significant increases in language and adaptive behavior in severely handicapped children.[67] More importantly, no other therapeutic modality had been found to be successful with these individuals touched by this musical approach.

The iso-moodic principle and entrainment theory began to dramatically shift the focus of research and clinical practice in music therapy. One of the initial paradigms in the profession concerned the effects of sedative vs. stimulative music. When results however proved that the structural components of music were inadequate to fully explain the influence of music on behavior, the field turned to qualities of the listener for its answers. In other words, the listener's own preferences, initial mood, and cultural matrix determined the majority of the responses.[68-69]

There appear to be at least five mechanisms involved in the effects of music on physical healing. All are perhaps operating simultaneously, giving music its unique power over the complete bodymind. The first, and perhaps most prolifically-studied level is the limbic, or emotional, response to music. Second, music elicits fantasy, thought, and imagery, and consequently, this level is the cortical, or cognitive response to music. Next, there is the thalamic response in which musical rhythms entrain rhythmic movements within the body. A newer area of research pertains to the direct stimulation by sound of peripheral and cutaneous nerves. Finally, group music-making involves spiritual, or psychosocial mechanisms, which, we will see in Chapter 6, play a major role in health maintenance. Entrainment is undoubtedly involved in the first three levels, but research on the latter two has only scratched the surface. For an overview of research on music and physical healing, see Table 4-3.

TABLE 4-3. *MUSIC AND PHYSICAL HEALTH*

1st Author	Date	Results
Goldstein	1980	Emotionally thrilling music increased endorphin production
Spingte	1991	Anxiolytic music decreased ACTH and endorphin production while increasing analgesia during surgery
Bartlett	1993	Preferred music significantly increased IL-1 and decreased cortisol over a control group in normals
Barker	1991	Preferred music was more effective than control condition in reducing pain and heart rate of patients undergoing debridement of burns
Stein	1991	Preferred music decreased anxiety during Caesarian deliveries more than white noise or control
Bonny	1983	Preferred anxiolytic music reduced pain and heart rate on coronary care units
Webster	1973	Music matched to age and heart rate levels of post-MI patients decreased heart rate and blood pressure over controls
Marks	1974	Wind instrument performance increased lung capacity in asthmatic children
Kibler	1983	Music was equivalent to progressive muscle relaxation in decreasing autonomic arousal
Lapp	1986	Preferred anxiolytic music as a placebo control was more effective than biofeedback treatment in reducing the frequency and intensity of migraine headaches
Reynolds	1984	Music was more effective than autogenics and biofeedback in reducing frontalis muscle tension
Fowler-Kerry	1987	Music was more effective than suggestion in eliminating the pain of immunization injections in children
Rider	1985	Music, imagery, and relaxation decreased levels of urinary corticosteroids and increased entrainment of biological circadian rhythms in shift-working nurses
Rider	1985	Entrainment music was more successful than preferred or anxiolytic music in decreasing pain and EMG tension in chronic pain patients

(continued)

TABLE 4-3. *MUSIC AND PHYSICAL HEALTH (continuation)*

1st Author	Date	Results
Rider	1989	Entrainment music and imagery of specific white blood cells effected changes in only the cell line which was imaged
Rider	1990	Entrainment music and imagery was more successful than same music alone (only after third week) inincreasing sIgA levels
Tsao	1991	Music equivalent to imagery in increasing sIgA
Fried	1990	Music just below heart rate induced diaphragmatic breathing
Schneider	1957	Stimulative music increased muscle control in spastic cerebral palsied children whereas sedative music did so in athetoid cerebral palsy
Shapiro	1995	Alternating hand taps alleviated PTSD symptoms
Li	1991	Music electroacupuncture was more effective than electro-acupuncture or acupuncture in rehabilitating hemiplegia patients
Seki	1983	Sounds applied through acupuncture needles which matched the power density spectra of nerve fibers superior to other non-matching sounds in reducing pain in cancer patients
Madsen	1965	High frequencies were more effective than lows in improving tactile discrimination in deaf subjects
Tomatis	1987	Psychosomatic, learning, and mental disorders were improved with high frequency stimulation
Rider	1991	Toning condition elicited a significantly higher immune response (sIgA) and a lower heart rate than the singing condtion; concentration highest after toning over all other conditions
Rider	1990	Live entrainment imagery session produced greater immune enhancement than after six weeks using taped version of same music
Bailey	1983	Live musical performance was more effective than taped renditions of the same songs in reducing anxiety and in-creasing vigor with cancer patients
Cassity	1976	Group musical performance increased peer acceptance and group cohesiveness
Munro	1978	Live musical experiences increased psychospiritual quality of life in terminally ill

Music Medicine and Emotion

It is impossible to separate the five specific components of the musical response without destroying the original stimulus we understand as music. Nevertheless, each of the five will be addressed to illuminate the breadth of the influence music has on behavior. Most of the research on altering physical health through music has centered upon the emotional effects. Even though the purpose in many studies was to use music as a distraction from a painful medical procedure, the fact that musical preferences have been found particularly effective implicates emotional mechanisms. Research conducted with hundreds of subjects and many different musical selections has demonstrated that listeners prefer music which matches their mood.[70]

One of the first reports to prove that the medicinal effects elicited by music were more than mere cognitive distraction was appropriately titled "Thrills in Response to Music and Other Stimuli."[57] Medical researcher Avram Goldstein, M.D. demonstrated that administering the opioid blocker naloxone significantly attenuated the thrill response generated in subjects listening to their most preferred musical selections. This demonstrated that part of the psychophysiological effect that emotionally charged music evokes is upon the endorphinergic system. As we have already seen, this system is intimately involved with the immune system and health.

While exciting music has been found to yield mild increases in endorphin-mediated thrill responses, relaxing music has been found to decrease endorphin levels during stressful surgical procedures. A group of physician researchers in Germany has determined that preferred anxiolytic (relaxing) music induced significant reductions in beta- endorphin during surgeries and labor/deliveries.[71] They also discovered that levels of the stress hormones ACTH and noradrenaline dropped when anxiolytic music was played during dental and surgical procedures. Furthermore, the needs for sedatives, analgesics, and anesthetics were reduced by 50% of the usual dosages.

Preferred music has been found successful in a number of medical interventions. One study demonstrated that preferred music elicited immediate, significant enhancement of immune responsivity in normal subjects as measured by increases in interleukin-1 and decreases in cortisol.[72] In another study, having burn patients choose their preferred music allowed them to significantly decrease pain and heart rate during debridement procedures.[73] In a study of music and birthing, preferred music was more successful than white noise or a control condition in decreasing anxiety in Caesarian deliveries.[74] Similarly chosen relaxation music has also been reported to reduce pain and heart rate on coronary care units.[75]

Music which was matched for the age group and for the heart rates of post myocardial infarction patients was found to decrease blood pressures and heart rates over control conditions.[76] Finally, preferential music activities involving the playing of wind instruments has been found to increase lung capacity in asthmatic children while decreasing clinical symptoms, hyperaeration, and barrel-chest deformities.[77]

Studies which have compared music to cognitive forms of relaxation have consistently demonstrated that music functions through a multitude of mechanisms. One of my first studies in the area of music medicine found that music was equivalent to progressive muscle relaxation in reducing autonomic arousal as measured by skin temperature.[78] Another researcher, intending to use preferred anxiolytic music as a placebo control, found that it worked even better than the biofeedback treatment condition in reducing the frequency and intensity of migraine headaches.[79] Music has also been demonstrated to be superior to the mental techniques of autogenics and biofeedback in reducing frontalis muscle tension.[80] Preferred music as a distraction has also been found to eliminate the pain of immunization injections in children more effectively than the cognitive technique of suggestion.[81]

Music and the Cognitive Response

Having discovered the importance of the emotional response in music medicine, I next attempted in my own studies to enhance the cognitive responsivity of music beyond that of mere distraction. I began to develop imagery and relaxation scripts that fit the particular types of music preferred by the patients. This combined intervention of music, relaxation and imagery was subsequently found to decrease levels of urinary corticosteroids and increase entrainment of biological circadian rhythms in stressed shift-working nurses.82

In working for a period of time with chronic back pain patients, I noticed early on that these patients with excruciating pain did not respond well to anxiolytic music which other patients had responded to successfully. Attempting to build upon the examples of entrainment which Altschuler, and Nordoff and Robbins had used so successfully with the emotionally and mentally impaired, I searched the repertoire of recorded music for examples of music which might first match the emotional intensity of pain which my back patients were experiencing, before it transitioned into music evocative of pain relief. Much to my chagrin, I could find no such music. There was music which started calmly and ended with intensity, but nothing which progressed in the opposite direction.

Finally, I decided to experiment with slightly different variations of the forms I was searching for through the use of improvisational music. Utilizing drums, xylophones, bells, zithers, and shakers, we found that with the pain patients we needed to start with music that briefly evoked imaginal qualities used to describe their pain. The most effective music contained a transition within two or three minutes into softer and smoother music with a more regular pulse, almost like a lullaby. The music during this latter stage was designed to symbolically represent, through the specific instruments, muscles relaxing and inflammation/pain subsiding.

Having a better idea of the form for this type of music, I went into a studio and recorded a multitrack version for research purposes. I labeled this type of music "entrainment" music. The "iso-moodic" principle upon which it was based seemed to work according to entrainment mechanisms which had been discovered in physics and biology centuries before. These mechanisms describe, for instance, the phase-locking of pendula and our own sleep-wake schedule. One rhythmic oscillation can influence, or entrain, another if their periods (cycles) are similar. We phase lock to the 24-hr. solar day even though our free-running rhythms are actually about an hour or two longer.

When I compared the effects of this entrainment music to traditional anxiolytic music and relaxation instructions without music, I found that the back pain patients had significantly greater decreases in both muscle tension (EMG) and reported back pain with the entrainment condition than with other more familiar types.[83] Somehow, the shift through more than one emotional state allowed for both tension and pain to be released, possibly through modulation of endorphinergic mechanisms.

We next began to pair this entrainment music with imagery to measure the effects upon the immune system. In so doing, we documented significant biological effects within the immune system.[84-85] (These studies are presented in more detail in Chapter 5.) While the immune- specific imagery was a dominant factor in producing these effects, the music by itself also stimulated significant immunological changes. Thus, the spontaneous imaginal shifts created by the music induced immunological enhancement, presumably by homeodynamic mechanisms.

One feature of the entrainment music process that we had noticed from the beginning was that the subjective effects of the patient were more profound when the music was improvised live. In this way, a closer match between the music and the patient's images of disease and immune system could be made. When we tested the antibody (secretory IgA) production of individual patients, it didn't matter whether a zither represented the cancer or the immune system— as long as an imagery shift was induced by the music, the immune system was still boosted.

Others began to confirm the premise we had formulated, except utilizing prerecorded music. One such group employed Pachelbel's Canon in D, which approximated the entrainment musical form in that it engaged a steady buildup in activity and intensity. This music was equally effective to imagery alone in increasing the immune response, as measured by secretory IgA.[86]

The Thalamic Response and EMDR Psychotherapy

Try to turn on a piece of jazz swing or rock & roll and not tap your fingers or foot. This uncontrollable urge is what is called the "thalamic response," mainly due to the presence of neurons in the thalamus which respond to specific tempos. From there the basal ganglia controls the actual motor responses. Again, musical entrainment plays a dominant role, for the tempos must be in a range which approximated the bodily tempos attempting to be influenced. Music which is rhythmically paced to a beat similar to one's respiration rate has been demonstrated to attenuate the breathing rate in a desirable direction. Fried has demonstrated that certain types of music, especially those just below the pulse rate, enhanced the kind of diaphragmatic breathing patterns which reduced the hyperventilation syndrome.[87] Conversely, music which was faster than the pulse rate had an accelerating effect on the breathing rate.

Another intriguing example of entrainment occurring within the thalamic response to music was discovered with cerebral palsied children. Some of these children studied were spastic, a condition involving tightly contracted limbs, while others were athetoid, evidenced by hypotonicity and slow writhing tremors. The amazing phenomenon which was observed was that the spastic children responded with greater muscular control to faster music, which in an indirect way, matched their hypertonicity, whereas the athetoid children had better coordination with slower music, again which seemed to match their hypotonicity.[88]

A revolutionary new technique in the treatment of post traumatic stress disorder (PTSD) is called "eye movement desensitization and reprocessing" (EMDR).[89] Although this technique involves other behaviors, such as imagery of the trauma and cognitive therapy to alter the associated maladaptive thoughts, the primary feature is alternating movements of lateralized body parts, such as the eyes, hands, or feet. These alternating movements have been found to provide a stabilization of the intense and disturbing flashbacks among PTSD victims. This technique has also been showing potential promise in the healing of somatic illnesses, including hypertension, headaches, and gastric ulcers, in these same survivors.[89-90]

Why this technique is being included in the music section of healing treatments is that the alternating left-right motor patterns of hand or feet movements has long been known by music therapists and musicians to alleviate anxiety and other disturbing feelings. When music therapists need music to build up emotional imagery, they look to music without a regular pulse. The rock 'n roll of adolescence and the mother's nurturing pat on the back are both examples of the emotionally dissipative effect of regularly pulsed stimulation. As will be discussed in the Homeodynamic Mechanisms section of music techniques, the alternating right-left patterns are involved in synchronizing the left and right cerebral hemispheres. Hence, music may have evolved from simple intuitive motor techniques designed to quell intense emotions.

Music Medicine and Nerve Stimulation

The mechanisms involved in this level of music medicine operate primarily through peripheral and cranial nerve stimulation rather than through the influence of brain structures.

In a very interesting application, music has been integrated directly into the clinical practice of acupuncture. By converting music into electrical impulses through a mechanical-to-electrical transducer, the musical signals have been electrically fed into the acupuncture needles. Experimenters have found that this procedure of music electroacupuncture remarkably enhanced both muscle strength and use in hemiplegia patients over traditional acupuncture or electroacupuncture without music.[91]

The reasoning for this extraordinary phenomenon has been demonstrated to be that music shares an identical feature with the conduction of electrical impulses along nerve fibers. It seems that such acoustical stimuli as music and babbling brooks (but not white noise) exhibit the same spectral power densities as the voltage fluctuations across the resting membrane of myelinated nerve fibers.[92] Furthermore, sounds applied through acupuncture needles, as in the above procedure, which matched the power density spectra of nerve fibers were found to be superior to other non-matching sounds in reducing pain in cancer patients. Thus, this particular use of music operates through entrainment mechanisms.

Other musical techniques which stimulate nerve conduction pathways involve the use of high frequency harmonics. High frequencies may be particularly important in enhancing the sensitivity of other nerve pathways. For example, high frequencies have been determined to be more effective than lows in improving tactile discrimination in deaf subjects.[93]

Two musical techniques which make particular use of high frequency overtones include toning (or chanting) and gonging. The chanting of low-pitched vowel sounds as mantras has been utilized for millennia in different religious and meditational traditions. The French physician Albert Tomatis made an interesting discovery when asked to consult at a monastery for symptoms of fatigue the monks were experiencing.[94] Dr. Tomatis could not find anything medically wrong with the monks and accordingly inquired as to any other environmental or behavioral changes that had been made which could account for the reported malaise. The only variable that had changed was the elimination of the prolific schedule of chanting for the purpose of increasing the amount of time in which other "more fruitful" activities could be pursued. Dr. Tomatis recommended that they perhaps reinstitute the chanting back into their regimen. Doing so promptly reinvigorated the tired monks.

When Tomatis began to try to understand the mechanisms involved in the therapeutic value of chanting, he found that all cranial nerves led to the ear. Furthermore, the 10th cranial, or vagus, nerve had an origination point on the outer surface of the eardrum which no one had been able to explain. The vagus nerve is involved in many psychosomatic diseases as it connects from the ear the lungs, heart, and stomach. Thus, acoustic vibrations were found to directly stimulate the autonomic nervous system and ameliorate medical conditions affected by stress.

As he began to study audiograms of many different diagnostic groups, Tomatis noted that individuals with mental disorders such as dyslexia and scizophrenia had pockets of reduced hearing efficiency in the higher frequencies. Furthermore, if he boosted these higher frequencies through special listening devices, often their mental disorders lessened.

I have experimentally studied the effects of toning on the human body by having subjects vocalize on a syllable and pitch of their choice for ten minutes. This type of toning seems to provide subjects with a continuous high frequency stimulation from the harmonics of the tone, perhaps chosen intuitively based on a subconscious perception of high frequency hearing loss. If so, this procedure would constitute a natural form of biofeedback. When compared to singing of familiar songs, we found that the toning condition elicited a significantly higher immune response (sIgA) and a lower heart rate than the singing condition.[95] The toning condition also elicited the lowest post test measures of confusion, suggesting that some enhancement of brain wave activity may have occurred. One researcher has discussed the possibility that chanting influences the vibration of cerebrospinal fluid in the ventricles of the brain.[96] Furthermore, certain resonance patterns created by the chanting purportedly enhance psychospiritual communication abilities.

Gongs elicit some of the greatest array of high frequency overtones than any other musical instrument. Although no experimental testing of gong listening has occurred, our own clinical results of profound psychological enhancement of imagery and emotions suggests that similar homeodynamic activation of the nervous system responses takes place.

This leads us to the last mechanism by which music affects the body.

Music Medicine, Social Support and Spirituality

Musical experiences also have the power to reduce physical symptomatology through group support, or sociospiritual, mechanisms. Especially in live performance mediums, the music becomes "that power greater than ourselves." When we compared the effect of live entrainment music versus a tape-recorded version of the same music, the live version elicited as high of an immunological boost after one session as it took for the recorded condition in a previous study to produce after six weeks of practice.[97] Hence, the subjects may have felt the addition of transpersonal effects on their immune system. This study matched the clinical data we had long observed in the enhancement of mental imagery and disease management following a session in which the music had been improvised around the patients' imagery descriptions of their disease and health.

Transpersonal, spiritual effects of live musical performance was also demonstrated as more effective than taped renditions of the same songs in reducing anxiety and increasing vigor with cancer patients.[98] Although not measuring medical outcomes, other studies have likewise supported the notion that group musical performance increases peer acceptance and group cohesiveness[99] and psychospiritual quality of life[100], factors which have been demonstrated in other social support research to correlate highly with positive health outcomes.

Homeodynamic Mechanisms of Music

Music produces several different types of shifts in the brain. Both hemispheric as well as frequency shifts have been documented by researchers. For an overview of the research documenting the homeodynamic mechanisms involved in music medicine, see Table 4-4.

TABLE 4-4. *HOMEODYNAMIC MECHANISMS OF MUSIC AND RHYTHM-BASED TREATMENTS*

1st Author	Date	Results
Neher	1961	Drumbeats produced alpha brain wave shifts
Nicosia	1994	EMDR psychotherapy increased synchronized alpha
Kabuto	1993	Enjoyment of either New Age or classical music induced increases in delta power and decreases in alpha-peak EEG frequency
Bruya	1984	EEG slowing and alpha production was dependent upon the subjective appraisal of the music as "relaxing"
Fried	1990	Following music listening, brain waves shifted to increased alpha and decreased theta
Satoh	1983	Surgery patients who listened to music had significantly more alpha brain wave production than controls; experimental group evidenced decreases in plasma levels of the stress hormones cortisol, ACTH, and beta-endorphin whereas the control group increased in these hormones.
Wagner	1977	Musicians exhibited more alpha brain wave activity when listening to music than nonmusicians
Goldstein	1993	Music listening activated the right hemisphere in musicians, whereas, nonmusicians registered left hemispheric activation
Dostalek	1979	Singing the syllable "OM" led to the appearance of theta and delta rhythms as well as increases in the amplitude of alpha and beta activity.

One of the classic studies in this area made the discovery that regularly-pulsed drum rhythms produced alpha brain wave shifts and trance-like states.[101] Although the proposed mechanism of "sonic-driving" has been convincingly refuted by Rouget[65], apparently any regular stimulus (using light or sound) at any frequency has the capability of inducing low frequency shifts. Rouget found that these trance states were utilized in many cultures to facilitate mental and physical healing. Bodily responses, such as foot taps, have been found to synchronize with rhythmic music, while at the same time inducing brain wave shifts alternating back and forth between beta and alpha.[102]

Brainwave analysis of eye movement desensitization and reprocessing (EMDR) psychotherapy has also demonstrated that alternating left-right motor patterns induces increased alpha activity and an increased coherence between left and right cerebral hemispheres, particularly in the theta and delta bands.[90] Hence, EMDR or any similar motor behaviors prompted by a stimulus such as music would qualify as homeodynamic due to this EEG shift coupled with increased brainwave resonance.

Corroborating Rouget's findings that nothing endemic to the musical structure itself relates to the psychophysiological shifts (other than the regularity of the musical beat), a number of studies seem to confirm that "stimulative" and "sedative" are words that should be applied to the relationship between the music and the listener rather than to the music itself. Unless the music is specifically composed to match one's emotional state, the familiarity with a piece of music is more likely to enable one to relax and enjoy the music than any structural element of the music.[68] One study found that when listeners enjoyed a piece of music (either classical or New Age), significant homeodynamic shifts were noted in the EEG.[103] These shifts primarily involved a slowing of brain wave activity, characterized by increases in delta power and decreases in alpha-peak frequency.

In a study of sedative and stimulative music types, neither type contributed more to EEG slowing, although the sedative music did elicit more significant increases in the ability to focus attention on a task.[104] In another study of New Age and classical music, the authors discovered that EEG slowing and alpha production was dependent upon the subjective appraisal of the music as "relaxing."[105] Fried's studies of music and the hyperventilation syndrome (discussed above) also demostrated that following music listening, brain waves shifted to increased alpha and decreased theta.[87]

One study demonstrated elegantly the connection between music, homeodynamic shifts, and the healing potential. In this study, music was presented to surgical patients immediately before the anesthesia was administered.[106] Results indicated that patients who listened to music had significantly more alpha brain wave production than the control patients. Furthermore, the experimental group evidenced decreases in plasma levels of the stress hormones cortisol, ACTH, and beta-endorphin whereas the control group increased in these hormones.

Musical experience also appears to increase the amount of brain wave slowing. In several studies, musicians have been shown to exhibit more alpha brain wave activity when listening to music than nonmusicians.[107-108] Musical training also seems to endow one to a particular kind of brain wave shift involving activation of the right hemisphere, whereas, nonmusicians tend to register left hemispheric activation shifts.[109-110]

One study has been conducted on the effects of chanting on brain wave activity.[111] Singing the syllable "OM" led to the appearance of theta and delta rhythms as well as increases in the amplitude of alpha and beta activity.

References

1. Somers, A.R. (1979). Marital status, health, and use of health services. *Journal of the American Medical Association, 241*, 1818– 1822.

2. Bartrop, R.W., Luckhurst, E., Lazarus, L., Kiloh, L.G., & Penny, R. (1977). Depressed lymphocyte function after bereavement. *Lancet, 1*, 834–836.

3. Renne, K.S. (1971). Health and marital experience in an urban population. *Journal of Marriage and the Family, 23*, 338–350.

4. Kiecolt-Glaser, J.K., Glaser, R., Dyer, C., Shuttleworth, E., Ogrocki, P., & Speicher, C.E. (1987). Chronic stress and immunity in family caregivers of Alzheimer's disease victims. *Psychosomatic Medicine, 49*, 523–535.

5. Glaser, R., Kiecolt-Glaser, J.K., Speicher, C.E., & Holliday, J.E. (1985). Stress, loneliness, and changes in herpesvirus latency. *Journal of Behavioral Medicine, 8*, 249–260.

6. Snyder, B.K., Roghmann, K.J., & Sigal, L.H. (1993). Stress and psychosocial factors: Effect on primary cellular immune response. *Journal of Behavioral Medicine, 16*, 143–161.

7. Greer, S., & Morris, T. (1975). Psychological attributes of women who develop breast cancer: A controlled study. *Journal of Psychosomatic Research, 19*, 147–153.

8. Shea, J.D.C., Burton, R., & Girgis, A. (1993). Negative affect, absorption, and immunity. *Physiology and Behavior, 53*, 449–457.

9. Scherg, H. (1987). Psychosocial factors and disease bias in breast cancer patients. *Psychosomatic Medicine, 49*, 302–312.

10. Temoshok, L. (1987). Personality, coping style, emotiona, and cancer: Toward an integrative model. *Cancer Surveys, 6*, 545–567.

11. Kneier, A.W., & Temoshok, L. (1984). Repressive coping reactions in patients with malignant melanoma as compared to cardiovascular patients. *Journal of Psychosomatic Research, 28*, 145–155.

12. Kiecolt-Glaser, J.K., Malarkey, W.B., Chee, M.A., Newton, T., Cacioppo, J.T., Mao, H.-Y., & Glaser, R. (1993). Negative behavior during marital conflict is associated with immunological down- regulation. *Psychosomatic Medicine, 55*, 395–409.

13. Knapp, P.H., Levy, E.M., Giorgi, R.G., Black, P.H., Fox, B.H., & Heeren, T.C. (1992). Short-term immunological effects of induced emotion. *Psychosomatic Medicine, 54*, 133–148.

14. Cousins, N. (1979). *Anatomy of an illness.* New York: W.W. Norton.

15. Berk, L. (1989). Laughter and immunity. *Advances, 6*(2), 5.

16. Dillon, K.M., Minchoff, B., & Baker, K.H. (1985–86). Positive emotional states and enhancement of the immune system. *International Journal of Psychiatry and Medicine, 15*, 13–17.

17. Martin, R.A., & Dobbin, J.P. (1988). Sense of humor, hassles, and immunoglobulin A: Evidence for a stress-moderating effect of humor. *International Journal of Psychiatry and Medicine, 18*, 93–105.

18. Melnuchuk, T. (1988). Emotions, brain, immunity, and health: A review. In M. Clynes & J. Panksepp (Eds.), *Emotions and psycho-pathology.* New York: Plenum Press.

19. Heijnen, C.J., & Ballieux, R.E. (1986). Influence of opioid peptides on the immune system. *Advances, 3*(4), 114–121.

20. Wybran, J., Appelboom, T., Famacy, J.P., & Govaerts, A. (1979). Suggestive evidence for receptors for morphine and methionine- enkaphalin on normal human blood T-lymphocytes. *Journal of Immunology, 123*, 1068–1070.

21. Weinstock, C. (1977). Notes on "spontaneous" regression of cancer. *American Society of Psychosomatic Dentistry and Medicine, 24*(4), 106–110.

22. Ikemi, Y., Nakagawa, S., Nakagawa, T., & Mineyasu, S. (1975). Psychosomatic consideration on cancer patients who have made a narrow escape from death. *Dynamische Psychiatrie, 31*, 77–92.

23. LeShan, L.L., & Gassmann, M.L. (1958). Some observations on psychotherapy with patients with neoplastic disease. *American Journal of Psychotherapy, 12*, 723–734.

24. LeShan, L.L. (1989). *Cancer as a turning point*. New York: Dutton.

25. Spiegel, D., Bloom, J.R., Kraemer, H.C., & Gottheil, E. (1989). Effect of psycho social treatment on survival of patients with metastatic breast cancer. *Lancet, 2*, 888–891.

26. Grossarth-Maticek, R., Schmidt, P., Vetter, H., & Arndt, S. (1984). Psycho therapy research in oncology. In P. Steptoe & A. Mathews (Eds.), *Healthcare and human behavior*. New York: Academic Press.

27. Solomon, G.F., Temoshok, L., O'Leary, A., & Zich, J. (1987). An intensive psychoimmunologic study of long-surviving persons with AIDS. *Annals of the New York Academy of Sciences, 496*, 647–655.

28. Frey, W.H., & Langeth, M. (1985). *Crying: The mystery of tears*. Houston: Winston Press

29. Pennebaker, J.W. (1988). *Personal communication*.

30. Pennebaker, J.W., Kiecolt-Glaser, J.K., & Glaser, R. (1988). Disclosure of traumas and immune function: Health implications for psychotherapy. *Journal of Consulting and Clinical Psychology, 56*, 239–245.

31. Pennebaker, J.W., Barger, S.D., & Tiebout, J. (1989). Disclosure of traumas and health among holocaust survivors. *Psychosomatic Medicine, 51*, 577–589.

32. Rider, M.S., & Kibler, V.E. (1990). Treating arthritis and lupus patients with music-mediated imagery and psychotherapy. *Arts in Psychotherapy, 17*(1), 29–33.

33. Clynes, M. (1977). *Sentics*. Garden City, NY: Anchor Press.

34. Spingte, R., Droh, R., Clynes, M., Mulders, A., & Hiby, A. (1988). [Emotion and sports sentic cycle: On the way of creating an emotional state for the enhancement of human performance]. In R. Spingte & R. Droh (Eds.), [*Pain and sports*]. Berlin: Springer- Verlag.

35. Redington, D.J., & Reidbord, S.P. (1992). Chaotic dynamics in autonomic nervous system activity of a patient during a psychotherapy session. *Biological Psychiatry, 31*(10), 993–1007.

36. Singer, D.H., Martin, G.J., Magid, N., Weiss, J.S., Schaad, J.W., Kehoe, R., Zheutlin, T., Fintel, D.J., Hsieh, A.M., & Lesch, M. (1988). Low heart rate variability and sudden cardiac death. *Journal of Electrocardiology, Sup.*, S46–S55.

37. Ori, Z., Monir, G., Weiss, J., Sayhouni, X., & Singer, D.H. (1992). Heart rate variability. *Ambulatory Electrocardiography, 10*(3), 499–537.

38. Lovallo, W.R., Pincomb, G.A., Brackett, D.J., & Wilson, M.F. (1990). Heart rate reactivity as a predictor of neuroendocrine responses to aversive and appetitive challenges. *Psychosomatic Medicine, 52*, 17–26.

39. McCraty, R., Atkinson, M., & Tiller, W.A. New electrophysiological correlates of mental and emotional states via heart rate variability studies. Unpublished manuscript, Institute of HeartMath, Boulder Creek, CA.

40. Temoshok, L. (1991). Malignant melanoma, AIDS, and the complex search for psychosocial mechanisms. *Advances, 7*(3), 20–28.

41. Morishige, H., & Reyher, J. (1975). Alpha rhythm during three conditions of visual imagery and emergent uncovering psychotherapy: The critical role of anxiety. *Journal of Abnormal Psychology, 84*(5), 531–538.

42. Aladzhalova, N.A., & Kamenetskii, S.L. (1974). [Superslow oscillations in the potential of the human brain during transition from the waking to the hypnotic state]. *Voprosy Psikhologii, 20*(1), 94–103.

43. Sobotka, S.S., Davidson, R.J., & Senulis, J.A. (1992). Anterior brain electrical asymmetries in response to reward and punishment. *Electroencephalography and Clinical Neurophysiology, 83*, 236–247.

44. Karle, W., Hopper, M., Switzer, A., Corriere, R., & Woldenberg, L. (1980). Effects of psychotherapy on REM latency and REM time. *Perceptual and Motor Skills, 51*, 319–324.

45. Scott, R., Karle, W., Switzer, A., Hart, J., Corriere, R., & Woldenberg, L. (1978). Psychophysiological correlates of the spontaneous K-complex. *Perceptual and Motor Skills,* 46, 271–287.

46. Hoffman, E. (1983). Long-term effects of psychotherapy on the EEG of neurotic patients: A follow-up study of primal patients. *Research Communications in Psychology, Psychiatry and Behavior,* 8(2), 171–185.

47. Karle, W., Corriere, R., & Hart, J. (1973). Psychophysiological changes in abreactive therapy—Study I: Primal therapy. *Psychotherapy: Theory, Research and Practice,* 10(2), 117–122.

48. Buysse, D.J., Kupfer, D.J., Frank, E., Monk, T.H., Ritenour, A., & Ehlers, C.L. (1992). Electroencephalographic sleep studies in depressed outpatients treated with interpersonal psychotherapy: I. Baseline studies in responders and nonresponders. *Psychiatry Research,* 40, 13–26.

49. Kupfer, D.J., Franf, E., McEachran, A.B., & Grochocinski, V.J. (1990). Delta sleep ratio: A biological correlate of early recurrence in unipolar affective disorder. *Archives of General Psychiatry,* 47, 1100–1105.

50. Engel-Sittenfeld, P., Engel, R.R., Huber, H.P., & Zangl, K. (1980). Active mechanisms of psychological therapy techniques in the treatment of chronic sleep disorders. *Zeitschrift fur Klinische Psychologie: Forschung und Praxis,* 9(1), 34–52.

51. Dovzhenko, A.R., Artemchuk, A.F., Bolotova, Z.N., Vorob'eva, T.M., & Manuilenko, I.A. (1990). Outpatient stress psychotherapy of patients with alcoholism. *Zhurnal Nevropatologii i Psikhiatrii Imeni S.S. Korsakova (Moskva),* 88(2), 94–97.

52. Semczuk, B. (1968). Studies on the influence of acoustic stimuli on respiratory movements. *Polish Medical Journal,* 7(5), 1090–1096.

53. Congreve, W. (1695). *Love for love.*

54. Zackheim, M. (1985). Tent of meeting. Artwork exhibited at the Museum of Art, Santa Fe, New Mexico, December, 1985.

55. Hykes, D. (1984). *Harmonic meetings.* Celestial Harmonies.

56. Stratton, V.N., & Zalanowski, A.H. (1989). The effects of music and paintings on mood. *Journal of Music Therapy,* 16(1), 30–41.

57. Goldstein, A. (1980). Thrills in response to music and other stimuli. *Physiological Psychology,* 8(1):126–129.

58. Atlas, D.H. Music hath charms to extend lifespan. Unpublished manuscript, University of California, San Diego, 1977.

59. Bonny, H.L., & Savary, L.M. (1973). *Music and your mind.* New York: Harper & Row.

60. Munroe, S. (1984). *Music therapy in palliative hospice care.* St. Louis: MMB Music.

61. Nordoff, P., & Robbins, C. (1977). *Creative music therapy.* New York: John Day Co.

62. Tyson, F. (1981). *Psychiatric music therapy.* New York: Creative Arts Rehabilitation Center.

63. Gaston, E.T. (1968). *Music in therapy.* New York: Macmillan.

64. Parry, D. (1976). *The music child* (film). Biracliff Manor, NY: Benchmark Films.

65. Rouget, G. (1985). *Music and trance.* Chicago: University of Chicago Press.

66. Altschuler, I. (1948). A psychiatrist's experience with music as a therapeutic agent. In D. Schullian (Ed.), *Music and medicine.* New York: Books for Libraries Press.

67. Nordoff, P., & Robbins, C. (1971). *Music therapy in special education.* New York: John Day Co.

68. Peretti, M. (1983). The effect of musical preference on anxiety as determined by GSR. *Acta Psychiatrica–Belgium,* 83(5), 437–442.

69. Eagle, C.T. (1971). Effects of existing mood and order of presentation of vocal and instrumental music on rated mood responses to that music. Unpublished doctoral dissertation, The University of Kansas.

70. Rider, M. (1987). Treating chronic disease and pain with music- mediated imagery. *The Arts in Psychotherapy, 14*(2),113–120.

71. Spingte,R.(1991).The neurophysiology of emotion and its therapeuticapplications in music therapy and music medicine. In C. Maranto (Ed.), *Applications of music in medicine,* 59–72.

72. Bartlett, D., Kaufman, D., & Smeltekop, R. (1993). The effects of music listening and perceived sensory experiences on the immune system as measured by interleukin-1 and cortisol. *Journal of Music Therapy, 30*(4), 194–209.

73. Barker, L.W. (1991). The use of music and relaxation techniques to reduce pain of burn patients during daily debridement. In C. Maranto (Ed.), *Applications of music in medicine,* 123–140.

74. Stein, A.M. (1991). Music to reduce anxiety during cesarean births. In C. Maranto (Ed.), *Applications of music in medicine,* 179–190.

75. Bonny, H.L. (1983). Music listening for intensive coronary care units: A pilot project. *Music Therapy, 3*(1), 4–16.

76. Webster, C. (1973). Relaxation, music and cardiology: The physiological and psychological consequences of their interrelation. *The Australian Occupational Therapy Journal,* January-March:9–20.

77. Marks, M.B. (1974). Musical wind instruments in rehabilitation of asthmatic children. *Annals of Allergy, 33*(6), 313–319.

78. Kibler, V.E., & Rider, M.S. (1983). Effects of progressive muscle relaxation and music on stress as measured by finger temperature response. *Journal of Clinical Psychology, 39*(2), 213–215.

79. Lapp, J.E. (1985). The effects of music and biofeedback on the frequency and intensity of migraine headaches. Unpublished manuscript, California State University.

80. Reynolds, S.B. (1984). Biofeedback, relaxation training, and music: Homeostasis for coping with stress. *Biofeedback and Self-Regulation, 9*(2), 169–179.

81. Fowler-Kerry, S., & Lander, J.R. (1987). Management of injection pain in children. *Pain, 30*(2), 169–175.

82. Rider, M.S., Floyd, J., & Kirkpatrick, J. (1985). The effect of music, imagery, and relaxation on adrenal corticosteroids and the re-entrainment of circadian rhythms. *Journal of Music Therapy, 22*(1), 46–58.

83. Rider, M.S. (1985). Entrainment mechanisms are involved in pain reduction, muscle relaxation, and music-mediated imagery. *Journal of Music Therapy, 22*(4), 183–192.

84. Rider, M.S., & Achterberg, J. (1989). Effect of music-assisted imagery on neutrophils and lymphocytes. *Biofeedback and Self-Regulation, 14*(3), 247–257.

85. Rider, M.S., Achterberg, J., Lawlis, G.F., Goven, A., Toledo, R., & Butler, J.R. (1990). Effect of immune system imagery on secretory IgA. *Biofeedback and Self-Regulation, 15*(4), 317–333.

86. Tsao, C.C., Gordon, T., Maranto, C.D., Lerman, C., & Murasko, D. (1991). The effects of music and directed biological imagery on immune response (sIgA). In C. Maranto (Ed.), *Applications of music in medicine,* 85–121.

87. Fried, R. (1990). Integrating music in breathing training and relaxation: I & II. *Biofeedback and Self-Regulation, 15*(2), 161–178.

88. Schneider, E.H. (1957). Relationships between musical experiences and certain aspects of cerebral palsied children's performance on selected tasks. In E.T. Gaston (Ed.), *Music therapy 1956.* Lawrence, Kansas: Allen Press.

89. Shapiro, F. (1995). *Eye movement desensitization and reprocessing.* NY: Guilford Press.

90. Nicosia, G.J. (1994). The quantitative analysis of electroencephalography representing a localized psychogenic amnesia and its resolution by eye movement deseEnsitization and reprocessing psychotherapy. Paper presented at International EMDR Conference, Sunnyvale, CA.

91. Shi-Jing, L., Hui-Ju, S., Guo, W., & Maranto, C.D. (1991). Music and medicine in China: The effects of music electro-acupuncture on cerebralhemiplegia. In C. Maranto (Ed.), *Applications of music in medicine*, 191–199.

92. Seki, H. (1983). Influence of music on memory and education, and the application of its underlying principles to acupuncture. *International Journal of Acupuncture and Electro-Therapeutics Research*, 8:1–16.

93. Madsen, C.K., & Mears, W.G. (1965). The effect of sound upon the tactile threshold of deaf subjects. *Journal of Music Therapy*, 2, 64–68.

94. Gilmor, T.M., Madaule, P., & Thompson, B. (Eds.). (1989). *About the Tomatis method*. Toronto: The Listening Centre Press.

95. Rider, M., Mickey, C., Weldin, C., & Hawkinson, R. (1991). The effects of toning, listening, and singing on psychophysiological responses. In C. Maranto (Ed.), *Applications of music in medicine*, 73–84.

96. Bentov, I. (1988). *Stalking the wild pendulum*. Rochester, VT: Inner Traditions.

97. Rider, M.S., & Weldin, C. (1990). Imagery, improvisation, and immunity. *The Arts in Psychotherapy*, 17, 211–216.

98. Bailey, L.M. (1983). The effects of live music versus tape-recorded music on hospitalized cancer patients. *Music Therapy*, 3(1), 17–28.

99. Cassity, M.D. (1976). The influence of a music therapy activity upon peer acceptance, group cohesiveness, and interpersonal relationships of adult psychiatric patients. *Journal of Music Therapy*, 13(2), 66–76.

100. Munro, S., & Mount, B. (1978). Music therapy in palliative care. *Canadian Medical Association Journal*, 119(9), 1029–1034.

101. Neher, A. (1961). Auditory driving observed with scalp electrodes in normal subjects. *Electroencephalography and Clinical Neurophysiology*, 13, 449–451.

102. Oswald, I. (1959). Experimental studies of rhythm, anxiety and cerebral vigilance. *The Journal of Mental Science*, 105(439):269–294.

103. Kabuto, M., Kageyama, T., & Nitta, H. (1993). EEG power spectrum changes due to listening to pleasant music and their relation to relaxation effects. *Nippon Eiseigaku Zasshi*, 48(4), 807–818.

104. Borling, J.E. (1981). The effects of sedative music on alpha rhythms and focused attention in high-creative and low-creative subjects. *Journal of Music Therapy*, 18(2), 101–108.

105. Bruya, M.A., & Severtsen, B. (1984). Evaluating the effects of music on electroencephalogram patterns of normal subjects. *Journal of Neurosurgical Nursing*, 16(2), 96–100.

106. Satoh, Y., Nagao, H., Ishihara, H., Oyama, T., & Spingte, R. (1983). An objective evaluation of anxiolytic effect of music for surgical patients. *Masui. Japanese Journal of Anesthesiology*, 32(10), 1206–1211.

107. Wagner, M.J., & Menzel, M.B. (1977). The effect of music listening and attentiveness training on the EEG's of musicians and non-musicians. *Journal of Music Therapy*, 14(4), 151–164.

108. Hodges, D.A. (1980). Neurophysiology and musical behavior. In D.A. Hodges, (Ed.), *Handbook of music psychology*, 195–224. Lawrence, KS: National Association for Music Therapy.

109. Goldstein, L. (1983). Some EEG correlates of behavioral traits and states in humans. *Research Communications in Psychology, Psychiatry and Behavior*, 8(2), 115–142.

110. Petsche, H., Pockberger, H., & Rappelsberger, P. (1985). [Music perception, EEG and musical training]. *EEG-EMG Zeitschrift fur Elektroenzephalographie, Elektromyographie und Verwandte Gebiete (Stuttgart)*, 16(4), 183–190.

111. Dostalek, C., Faber, J., Krasa, H., Roldan, F., & Vele, F. (1979). [Meditational yoga exercises in EEG and EMG]. *Ceskoslovenska psychologie*, 23, 61–65.

CHAPTER FIVE

Health Benefits of Mental Shifting

In this chapter, I will examine healing techniques in which attitudes and mental states are utilized to impact physical disease. The mental healing techniques to be discussed include 1) biofeedback and relaxation, 2) cognitive therapy, 3) hypnosis, and 4) meditation and imagery. Because these techniques overlap quite frequently in both research and practice, only one section demonstrating the inherent homeodynamic shifts for all approaches combined will be included at the end of the chapter.

In discussing the various forms of mental treatments used for physical healing, I will adopt the model of a grid in which the techniques are divided into the employment of internal versus external feedback and secondarily into either conscious or unconscious utilization of the techniques. As seen in Figure 5-1, cognitive therapy employs the use of statements which are consciously chosen and repeated, and which are accomplished internally by the patient. In other words, the patient uses no outside source of feedback. Biofeedback and relaxation on the other hand require, at least initially, an external source of feedback, whether it is the guiding voice of a therapist or tape in the case of relaxation, or a biofeedback monitor. Even when these techniques have become learned or conditioned by the patient, what has been integrated is often the voice of the relaxation instructor or the visual image of the biofeedback monitor itself. Still, the patient is utilizing, largely, conscious mechanisms because of the predictable course of the relaxation instructions as well as the criteria to be achieved in biofeedback treatment.

The techniques of imagery/meditation and hypnosis, however, employ mechanisms which would be described as involving the unconscious, or primary process thinking. The course of treatment is largely unpredictable. Even if I am guiding a patient during hypnosis with a familiar script, I often wait for unconscious signals of my own to guide me down unfamiliar deviations. Amazingly, these often turn out to be familiar to the patient, once awakened. Whether this is a telepathic event I am uncertain, although I do not consider myself a psychic person. I do know that these phenomena are quite common in therapeutic settings if one is sensitive to them, and they will be addressed from both research and clinical perspectives in the next chapter. The subtle difference between hypnosis and imagery/meditation is that an external source (the therapist) is providing the feedback with hypnosis whereas in the case of the latter, the patient derives unique information from primarily internal sources, with little external guiding.

	External	Internal
Conscious	Biofeedback, Relaxation	Cognitive Therapy
Unconscious	Hypnosis	Imagery/Meditation

Figure 5-1. Organization of mental techniques utilized for physical healing

Biofeedback and Relaxation

I would consider biofeedback and relaxation as the most basic of the mental techniques, and often the most easily utilizable. Due to the externally-referenced, conscious mechanisms employed, patients with higher levels of defensiveness can gain some symptom relief with these methods. The patient who is paranoid that he is going to be hypnotized will be more receptive to the predictable nature of relaxation instructions. And, the defiant patient with a personality disorder secondary to health problems, who "will not" make positive affirmations about her body, will often allow biofeedback monitoring to take place as an objective and gentle form of confrontation.

There are still clients for whom even biofeedback and relaxation procedures trigger abreactive and cathartic reactions too powerful too gain any meaningful results yet from these techniques. When this happens, one simply drops back to more fundamental forms of therapy utilizing emotional or even physical techniques to provide the appropriate forms of release until higher levels of treatment can be initiated.

Biofeedback and relaxation are both used in the cultivation of "low arousal." Although biofeedback has other uses, for example in the rehabilitation of paralyzed limbs, our concern here is only for the decrease of sympathetic nervous system activity and/or the increase of parasympathetic activity.

Biofeedback and relaxation both sometimes involve physical processes, such as the tensing and relaxing of muscle groups as in progressive muscle relaxation, or the lowering of a muscle's electrical output through electromyographic (EMG) biofeedback. More importantly, however, biofeedback and relaxation both involve the conditioning of a learned response which the patient strives to achieve with each practice session. This learned response is a mental state which some refer to as the "blank slate," in which no thought activity seems to be occurring. This is why these techniques are considered here to be mental therapies.

I also consider biofeedback and relaxation to be the most basic of the mental techniques because there is some crossovers with the physical level. One can observe a patient during relaxation as their musculature releases, allowing gravity to act unopposed on the body. During biofeedback, one may lose perception of sensation and movement in muscle groups as electrical activity of muscles becomes negligible. Some patients almost become frightened, as if their limbs had become paralyzed, as they suddenly flex a muscle just to be sure that this has not happened.

As can be seen in Table 5-1, biofeedback and relaxation have been effective in treating disorders not only of the musculoskeletal system, but also vascular, endocrinological, and immunological disorders as well. More attention is given to the treatment of immunological disorders as they are the area of most concern in this book.

TABLE 5-1. *BIOFEEDBACK/RELAXATION AND PHYSICAL HEALING*

1st Author	Date	Results
Figueroa	1982	Relaxation and stress inoculation more effective than psychotherapy in reducing frequency and intensity of tension headaches, and in reducing medication
Haynes	1975	EMG biofeedback as effective as relaxation in reducing intensity, frequency, and duration of tension headache activity
Gauthier	1981	Thermal biofeedback effective in reducing frequency, intensity, and duration of migraine activity as well as medication, regardless of whether biofeedback site was temporal artery or finger, and regardless of whether patient practiced cooling or warming
Blanchard	1975	Hand warming enabled Raynaud's patient's symptoms to entirely disappear
Elder	1973	Diastolic blood pressure biofeedback effective in reducing both systolic and diastolic blood pressures in hypertensives over controls, but moreso when verbal praise added to feedback
Blanchard	1975	Systolic biofeedback and rest both effective in reducing systolic blood pressure in hypertensives, but biofeedback more significantly so
Khan	1973	Biofeedback to increase forced expiratory volume decreased medication, ER visits, frequency of attacks, and number of hospitalizations in asthmatic children
Peavey	1985	Thermal and EMG biofeedback increased phagocytic activity in neutrophils in high-stress group
Shulimson	1987	Thermal biofeedback successful in healing "nonhealing" diabetic mulcers

(continued)

TABLE 5-1. *BIOFEEDBACK/RELAXATION AND PHYSICAL HEALING*
(continuation)

1st Author	Date	Results
Auerbach	1992	Thermal biofeedback, imagery, and hypnosis decreased HIV-related symptoms (fever, pain, fatigue, nausea, and insomnia) in seropositive gay men
Rider	1985	Relaxation, imagery, and music tape reduced circadian amplitude and mean level of adrenal corticosteroids in high-stress, shift-working nurses over non-tape listening days; corticosteroid and body temperature circadian rhythms more entrained on tape-listening days
McGrady	1992	Biofeedback-assisted relaxation increased lymphocyte blastogenesis in normal subjects
Kiecolt-Glaser	1985	Relaxation increased natural killer cell activity over social contact or no treatment in a group of geriatrics
Zachariae	1990	relaxation and imagery increased natural killer cell activity in group of normal subjects
Gruber	1993	Relaxation, biofeedback, and imagery more effective than control group in increasing natural killer cell activity and lymphocyte responsiveness in breast cancer patients
Peniston	1989	Alpha/theta EEG and thermal biofeedback decreased depression, B-endorphins, and relapse rates in alcoholics over no-treatment controls
Lubar	1989	EEG biofeedback increased attention in ADD children

The efficacy of biofeedback and relaxation was initially achieved by focusing awareness upon stress pathways directly involved with the symptoms and then learning to alter that pathway. Consequently, relaxation has yielded superior results to the more indirect technique of psychotherapy in reducing the frequency and intensity of tension headaches.[1] Progressive muscle relaxation and EMG biofeedback have proven equally effective in eradicating tension headaches[2]

In like manner, monitoring and learning to modulate peripheral temperature has been most successful with vasospastic diseases such as migraine headache[3] and Raunaud's syndrome.[4] On the other hand, the regulation of hypertension has been demonstrated most effectively through blood pressure biofeedback.[5-6] Finally, pulmonary diseases such as asthma have responded well to biofeedback in which the forced expiratory volume is monitored[7]

As we begin to explore the effect of biofeedback and relaxation on the immune system, we find that there is no immediately accessible immunological pathway that can be monitored and thereby operantly conditioned. I once had a surplus of radial immunodiffusion plates for the measurement of secretory IgA that were unneeded for studies in my lab. Even though the assay took a couple of days to culture and therefore the feedback not immediate, I still began to use them as pre/post tests for medical patients who were undergoing some combination of relaxation/ biofeedback/imagery treatment. As crude as it was, it still gave patients feedback about the relationship between their level of relaxation reached that day and its effect upon their humoral immune system.

Since the immune system travels by way of the vascular system, one of the next most direct pathways to our natural defenses would likely be through our bloodstream. Several studies have indeed verified this. A combination of thermal biofeedback, imagery, and hypnosis has accomplished the difficult task of decreasing HIV-related symptoms in one of the deadliest diseases of the immune system.[8] In another, thermal and EMG biofeedback with high-stressed individuals was successful in increasing phagocytic activity in neutrophils.[9] Finally, thermal biofeedback applied at the site of "nonhealing" diabetic ulcers enabled them to heal at a faster rate.[10]

Another approach to operant control of the immune system, albeit somewhat slower, has come through lessening the immunosuppressive effects of adrenal "stress" hormones through generalized relaxation. We pioneered some of the early work in this area, finding that relaxation/imagery/music tapes helped reduce adrenal corticosteroids in shift working nurses.[11] Furthermore, the circadian rhythms of these stress hormones became significantly more entrained with their body temperature rhythms when they relaxed.

Many studies have since demonstrated the immune enhancement conferred through relaxation and general biofeedback procedures. In one of the best demonstrations with clinical groups, lymphocyte blastogenesis, humoral immunity, and natural killer cell activity all increased significantly in breast cancer patients who participated in EMG biofeedback-assisted relaxation as compared to control patients.[12] Similar procedures were also found to increase lymphocyte blastogenesis in normal subjects after just four weeks.[13] Natural killer cell activity has been increased with both normal subjects[14] and geriatrics[15] after approximately ten sessions of relaxation training. The geriatric group also expressed better humoral immune responses than either a social contact group or a control group. EEG biofeedback, perhaps the quintessential homeodynamic treatment, has initially revealed positive results in decreasing depression, beta-endorphins, and relapse rates in alcoholic patients.[16] During this treatment, brain wave shifts into lower frequency activity were sought. EEG biofeedback treatment has also been used successfully in children with attention deficit disorder (ADD), with increases in frequency being the criterion.[17] Interestingly, these two populations of depressed and ADD patients were both identified in Chapter 1 for their higher rate of immunological diseases. Although not yet validated, homeodynamic shifts initiated by EEG biofeedback undoubtedly lead to improved immune responsivity.

Cognitive Therapy

Cognitive therapy represents the appraisal of events happening to oneself and attitudes about oneself. Research on cognitive therapy has demonstrated great efficacy in the treatment of depression, primarily by changing negative thoughts about oneself to positive.[18]

In the area of physical healing, negative appraisals can refer to the erroneous thoughts that accompany the presence of physical symptoms, for example, that such symptoms imply the presence of tissue damage, that one should reduce physical activity, or that one is being punished for some transgression. I have witnessed quite often in my own practice the mental negation of body parts following a history of sexual abuse, particularly in the pelvic/genital areas. This "organ neglect," as I refer to it, can occur when a person turns off positive intentions or love to certain areas of the body in an attempt to forget the previous abuse or feelings connected with it.

Other maladaptive thoughts which negatively influence the body and its attempts to physically heal concern certain needs which also become neglected, often due to a lack of psychological nurturing in the formative years. These I refer to as the patient's "Bill of Rights" or "just deserves," and include such statements as "I deserve to be comfortable,...to relax,...to enjoy myself,...to feel physically good,... and to take in as much air as anybody else."

As seen in Table 5-1, cognitive therapy treatments have been found to be effective with a variety of chronic diseases and syndromes. In my own practice of cognitive therapy, I have found patients at times to feel it is too simplistic or gimmicky. The association of cognitive therapy with the codependent, effeminate character on Saturday Night Live, Stewart Smalley, has added even more suspicion to some patients' initial attempts with this form of therapy. However, even as a former skeptic, I have found cognitive therapy to be extremely quick and effective in altering negative attitudes affecting symptoms as well as the symptoms themselves.

Cognitive therapy probably forms the most basic, conscious, internalized method for altering maladaptive beliefs which might affect one's physical as well as emotional and mental health. I have made contracts with many disbelieving patients in which if they pledged for one month to make their daily positive affirmations, that not only would they experience changes in their maladaptive thoughts, but that secondly, they would receive feedback from external sources about the validity of their statements. Without exception, no patient has ever failed to validate these claims having complied with their contracts.

For example, from a psychological perspective, learning to like oneself would result in an increased self-esteem on an internal level, and increased feedback from others that one is liked. From a physical healing perspective, verbal self-talk of a positive nature can go far in reversing negative internalized images of body parts. What I find is that after the age of about 16 (which incidentally is the age of emancipation as an adult), no external validation of one's body (or psyche) is very lasting. Even if the injured psyche can tolerate a compliment (which it usually can't), the positive reinforcement is very short-lived, and requires constant repetition. The anorectic or bulimic with a distorted body image, or the cancer or hypertensive patient who experienced a lack of childhood physical nurturing have to verbally affirm their own bodies, their own attractiveness, their own right to be in the world before physiological symptoms begin to vanish. Cognitive therapy is sometimes a prerequisite to the unconscious initiation of health imagery, which remains blank until the daily ritual of self-affirmation begins to shake loose the barriers.

TABLE 5-2. *COGNITIVE THERAPY AND PHYSICAL HEALING*

1st Author	Date	Results
Coates	1992	Appraisal of quality of life predicted survival duration in breast cancer patients
Achterberg	1984	Appraisal of internal health locus of control predicted successful management of disease and health better than external or random locus of control
Luthe	1969	Autogenics phrases led to clinical improvement in over 2,400 cases of both acute and chronic diseases including asthma, headaches, surgical procedures, gastritis, diabetes, arthritis.
Surwit	1978	Autogenic training and biofeedback reduced attacks of Raynaud's disease; biofeedback plus autogenics no more effective than autogenics alone in raising skin temperature
Bradley	1985	Cognitive therapy with biofeedback as effective with rheumatoid arthritis patients as social support group therapy in decreasing anxiety and depression, but more effective in decreasing pain and titers of rheumatoid factor
Achmon	1989	Cognitive therapy and biofeedback both effective in reducing blood pressure in essential hypertensives; biofeedback more so with blood pressure but cognitive therapy more so with anger management
Esterling	1992	Cognitive behavioral stress management equally effective as aerobic exercise in improving immune functioning in a group of asymptomatic gay men awaiting HIV-1 serostatus notification, as determined by decreased titers to Epstein-Barr viral capsid antigen and Herpes virus type-6
Butler	1991	Cognitive therapy led to significant improvements in overall disability, fatigue, somatic, and psychiatric symptoms in chronic fatigue patients
Blanchard	1988	Cognitive therapy with biofeedback and relaxation led to 50% reduction in symptoms in half of a group of irritable bowel patients
Booth	1973	Cognitive validation led to temporary remission in a case of terminal leukemia
Ikemi	1975	Cognitive validation led to complete remission in a case of maxilla cancer

The cognitive revolution has made quite an impact upon the world of physical disease and healing. The fact that several assessments of attitude predict prognosis of disease factors speaks highly of the power of mental phenomena. One oncology research group found that when breast cancer patients assessed their "quality of life" using visual analog scales, it predicted their survival duration.[19] In other words, those who cognitively appraised their quality of life as being higher, lived significantly longer.

Others have documented the connection between appraisal of one's "health locus of control" and incidence of disease. This test, called the Health Attribution Test, determined whether one appraised illness as being under internal, external, or random control.[20] Those who scored higher on the internal dimension had a significantly better chance of being physically healthier.

One of the early predecessors to cognitive therapy for physical disorders was autogenic therapy. Developed by the German physician J.H. Schultz and reported in a seven volume series edited by Wolfgang Luthe, autogenic therapy employed the use of statements regarding suggestions of heaviness and warmth in the limbs, regularity of heart rate and breathing, warmth of the solar plexus, and coolness of the forehead.[21] By repeating these statements over and over, a state of self-regulation was found to result which was documented in over 2,400 cases by these two authors. Significant clinical improvements were found to occur for both acute and chronic diseases, including asthma, headaches, surgical procedures, gastritis, diabetes, and arthritis. By taking physiological measurements of their patients, Schultz and Luthe discovered that these clinical improvements were not just placebo effects, but involved positive changes in immunological, endocrinological, muscular, and cardiovascular status.

Autogenics may be utilizing some of the same cognitive mechanisms as biofeedback. It has been demonstrated that autogenics alone was just as effective in reducing Raynaud's attacks as autogenics combined with thermal biofeedback.[22]

Traditional cognitive therapy has been utilized successfully in the treatment of a variety of physical disorders. This type of therapy involves the reprogramming of maladaptive thoughts about one's self-esteem and/or expectations about futuristic events. Such treatment typically involves the patient reciting statements such as "Everything is going to be O.K.," "I am worthwhile," "I love myself," "I am doing the best job I can," and "I forgive myself." Part of the therapy first entails discovering the particular maladaptive thought pattern the patient is unconsciously using.

Cognitive therapy when combined with biofeedback has been shown to be superior to social support in managing pain behavior.[23] Rheumatoid arthritis patients were randomly divided into three groups: either group cognitive therapy with thermal biofeedback, social support group therapy, or no-contact controls. Patients in both treatment groups had similar decreases in trait anxiety and depression. However, the cognitive- behavioral patients had significantly greater decreases in reported pain behaviors and titers of rheumatoid factor.

In a study of different treatment approaches for essential hypertension, cognitive therapy was compared with biofeedback.[24] The cognitive therapy was designed to control anger by assisting in lowering "general anger" and providing an understanding of appropriate expression of anger in specific situations. Results indicated that after 17 weeks, patients in both treatment groups had significantly lower blood pressure readings as compared to controls. Although patients in the cognitive therapy group learned to manage their anger better than the biofeedback patients, the latter group had significantly lower blood pressure readings than those in the cognitive therapy group.

Cognitive therapy has also been utilized to improve the immune functioning of a group of asymptomatic gay men awaiting HIV-1 serostatus notification.[25] HIV-1 seropositive individuals were found to exhibit decreased immune functioning over their seronegative counterparts as determined by higher titers of Epstein-Barr viral capsid antigen (EBV- VCA), lower blastogenesis to PHA, and lower CD4 cell counts. The only immune parameter not different between the two groups was Herpes virus type-6 (HHV-6) antibody titers. Following five weeks of treatment with either cognitive behavioral stress management or aerobic exercise, both groups manifested significant decreases in EBV-VCA and HHV-6 antibody titers as compared to assessment-only controls.

Cognitive therapy has also been shown to be effective in the treatment of the complex and controversial group of symptoms called chronic fatigue syndrome.[26] The maladaptive thoughts discovered in this study about this disease were that physical symptoms always imply tissue damage, and that physical activities will exacerbate these symptoms. Cognitive therapy to alter these thoughts led to significant improvements in overall disability, fatigue, somatic, and psychiatric symptoms.

Undoubtedly, combinational approaches offer the advantage of "taking the best of" each of the treatments or insuring that each participant is going to respond to at least one dimension of the treatment. One study utilized a multicomponent treatment of irritable bowel syndrome involving cognitive therapy along with relaxation and biofeedback.[27] Results indicated that half of the patients achieved a 50% reduction in symptoms, which lasted up to two years.

Selected case reports have suggested that cognitive therapy interventions were responsible for some medically documented remissions of cancer. In one, the famous composer, Bela Bartok, was on his death bed in the hospital with terminal leukemia. He had been very despondent over the lack of response to his work in America. While in the hospital, Serge Koussevitzky commissioned him to write a work for the Boston Symphony. This validation rekindled not only his spirit, but sent his leukemia into remission for several more years while he composed his most successful work, the "Concerto for Orchestra."[28]

Another case study revealed a self-punitive man working in a religious sect in Japan. Following his diagnosis with maxilla cancer, he visited the sect leader, who validated his invaluable importance to the sect. This affirmation was evidently internalized as documented by his subsequent cure from his cancer.[29]

Hypnosis

Hypnosis has probably stirred up as much controversy as any technique in psychology. But, like each of the techniques discussed heretofore in this chapter, hypnosis depends to some degree on the development of the capacity to utilize relaxation skills as well as the elimination of enough defensiveness to begin to surrender oneself to verbalized commands and suggestions. With cognitive therapy, however, these verbal affirmations were under the control of the patient. The patient, in fact, does not have to believe in the concept of cognitive therapy for it to work, only comply with the homework.

As we move down the consciousness ladder to hypnosis and imagery, however, a fundamental belief and trust must be able to develop between the patient, the therapist, and the techniques. Otherwise, projective therapy techniques work nicely in elucidating certain repressed feelings which the resistant patient is defending against. Obviously, if the patient has never participated in such an intimate bond, then these techniques must wait for the proper timing.

Hypnosis is definitely the most intimate relationship between patient and therapist on the unconscious level. It has many commonalities with techniques to be discussed in the next chapter on social support, spiritual connectedness, and healing at a distance. Many therapists may consider hypnosis as a technique involving one-way control of a patient through use of a standardized script. However, information is actually being passed in many directions in this particular realm. Whether I am using my voice or a musical instrument to guide the patient, I find that I am responding all the while to very discrete and subtle information coming presumably from the patient. I say "presumably" because there are certainly other possibilities from whence the feedback is derived. Yet, when I reawaken the patient at the end of the hypnosis session, I almost always find that there was some element I was responding to during my induction which the patient goes on to describe in detail. For example, during a standardized script, the notion of a rose might pop into my head, which I will proceed to include in some unobtrusive way into the hypnotic induction, only to discover afterwards that the patient had been thinking of a rose all along. Phenomenologically, there is some unconscious feedback loop which hypnosis taps into. I have heard many hypnotherapists acknowledge the presence of this unconscious communication loop, without any of us claiming to possess psychic abilities, so I believe that these observations inductively prove the existence of some as yet unexplainable mechanism.

The literature suggests that there are two fundamental components underlying hypnosis. The first is a placebo mechanism, which underscores the importance of belief or expectancy that the suggestions made during hypnosis will occur. Research has demonstrated that this placebo mechanism operates via endorphinergic pathways. In one study the pain relief transmitted to dental patients with placebo was eliminated through an endorphin-blocking drug called nalaxone.[30] Placebo and hypnosis have both been found to exhibit the "law of thirds." One-third of the population responds well to both placebo and hypnosis, one-third responds in a mediocre fashion, and a third very little at all. Thus, expectancy plays a large roll in determining suggestibility.

The second mechanism involves a perceptual dissociation from sensory stimuli. This dissociative process has been found not to rely on endorphinergic mechanisms.[31] In an attempt to isolate and compare these two components, however, neither hypnotic induction without suggestion nor suggestion without induction alone were any better than the other in attenuating pain.[32] Furthermore, pain reactions were modulated far less than when the two components were combined. Even acupuncture may be more closely linked with imagery and placebo analgesia, for its effects can also be reversed with naloxone.[33] While the placebo component of hypnosis probably involves endorphinergic mechanisms, the induction component of hypnosis has been found to attenuate anxiety and anxiety-induced plasma cortisol levels.[34] Some association has even been made between the classic hypnosis "eye-roll" maneuver and optimum functioning of the pituitary gland, which controls adrenal activity.[35] Therefore, hypnosis is really a combination of relaxation and placebo.

But hypnosis goes further than mere relaxation, as Figure 5-1 suggests. A patient can relax muscles and learn to dilate blood vessels with some kind of feedback mechanism. Yet, the focus of someone under hypnosis is narrowed to a pinpoint so that very little else is being attended to. The patient may be able to perceive extraneous sensory stimuli, yet is aware only of the instructions being given. Once I had an extremely loud fire alarm go off in a building while a patient was under hypnosis. The alarm blared for a good five minutes, but when the patient reawakened, she could not recall the alarm at all.

Music is a very powerful hypnotic. And while it has been accused of programming negative messages to alienated youth, music has been used for millennia in ancient cultures to induce trance states conducive to healing. I utilize a variety of such musical instruments from gongs to drums to the human voice to teach patients how to enter the world of unconscious mental focus. Many musicians I have worked with had interestingly lost the ability to enter this unconscious world due to the formal musical training they had pursued. They were utilizing a more conscious, analytical mode of thinking. These same musicians also seemed to have lost the ability to use their own musical instruments to "play." Instead of "playing" their instrument as a child may have done, they now "performed" their instrument. One can probably find no purer state of hypnosis than to observe children at "play." They are in dream worlds that often completely exclude knowledge of reality or the present, much to the chagrin of parents at times. Undoubtedly, part of the movement to "find your lost child" may be the reawakening of lost abilities to undergo hypnosis. I have found many addictive behaviors to be maladaptive attempts to recreate similar hypnotic states that may have been familiar during more carefree, playful times during childhood. There is also a spiritual aspect to addictive behaviors which will be discussed in the next chapter.

Nevertheless, hypnosis involves possibly a third mechanism. This is especially evident in the demonstrated abilities under hypnosis to both turn on and off bleeding.[36] Control of blood flow may be the essential mechanism in the hypnotic 1) removal of warts, 2) inhibition of the immediate type of skin hypersensitivity, and 3) cancer regression. The way in which hypnosis influences both vascular and immunological events may involve the aforementioned pituitary/adrenal pathway, as the production of norepinephrine and cortisol has both immediate and long-term effects upon these systems. However, Becker's work has demonstrated that hypnotic induction involves a shift in the direct current polarity of the skin.[37] The presence of suggestions may be much more effective when presented under this change of polarity. Researchers have shown that learning is enhanced when presented to subjects just following particular types of polarity shifts.[38] And, because immune cells learn and respond to electrical changes, they may be more teachable during hypnotic states. Therefore, this proposed third mechanism of hypnosis is hypothesized to operate via the D.C. electrical system of the body.

Table 5-3 contains some of the important studies demonstrating the effectiveness of hypnosis on physiological healing, with particular emphasis upon the immune system.

TABLE 5-3. *HYPNOSIS AND PHYSICAL HEALING*

1st Author	Date	Results
Sears	1932	Hypnosis reduced experimentally-induced pain in normal subjects more so than without hypnosis
Wolfe	1962	Hypnosis reduced pain in cases of terminal cancer
Lea	1960	Intractable pain patients were significantly improved and most taken off pain medications following hypnotherapy
Friedman	1977	Hypnosis more effective than biofeedback in reducing blood pressure in hypertensives
Evans	1988	Hypnosis during anesthesia decreased postoperative days, pyrexia, and gastrointestinal problems following surgery
Sinclair-Gieben	1959	Hypnosis directed to only one side of patients' bodies with bilateral warts resulted in wart removal on only the side focused on
Spanos	1990	In a comparison of hypnosis, topical treatment with salicylic acid, and placebo with a no-treatment control condition in the removal of warts, only the hypnotic subjects had lost significantly more warts than the control subjects.
Koldys	1991	In a case of epidermolysis bullose, hypnosis and imagery decreased painful skin blistering and itching; patient cut dosages in half of her three immunosuppressant drugs
Zachariae	1993	Immediate type of hypersensitivity reactions to known allergens was measured in which subjects were hypnotized to either increase or decrease their response during sensitization; double blind testing one month later confirmed the hypnotically-induced differences between the groups given opposite suggestions

(continued)

TABLE 5-3. *HYPNOSIS AND PHYSICAL HEALING (continuation)*

1st Author	Date	Results
Smith	1983	Tuberculin skin test reduced with only placebo
Black	1963	The Mantoux tuberculin skin test was found to be smaller in size in subjects hypnotized to inhibit their response
Zachariae	1991	Hypnosis was found to alter monocytic chemotactic activity in a group of subjects asked to experience different emotional states
British TB Association	1968	Hypnosis improved asthma symptoms in a greater number of patients as compared to the control group
Smith	1981	Hypnosis effected a higher tolerance in a metacholine challenge test than no treatment in asthmatics
Gravitz	1985	Hypnosis for pain control was followed by remission in a case of breast cancer
Bowers	1978	Age regression hypnosis was involved in remission in a case of metastatic testicular cancer

Perhaps the most successful use of hypnosis with physical problems involves the remediation of pain. This is because the motivation to remove pain may be higher than with other disorders which don't involve physical pain. In the laboratory, investigators have found that hypnotized subjects manifested less pain reactions than nonhypnotized subjects.[39-40] Clinical evidence has demonstrated that hypnosis has been able to elicit pain relief in cases of terminal cancer.[41] Patients with intractable pain have been significantly improved and most taken off pain medications following hypnotherapy.[42] Pain shown to be unresponsive to surgery has been effectively eliminated with hypnosis.[43] Examples of body-specific analgesias, such as those employing the "glove" technique, have been reported, as well as complete analgesia during surgical and dental procedures.

Another physical condition which has been shown to be readily influenced by hypnosis is dermatological pathology. As in the hypnotherapeutic treatment of pain, the affected areas of the body seem to respond only when they are specifically attended to. For example, patients with bilateral warts have had their condition ameliorated unilaterally when hypnotic suggestions were directed to only one side of their body.[44] Some have suggested that the expectation for treatment success is correlated with actual improvement.[45] However, one study compared hypnosis, topical treatment with salicylic acid, and placebo against a no-treatment control condition in the removal of warts.[46] All three treatment conditions elicited the same measured degree of expectation of success. At the six-week follow-up however, only the hypnotic subjects had lost significantly more warts than the control subjects.

Hypnosis has also been found to be highly successful in the treatment of other skin conditions, including eczema, psoriasis, acne, dermatitis, urticaria, and pruritus.[47-48] In one case of epidermolysis bullose, an autoimmune disease in which the immune system attacks the skin, hypnosis and imagery were used to decrease painful skin blistering and itching, and reeducate the immune system to stop eating the collagen.[49] Further results indicated that this patient was able to cut the dosage in half of her three immunosuppressant drugs.

The mechanism behind the hypnotically induced changes in dermatological conditions implies that the immune system is involved, especially in the last-reported case of the autoimmune disease, epidermolysis bullose. Further evidence of immune system involvement comes from studies of the immediate type of hypersensitivity reactions. Cutaneous reactivity to challenge with known allergens was measured in one study in which subjects were hypnotized to either increase or decrease their response during sensitization.[50] Double blind testing one month later confirmed the hypnotically-induced differences between the groups given opposite suggestions. In another study, the Mantoux tuberculin skin test was found to be smaller in size in subjects hypnotized to inhibit their response.[51] Histological analysis of biopsies from these subjects suggested that the observed phenomenon was due to vascular changes rather than immunological changes. However, hypnosis was found to alter monocytic chemotactic activity in another study in which a group of subjects were asked to experience different emotional states.[52]

Asthma is another condition involving the immune system which has been found to be amenable to hypnosis treatment. A large study conducted by the British Tuberculosis Association found improvement in asthma symptoms in a significantly greater number of patients as compared to the control group.[53] Another study of asthmatics demonstrated that hypnosis effected a higher tolerance in a metacholine challenge test than no treatment.[54]

Of critical importance to this book are several citations evidencing remission from cancer due to hypnosis. Although the reports are case studies, medical documentation confirmed the presence of spontaneous remission. In one report of an intervention conducted in 1846, prior to the use of ether anesthesia, a patient was being hypnotically prepared in pain control for several days prior to her scheduled surgery for breast cancer.[55] When she went in for surgery, fully hypnotized, the four surgeons refused to operate as the cancer had completely remissed.

A second case study reported on the use of age regression hypnotherapy with a patient with testicular cancer and pulmonary metastases.[56] During the age regression, the patient, who had experienced much abandonment in his life, remembered a loving relative who had since died. This intervention created a major psychological shift in the patient which was followed by complete remission of his cancer.

Imagery and Meditation

Imagery and meditation are natural extensions of the techniques of hypnosis and relaxation/biofeedback. Instead of accomplishing the learning through external feedback mechanisms, imagery and meditation utilize more internalized, unconscious feedback systems. Unlike hypnosis, practically everyone can be taught imagery skills. However, there are individuals called alexithymic which have a very concrete, static, and two-dimensional imagery capability at first. Alexithymic individuals have had suppressed feelings for so long that they are not only "without words for feelings," but practically unaware of feelings altogether. This relationship elucidates the close connection between imagery and the emotions.

Some psychologists, such as Peter Lang, have conducted award-winning research on the validation of these intimate connections between imagery and the emotions.[57] Joseph Shor utilized brief imagery exercises as projection techniques into the emotional soul of patients less in touch with their feelings.[58] Jeanne Achterberg has discussed the brain research findings that imagery utilizes more right cerebral hemispheric activity, which in turn has prolific connections with the emotion center of the brain—the limbic system.[59]

Mind-body critics have suggested that imagery is not directly responsible for cell-specific physiological responses, but rather that it is, at best, a reflection of how well someone is relaxed. While I would agree that imagery vividness is associated with the depth of relaxation, it may act to assist in the relaxation rather than the other way around. I have seen people experience deep levels of relaxation without generating any imagery. Imagery, on the other hand, has been found to yield cell- specific results in several studies, guiding cells to accomplish feats not normally associated with general relaxation.

Imagery and meditation are the unbridled experiences of the mind on its simultaneous journey through the body and the cosmos. As we will see in the next chapter, imagery is highly amenable to transpersonal influences. Imagery contains none of the distortion of dreams and therefore contains important information relating to past, present, and future. Probably nowhere does the dynamic spirit of the bodymind become as manifest as it does through imagery and meditation. For an overview of research on the use of imagery and meditation on physical healing, see Table 5-4.

TABLE 5-4. *IMAGERY/MEDITATION AND PHYSICAL HEALING*

1st Author	Date	Results
Orme-Johnson	1987	Meditation led to 50% fewer inpatient and outpatient medical visits for children and young adults, 70% reduction in older adults; by disease category, reduction in admissions were 87% for cardiovascular and nervous system diseases, 55% for malignancies, and 30% for infectious diseases

(continued)

TABLE 5-4. *IMAGERY/MEDITATION AND PHYSICAL HEALING (continuation)*

1st Author	Date	Results
Fernandez	1989	Meta-analysis of a variety of cognitive-behavioral techniques used for pain management concluded that imagery was found to be associated with the greatest amount of pain-relief
Achterberg	1977; 1984	Concurrent blood chemistries and prediction of subsequent disease status of cancer patients were most highly correlated with mental imagery of one's disease/health
Meares	1976	Reported case studies medically documenting cancer remissions following imagery and deep meditation
Andrews	1990	Imagery decreased frequency of aphthous stomatitis ulcers
Zachariae	1990	Imagery increased natural killer cell activity in normal subjects
Jasnoski	1988	Imagery equal to relaxation in increasing secretory IgA over control group with only one training/testing session
Rider	1990	Imagery increased production of secretory IgA in normal subjects; imagery equal to relaxation at initial session in increasing sIgA, but greater than relaxation at weeks three and six.
Schneider	1983	Imagery of "contrary" activity in neutrophils resulted in their becoming more adhesive but not attaching to blood vessel walls, making them available for venepuncture
Rider	1989	Imagery of specific leukocyte subtypes led to quantitative changes in only that subtype
Smith	1983	Imagery enabled the suppression of tuberculin skin test
Smith	1985; 1989	Imagery selectively suppressed or enhanced skin test response and in vitro lymphocyte stimulation test for varicella zoster

Meditation has been found to be highly successful in reducing and preventing physical disease. When transcendental meditators (TM) were compared to a normative base of members of the same insurance carrier, the TM group was discovered to have 70% fewer inpatient and outpatient medical visits for older adults and a 50% drop for children and young adults.[60] Meditation seemed to have its greatest effect on cardiovascular diseases, with an 87% reduction in admissions. Cancer admissions were reduced by 55% in the TM group and infectious diseases witnessed a 30% decline.

Imagery has shared an equally impressive victory over physical illness. Imagery as a distraction technique has been utilized for many years. In a meta-analysis of a variety of cognitive-behavioral techniques used for pain management, imagery was determined to be associated with the greatest amount of pain relief.[61]

Once the association between imagery and the immune system began to be explored, a momentous finding emerged. A group of pioneers of imagery medicine composed of Drs. Achterberg, Lawlis, Simonton, and Simonton concluded that of a host of psychological and blood chemistry variables, "imagery of a positive outcome" was the most highly correlated with survivability from terminal cancer.[62] The important features of one's imagery were discovered to be "vividness," "activity," and the overall "perceived effectiveness." Another feature associated with survivors, and that may be germane to the harmonic organization hypothesis of homeodynamism, was the presence during the imagery of bright colors as opposed to pastels.[63] When imagery scores were used as a cutoff between those who were high and low, 93% of the stage IV cancer patients who were low imagers had cancer progression or died. On the other hand, 100% of the high imagers showed no evidence of new disease or went into remission.[64]

Many medically-documented case studies have been reported on the use of meditation and imagery in the remission of cancer.[65-70] By having his patients use visualization exercises similar to those of the Simontons' while in a state of deep meditation, Meares reported that 10% of his cancer patients regressed and another 20% evidenced marked slowing of cancer growth.

Another disease involving the immune system, recurrent aphthous stomatitis, has been resistant to most therapeutic regimens. However, imagery was found to have a profound curative effect on ulcer recurrence for all subjects participating in one study.[71]

Many more recent studies on imagery have demonstrated a wide variety of effects on specific components of the immune system in normal subjects, including increased natural killer cell activity[72] and sIgA.[73] We also demonstrated increases in sIgA production which were equal to those elicited by music-mediated relaxation. However, the imagery group surpassed the relaxation group after three weeks of training, suggesting that imagery allows for a more advanced type of conditioning of the immune system than is available by relaxation alone.[74]

This superiority of imagery over relaxation has been demonstrated in another study in which subjects imaged their neutrophils becoming more adherent.[75] Pre- and post test venipunctures indicated that there was no change in neutrophil adherence but that the neutrophil count declined. Hypothesizing that the neutrophil counts decreased due to their increased adherence, the group then had the subjects image their neutrophils behaving in a way that was foreign to their normal way of acting, by becoming more adherent but staying in the bloodstream and not sticking to the blood vessel walls. This in fact happened as witnessed by the increased adherence in neutrophils this time without any change in count. Somehow, the message to behave in a novel way was communicated directly to these white blood cells in an extremely fast-acting manner.

Based on the exciting results from Schneider's group, we conducted a study which taught subjects in one group to focus imagery on neutrophil activity while another group was trained to image a different white blood cell—lymphocytes.[76] After subjects had reached a point in which an imagery shift had been experienced, as measured by an increase in vividness, activity, content, etc., white blood count differentials were run before and after a 20-minute imagery session. Amazingly, only the blood cell which was focused on changed significantly for both groups, indicating again that an immediate biological effect was able to be communicated to the immune system.

Dr. Richard Smith of the University of Arkansas Medical School conducted a fascinating series of studies which corroborated the presence of this communication system with subjects' responses to delayed-type hypersensitivity skin tests. In one study a group of tuberculin-positive subjects was administered tuberculin on one arm and saline on the other for 5 months. When the vials were switched without the subjects' knowledge, the tuberculin skin responses were significantly lower due to the subjects' expectation (imagery) that there would be no reaction.[77] In another set of experiments, subjects were taught to use imagery to enhance or suppress their skin response to varicella zoster, the viral agent for chicken pox. Results indicated that both the skin tests and the lymphocyte stimulation assays were in the direction of the imagery.[78-79]

Mental Healing Techniques and Neurophysiological Shifts

Although it may sound a bit paradoxical, thinking is not necessarily associated with shifts in electrical activity of the brain. In fact, fast-wave, unsynchronized beta activity is the predominant brain wave pattern for normal thought. Although there are shifts with each particular thought, these are so small that they get washed out due to the background noise consisting of similar micro-shifts occurring everywhere else in the brain. Yet, when a person is engaged in any of the mental healing techniques described in this chapter, profound frequency and coherence shifts are found which satisfy their fulfillment of the criteria under homeodynamic theory. For an overview of the research on the neurophysiological shifts associated with these techniques, see Table 5-5.

TABLE 5-5. *MENTAL HEALING TECHNIQUES AND NEUROPHYSIOLOGICAL SHIFTS*

1st Author	Date	Results
Tebecis	1976–1977	Autogenics training led to increases in slow-wave and decreases in fast-wave EEG activity
Lubar	1989	Autogenics increased theta-wave EEG activity
Ikemi	1988	Autogenics increased theta-wave and decreased beta-wave EEG activity
Luthe	1959	Autogenics led to increased alpha activity with increases in alpha frequency as well

(continued)

TABLE 5-5. *MENTAL HEALING TECHNIQUES AND*
NEUROPHYSIOLOGICAL SHIFTS (continuation)

1st Author	Date	Results
Morse	1977	Relaxation, meditation, and hypnosis were each shown to exhibit periodic brain wave slowing into alpha as compared with alertness
Fried	1987	Relaxation associated with deep breathing elicited increases in alpha and decreases in theta
Barabasz	1982	Restricted environmental stimulation increased alpha EEG activity
Gellhorn	1972	Close association demonstrated between ergotrophic functions such as high EMG levels and fast desynchronized EEG activity, and vice versa
Peniston	1989	Hand-warming biofeedback used as a way of stimulating alpha/theta brain wave shifts
Morgan	1974	High hypnotizable subjects showed more alpha EEG activity during music, imagery, and hypnosis than low hypnotizables
MacLeod	1982	Hypnosis increased alpha EEG activity with shift from left to right hemisphere
Evans	1982	High hypnotizables found to exhibit increased alpha brain wave productivity
Bauer	1980	Hypnosis stimulated decreased alpha and increased beta EEG activity
Raikov	1983	Regression hypnosis increased theta and delta EEG activity
Tebecis	1975	Hypnosis increased theta EEG activity
Sabourin	1990–1991	Hypnosis increased theta EEG activity
Banquet	1973	Meditation induced synchronized brain wave activity
Glueck	1978	Meditation induced interhemispheric coherence in psychiatric patients
Jevning	1992	Review of meditation studies finding increased EEG synchrony
Walter	1970	Imagery elicited alpha blocking and increased beta EEG activity
Rugg	1982	Imagery of specific objects increased beta EEG activity

Very little data is available on EEG shifts during the cognitive therapy task of repeating verbal affirmations. On the other hand, autogenics training has many similarities with cognitive therapy through its repeated suggestions about body functions. Experimentally controlled studies have demonstrated significant increases in slow brainwave activity and decreases in beta-wave activity after $4\frac{1}{2}$ months of autogenics training.[80] Increases in theta activity have been reported in patients who engaged in the repetition of autogenic phrases.[17] In another study employing autogenic-like techniques in a paradigm called "self-regulation method," again decreases were noted in the beta-band along with increases in the theta-band.[81] Autogenics has been shown to have some similarities to sleep through the increased alpha activity. However, during sleep, the principal alpha frequency decreased whereas autogenics was characterized by an increase in alpha frequency, the so-called "autogenic shift."[21]

An abundant amount of data exists on the elicitation of EEG shifts of various types during relaxation and biofeedback. The most common frequency shifts observed during states of hypoarousal due to relaxation induction include increases in alpha brainwave production and decreases in mean theta production, although transient theta waves may still be present.[82-83] Even restricted environmental stimulation has been found to elicit alpha-band activity.[84] Therefore, a shift from beta to alpha brainwave activity is inherent in most relaxation-oriented techniques. In describing the alpha EEG rhythm, standard electroencephalography texts in fact relate it to conditions of "physical relaxation" and "mental inactivity."[85]

Biofeedback as a relaxation technique has its roots in the decrease of ergotropic, or sympathetic autonomic activity and the increase of trophotropic, or parasympathetic activity. Increasing trophotropic activity through such biofeedback procedures as hand-warming, EMG lowering, and hand-drying (galvanic skin response) therefore has a close relationship with the elicitation of synchronized, slow brain wave activity.[86]

In one study of biofeedback in which the EEG was used as both the independent and dependent variable, Peniston and Kulkosky administered alpha/theta EEG and finger temperature training to depressed alcoholics.[16] Alpha\theta feedback was received auditorily from brainmap site O1. Results indicated that alpha and theta activity increased 12-fold and 7-fold, respectively, in the experimental group while no increase was exhibited in the controls (also alcoholics). B-endorphins were significantly higher in the controls than the experimentals following treatment. Clinical data indicated that after biofeedback, the treatment group was significantly less depressed than the controls, and experienced a relapse rate of 20% as opposed to 80% in the controls.

The further implication for a connection between immune and CNS activity can be derived from this study. One of the important health benefits of brainwave shifting for depressives may be to lower endorphins, which if chronically-elevated, can have deleterious effects upon the immune system. The hypothesis of homeodynamic theory is that static overusage of any particular brainwave (beta in the case of depressives and alcoholics) will increase stress and its concomitant elevation of endorphins.

Hypnosis has demonstrated some features of EEG activity which are somewhat unique from relaxation, biofeedback, meditation, and imagery. Although many studies have reported the more traditional increases in alpha-band production[87-88], others have reported the opposite finding of decreased alpha[89] or increases in production of theta-band activity.[90-92] Some have reported increases in alpha activity in the right hemisphere following hypnosis.[93] Whether the alpha activity increased or decreased, the important homeodynamic feature of all of the EEG studies of hypnosis is that the predominant baseline brainwave frequency changed following induction.

One other feature of the hypnosis literature bears some resemblance to the studies of CNS activity during autogenics training. As opposed to the techniques of relaxation/biofeedback and meditation/imagery, far more theta-band activity was found in the hypnosis and cognitive therapy conditions. This fact possibly relates to the verbalized content, whether from internal or external sources, of the induction procedure. It is possible that any regularly occurring phrase, or stimulus for that matter, may tend to produce activity in either the alpha-band or theta-band, or both. Various researchers have shown that regular pulse-trains of light flashes[94] or sounds[95] are capable of producing theta and alpha brainwaves. Perhaps, then, the consistency of the stimulus, whether voice, light, or drumbeat, contributes to the productivity of not only alpha, but especially theta-band activity.

Two other possibilities exist in explaining the high prevalence of theta brainwave activity during hypnosis and cognitive therapy. The existence of verbalized phrases, whether spoken by the patient during cognitive therapy, or internalized as verbalizations during hypnotic induction, may induce some kind of hyperventilation response due to the possible interruption of breathing patterns. Hyperventilation has been found to cause higher incidences of theta, due to a transient hypocapnic (reduced carbon dioxide) condition in the cerebral vascular bed.[83]

The other explanation has to do with the ontogeny of EEG rhythms in the development of the human body. Theta and alpha rhythms predominate in young children until puberty, when faster beta rhythms begin to take over.[96] Hypnosis and cognitive therapy (particularly autogenic training) may induce a regressed brainwave state back to some time period during childhood when the individual was very receptive to suggestions by adults and other figures of authority. Evidence for this explanation has been demonstrated through the high percentages of theta and delta activity yielded following age-regression hypnosis.[90] Although rarely experienced by adults except in deep sleep, delta waves are commonly found in awake babies. Therefore, the healing role of hypnosis and cognitive therapy may reside in the brainwave shifts underlying the capacity to regress, as opposed to the ability to experience hypoarousal.

Meditation and imagery also appear to produce their healing effects through homeodynamic brainwave shifts. These shifts are somewhat different from those experienced in cognitive therapy or hypnosis, however. In meditation, the frequency shifts have been found to have spanned a large range of activity, from alpha, to theta, to fast beta, and back to alpha.[97] Meditation has in fact been found in one study to exhibit a wide range of frequency activity which the investigators proposed was similar to the different sleep stages.[98] Sidestepping the debate over whether meditation and sleep differ is the presence of a dynamic range of activity relevant to the healing properties of both meditation and sleep.

However, the feature of meditation which appears different from sleep is the high amount of synchronized activity, especially in the beta-band, which has been reported in meditation.[97,99-100] This synchronization of EEG activity, or coherence as it is sometimes referred to, represents the homeoresonant properties of homeodynamic theory.

Like many of the mental techniques for achieving physical healing, it is difficult to tease apart imagery from meditation, hypnosis, and relaxation, as one can hardly not experience prolific imagery during these other forms of hypoarousal. The specific topic of brain activity while a patient is undergoing spontaneous or healing-specific imagery has not been reported in the literature. Brain studies of the act of imagining specific objects requested by the experimenter have been conducted and generally show a blocking of alpha and an increase in beta-band activity.[96,101]

We witnessed this alpha-blocking phenomenon in the brainmapping study we conducted on our own patients with immune disturbances. One of the tasks consisted of their own spontaneous images of the healing process occurring within their bodies. Whereas the eyes closed conditions consisted of fairly constant synchronized, slow wave activity, the EEG recordings of these images were marked not just by alpha-blocking, but by alternating shifts between alpha and beta-band frequencies. This imagery- based activity also differed from active thought, which was characterized by more continuous beta activity. During the imaging tasks, rhythms alternating between about two seconds of alpha and about two seconds of beta were not uncommon. This suggests the presence of a very slow rhythm with a frequency of about .25 Hz. However, this rhythm is much faster, and therefore dynamic, than that of a continuously alert or relaxed EEG which would contain an alpha burst (in the case of alertness) or a beta burst (in the case of relaxation) perhaps every ten seconds, yielding a rhythm of about .1 Hz.

The implication is that for the bodymind to be constructing images which create and recreate physical health, a certain rhythmic language of brainwave activity consisting of alpha and then beta bursts needs to exist. If one thinks of beta as the drumbeat and alpha as the silence in between, you have a rhythmic structure with which practically any musical landscape can be embroidered. One neurophysiologist has demonstrated that the mental image is analogous to the frames of a motion picture.[102] Applying what we know from our own research, alpha-band activity is perhaps like the boundaries separating each motion picture frame. If too much beta activity is present, the motion picture reels by too fast to make any sense of; however, if too much alpha exists, the screen goes blank and nothing at all is perceived.

EEG and Imagery: The Good, the Blank, and the Ugly

In our EEG studies of mental imagery, patient imagery turned out to be different from that of healthy controls in several interesting ways. First, in analyzing the frequency of images which spontaneously arose during a 5-minute period, healthy controls consistently yielded about 10 images, with the images becoming more prolific as time increased. Patients' imagery tended to fall into one of two groups. One group had a low number of images, which may have started out blank or, when content appeared, was emotionally uncomfortable or "ugly." This group tended to be a posttraumatic stress disorder group composed of individuals who had experienced some type of emotional or physical trauma, such as sexual abuse, which had been left unresolved. This group required more of a psychotherapy-based approach to therapy, to discharge the feelings associated with their unresolved trauma.

The second patient group had a high number of images which was higher than the controls' frequency. The pattern of imagery emergence was different from the controls as well. The images of this second patient group, as opposed to the control group, became less prolific over time. This group tended to be a high-stress group which simply needed to take the time to slow down. These individuals required more of a stress management/psychoeducational approach to therapy, emphasizing the actual role of the organs in the body during both stress and health.

Already reported in Chapter 2 on functional resonance between body, brain, and mind is the finding in our EEG studies of uni-harmonic organization of brainwaves in the healthy controls while engaged in the mental imagery task. The patients were found to demonstrate a bi-harmonic spectral organization containing two fundamental centers, each of lower voltage.

An analysis of the images of both patients and controls was conducted, comparing those which were rated "good or effective" with those rated "ugly, blank, or ineffective." This analysis indicated some intriguing features of mental imagery. Perhaps the most important feature relates to the reason that imagery is such a useful prognostic and treatment approach to immune disorders. Good images yielded more electrical activity in the brain, especially at the slower brainwave frequencies. As we have seen, this electrical activity is important in stimulating both normal cell-to-cell communication through the regulation of ionic channels, and the immune system.

As can be seen in the brain map of alpha activity in Figure 2102 BIM, this fibromyalgia patient has a total of 6 electrode sites at an amplitude over 4 uv during her attempted image of healing in which only "blackness" appeared. During an image which this patient described as more successful, 12 electrode sites reach 4 uv amplitude both frontally and occipitally (see Figure 2102 GIM). A slowing of the alpha frequency from 9 Hz to around eight also characterizes the "good" image.

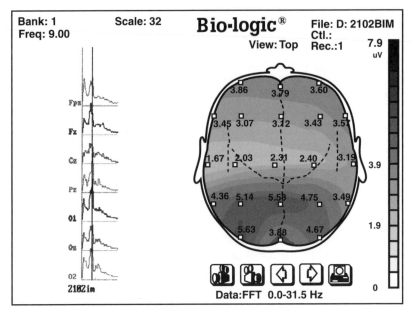

Figure 2102 BIM. *Spectral analysis and alpha brain map of fibromyalgia patients during ineffective image.*

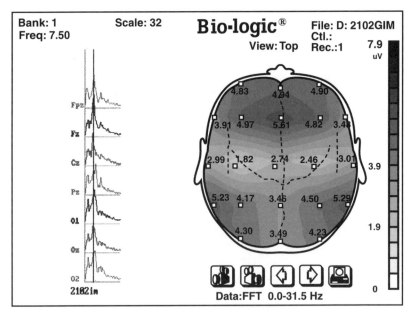

Figure 2102 GIM. *Spectral analysis and alpha brain map of fibromyaalgra patient during good image*

A rheumatoid arthritis patient in Figure 2104 BIM is unable to reach 4 uv amplitude for an uncomfortable image she describes as "trying to cool the hot pain" of her disease. In Figure 2104 GIM she successfully reaches higher voltages frontally and occipitally (in the alpha frequency band) during a more effective image she describes as "cool bubbles bathing her body."

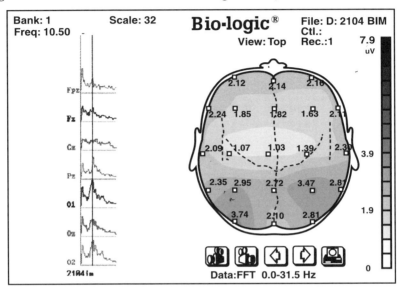

Figure 2104 BIM. *Spectral analysis and alpha brain map of rheumatoid arthritis patient during ineffective image.*

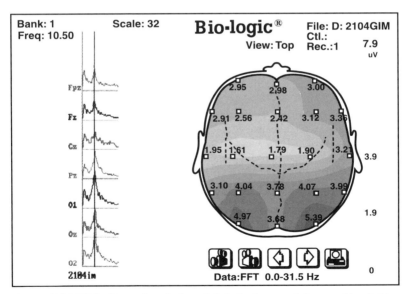

Figure 2104 GIM. *Spectral analysis and alpha brain map of rheumatoid arthritis patient during good image.*

A final pertinent feature of the brain research surrounding mental imagery is that images activate the area of the brain normally responsible for actually sensing the imaged stimulus.[103-104] For example, imagining the big toe activates that area of the motor cortex, while imagining a beautiful landscape activates the visual cortex. Furthermore, activity of one's health-specific imagery has been found to be highly correlated with the production of the desired results.[64] Integrating this information, creating health apparently requires the dynamic stimulation of different parts of the brain, corresponding to those "motion picture frames" making up the movie occurring in one's bodymind. Imagery apparently elicits just this sort of dynamic EEG activity through the presence of the .25 Hz rhythm relating to the variability in frequency bands. Because the brain activity underlying this motion picture is coherent, or synchronous, again highlights the homeodynamic nature of mental imagery as a healing technique

References

1. Figueroa, J.L. (1982). Group treatment of chronic tension headaches: A comparative treatment study. *Behavior Modification, 6*, 229–239.

2. Haynes, S.N., Griffin, P., Mooney, D., & Parise, M. (1975). Electromyographic biofeedback and relaxation instructions in the treatment of muscle contraction headaches. *Behavior Therapy, 6*, 672–678.

3. Gauthier, J., Bois, R., Allaire, D., & Drolet, M. (1981). Evaluation of skin temperature biofeedback training at two different sites for migraine. *Journal of Behavioral Medicine, 4*, 407–420.

4. Blanchard, E.B., & Haynes, M.R. (1975). Biofeedback treatment of a case of Raynaud's disease. *Journal of Behavior Therapy and Experimental Psychiatry, 6*, 230–234.

5. Blanchard, E.B., Young, L.D., & Haynes, M.R. (1975). A simple feedback system for the treatment of elevated blood pressure. *Behavior Therapy, 6*, 241–245.

6. Elder, S.T., Ruiz, Z.R., Deabler, H.L., & Dillenkoffer, R.L. (1973). Instrumental conditioning of diastolic blood pressure in essential hypertensive patients. *Journal of Applied Behavior Analysis, 6*, 377–382.

7. Khan, A.U., Staerk, M., & Bonk, C. (1973). Role of counter- conditioning in the treatment of asthma. *Journal of Psychosomatic Research, 17*, 389–392.

8. Auerbach, J.E., Oleson, T.D., & Solomon, G.F. (1992). A behavioral medicine intervention as an adjunctive treatment for HIV-related illness. *Psychology and Health, 6*, 325–334.

9. Peavey, B.S., Lawlis, G.F., & Goven, A. (1985). Biofeedback-assisted relaxation: Effects on phagocytic capacity. *Biofeedback and Self- Regulation, 10*, 33–47.

10. Shulimson, A.D., Lawrence, P.F., & Iacono, C.U. (1987). The effect of thermal biofeedback-mediated relaxation training on healing. *Biofeedback and Self-Regulation, 11*, 311–319.

11. Rider, M.S., Floyd, J., & Kirkpatrick, J. (1985). The effect of music, imagery, and relaxation on adrenal corticosteroids and the re-entrainment of circadian rhythms. *Journal of Music Therapy, 22*(1), 46–58.

12. Gruber, B.L., Hersh, S.P., Hall, N.R.S., Waletzky, L.R., Kunz, J.F., Carpenter, J.K., Kverno, K.S., & Weiss, S.M. (1993). Immunological responses of breast cancer patients to behavioral interventions. *Biofeedback and Self-Regulation, 18*(1), 1–21.

13. McGrady, A., Conran, P., Dickey, D., Garman, D., Farris, E., & Schumann-Brzezinski, C. (1992). The effects of biofeedback- assisted relaxation on cell-mediated immunity, cortisol, and white blood cell count in healthy adult subjects. *Journal of Behavioral Medicine, 15*(4), 343–354.

14. Zachariae, R., Kristensen, J.S., Hokland, P., Ellegaard, J., Metze, E., & Hokland, M. (1990). Effect of psychological intervention in the form of relaxation and guided imagery on cellular immune function in normal healthy subjects. *Psychotherapy and Psychosomatics, 54,* 32–39.

15. Kiecolt-Glaser, J.K., Glaser, R., Williger, D., Stout, J., Messick, G., Sheppard, S., Ricker, D., Romisher, S.C., Briner, W., Bonnell, G., & Donnerberg, R. (1985). Psychological enhancement of immunocompetence in a geriatric population. *Health Psychology, 4,* 25–41.

16. Peniston, E.G., & Kulkosky, P.J. (1989). Alpha-theta brainwave training and beta-endorphin levels in alcoholics. *Alcoholism: Clinical and Experimental Research, 13*(2), 271–279.

17. Lubar, J.F. (1989). Electroencephalographic biofeedback and neurological applications. In J.V. Basmajian (Ed.), *Biofeedback.* Baltimore: Williams & Wilkins.

18. Beck, A.T. (1976). *Cognitive therapy and the emotional disorders.* NY: New American Library.

19. Coates, A., Gebski, V., Signorini, D., Murray, P., McNeil, D., Byrne, M., & Forbes, J.F. (1992). Prognostic value of quality-of-life scores during chemotherapy for advanced breast cancer. *Journal of Clinical Oncology, 10*(12), 1833–1838.

20. Achterberg, J., & Lawlis, G.F. (1984). *Health attribution test.* Champaigne, IL: Institute for Personality and Ability Testing.

21. Luthe, W. (1969). *Autogenic therapy,* vol. 1-7. NY: Grune & Stratton.

22. Surwit, R.S., Pilon, R.N., & Fenton, C.H. (1978). Behavioral treatment of Raynaud's disease. *Journal of Behavioral Medicine, 1,* 323–335.

23. Bradley, L.A., Turner, R.A., Young, L.D., Agudelo, C.A., Anderson, K.O., & McDaniel, L.K. (1985). Effects of cognitive-behavioral therapy on pain behavior of rheumatoid arthritis (RA) patients. *Scandinavian Journal of Behaviour Therapy, 14*(2), 51–64.

24. Achmon, J., Granek, M., Golomb, M., & Hart, J. (1989). Behavioral treatment of essential hypertension: A comparison between cognitive therapy and biofeedback of heart rate. *Psychosomatic Medicine, 51,* 152–164.

25. Esterling, B.A., Antoni, M.H., Schneiderman, N., Carver, C.S., LaPerriere, A., Ironson, G., Klimas, N.G., & Fletcher, M.A. (1992). Psychosocial modulation of antibody to Epstein-Barr viral capsid antigen and human herpesvirus type-6 in HIV-1-infected and at-risk gay men. *Psychosomatic Medicine, 54,* 354–371.

26. Butler, S., Chalder, T., Ron, M., & Wessely, S. (1991). Cognitive behavior therapy in chronic fatigue syndrome. *Journal of Neurology, Neurosurgery, and Psyhiatry, 54,* 153–158.

27. Blanchard, E.B., Schwarz, S.P., & Neff, D.F. (1988). Two-year follow-up of behavioral treatment of irritable bowel syndrome. *Behavior Therapy, 19,* 67–73.

28. Booth, G. (1973). Psychobiological aspects of spontaneous regressions of cancer. *American Academy of Psychoanalysis Journal, 1*(3), 303–317.

29. Ikemi, Y., Nakagawa, S., Nakagawa, T., & Mineyasu, S. (1975). Psychosomatic consideration on cancer patients who have made a narrow escape from death. *Dynamische Psychiatrie, 31,* 77–92.

30. Levine, J.D., Gordon, N.C., & Fields, H.L. (1978). The mechanism of placebo analgesia. *Lancet,* September 23, 654–657.

31. McGlashan, T.H., Evans, F.J., & Orne, M.T. (1969). The nature of hypnotic analgesia and placebo response to experimental pain. *Psychosomatic Medicine, 31*(3), 227–246.

32. Evans, M.D., & Paul, G. (1970). Effects of hypnotically suggested analgesia on physiological and subjective responses to cold stress. *Journal of Consulting and Clinical Psychology, 35,* 362–371.

33. Mayer, D.J., Price, D.D., Rafii, A., & Barber, J. (1976). Acupuncture hypalgesia: Evidence for activation of a central control system as a mechanism of action. In J.J. Bonica, & D. Albe-Fessard (Eds.), *Advances in pain research and therapy, Vol. 1.* NY: Raven Press.

34. Black, S., & Friedman, M. (1968). Effects of emotion and pain on adrenocortical function investigated by hypnosis. *British Medical Journal, 1,* 477–481.

35. Leskowitz, E. (1988). The "third eye": A psychoendocrine model of hypnotizability. *American Journal of Clinical Hypnosis, 30,* 209–215.

36. Crasilneck, H.B., & Hall, J.A. (1985). *Clinical hypnosis.* Orlando, FL: Grune & Stratton.

37. Becker, R.O. (1985). *The body electric.* NY: William Morrow & Co.

38. Stamm, J.S., Whipple, S.C., & Born, J. (1987). Effects of spontaneous cortical slow potentials on semantic information processing. *International Journal of Psychophysiology, 5,* 11–18.

39. Sears, R. (1932). An experimental study of hypnotic anesthesia. *Journal of Experimental Psychology, 15,* 1–22.

40. Hilgard, E.R. (1967). The use of pain-state reports in the study of hypnotic analgesia to the pain of ice water. *Journal of Nervous and Mental Disease, 144,* 506–513.

41. Wolfe, L.S. (1962). Hypnosis and pain: A clinical instance. *American Journal of Clinical Hypnosis, 4,* 193–194.

42. Lea, P.A., Ware, P.D., & Monroe, R.R. (1960). The hypnotic control of intractable pain. *American Journal of Clinical Hypnosis, 3,* 5–8.

43. Cheek, D.B. (1966). Therapy of persistent pain states. I. Neck and shoulder pain of five years duration. *American Journal of Clinical Hypnosis, 8,* 281–286.

44. Sinclair-Gieben, A.H.C., & Chalmers, D. (1959). Treatment of warts by hypnosis. *Lancet, 2,* 480–482.

45. Johnson, R.F., & Barber, T.X. (1978). Hypnosis, suggestion, and warts: An experimental investigation implicating the importance of "believed-in efficacy." American *Journal of Clinical Hypnosis, 20,* 165–174.

46. Spanos, N.P., Williams, V., & Gwynn, M.I. (1990). Effects of hypnotic, placebo, and salicylic acid treatments on wart regression. *Psychosomatic Medicine, 52,* 109–114.

47. Mason, A.A. (1952). A case of congenital ichthyosiform erythroderma of broc treated by hypnosis. *British Medical Journal, 2,* 422–423.

48. Sampson, R.N. (1990). Hypnotherapy in a case of pruritus and Guillain-Barre syndrome. *American Journal of Clinical Hypnosis, 32,* 168–173.

49. Lightfoot, M.J., & Koldys, K.W. (1991). Applying the mind to EBA— A story of patient-doctor cooperation. *Advances, 7*(4), 3–15.

50. Zachariae, R., & Bjerring, P. (1993). Increase and decrease of delayed cutaneous reactions obtained by hypnotic suggestions during sensitization. *Allergy, 48,* 6–11.

51. Black, S., Humphrey, J.H., & Niven, J.S.F. (1963). Inhibition of Mantoux reaction by direct suggestion under hypnosis. *British Medical Journal, 5346,* 1649–1652.

52. Zachariae, R., Bjerring, P., Zachariae, C., Arendt-Nielsen, L., Nielsen, T., Eldrup, E., Larsen, C.S., & Gotliebsen, K. (1991). Monocyte chemotactic activity in sera after hypnotically-induced emotional states. *Scandinavian Journal of Immunology, 34,* 71–79.

53. British Tuberculosis Association. (1968). *Hypnosis for asthma: A controlled trial.* A report of the research committee of the British Tuberculosis Association, 4:71–76.

54. Smith, L.J., Wain, H.J., & Evans, R. (1981). The effects of hypnosis on bronchial response to methacholine in asthma. *Journal of Allergy and Clinical Immunology, 67:*44.

55. Gravitz, M.A. (1985). An 1846 report of tumor remission associated with hypnosis. *American Journal of Clinical Hypnosis, 28*(1), 16–19.

56. Bowers, M.K., & Weinstock, C. (1978). A case of healing in malignancy. *American Academy of Psychoanalysis, 6*(3), 393–402.

57. Lang, P.J. (1979). A bio-informational theory of emotional imagery. *Psychophysiology, 16*(6), 495–512.

58. Shorr, J.E. (1972). *Psycho-imagination therapy : the integration of phenomenology and imagination.* NY: Intercontinental Medical Book Corporation.

59. Achterberg, J., & Lawlis, G.F. (1980). *Bridges of the bodymind.* Champaign, IL: Institute for Personality and Ability Testing.

60. Orme-Johnson, D. (1987). Medical care utilization and the transcendental meditation program. *Psychosomatic Medicine, 49,* 493-507.

61. Fernandez, E., & Turk, D.C. (1989). The utility of cognitive coping strategies for altering pain perception: a meta-analysis. *Pain, 38,* 123-135.

62. Achterberg, J., Lawlis, G.F., Simonton, O.C., & Simonton, S. (1977). Psychological factors and blood chemistries as disease outcome predictors for cancer patients. *Multivariate Experimental Clinical Research, 3,* 107-122.

63. Achterberg, J. (1985). *Imagery in healing: Shamanism and modern medicine.* Boston: New Science Library.

64. Achterberg, J., & Lawlis, G.F. (1984). *Imagery and disease.* Champaign, IL: Institute for Personality and Ability Testing.

65. Meares, A. (1976). Regression of cancer after intensive meditation. *Medical Journal of Australia, 2,* 184.

66. Meares, A. (1978a). Vivid visualization and dim visual awareness in the regression of cancer in meditation. *American Society of Psychosomatic Dentistry and Medicine. Journal, 25,* 85-88.

67. Meares, A. (1978b). Regression of osteogenic sarcoma metastases associated with intensive meditation. *Medical Journal of Australia, 2*(Oct. 21), 433.

68. Meares, A. (1979). The psychological treatment of cancer: The patient's confusion of the time for living with the time for dying. *Australian Family Physician, 8,* 801-805.

69. Meares, A. (1980). Remission of massive metastasis from undifferentiated carcinoma of the lung associated with intensive meditation. *American Society of Psychosomatic Dentistry and Medicine. Journal, 27,* 40-41.

70. Meares, A. (1981). Regression of recurrence of carcinoma of the breast at mastectomy site associated with intensive meditation. *Australian Family Physician, 10,* 218-219.

71. Andrews, V.H., & Hall, H.H. (1990). The effects of relaxation/ imagery training on recurrent aphthous stomatitis: A preliminary study. *Psychosomatic Medicine, 52,* 526-535.

72. Zachariae, R., Kristensen, J.S., Hokland, P., Ellegaard, J., Metze, E., & Hokland, M. (1990). Effect of psychological intervention in the form of relaxation and guided imagery on cellular immune function in normal healthy subjects. *Psychotherapy and Psychosomatics, 54,* 32-39.

73. Jasnoski, M.L., & Kugler, J. (198?). Relaxation, imagery, and neuroimmunomodulation. *Annals of the New York Academy of Sciences, 496,* 722-730.

74. Rider, M.S., Achterberg, J., Lawlis, G.F., Goven, A., Toledo, R., & Butler, J.R. (1990). Effect of immune system imagery on secretory IgA. *Biofeedback and Self-Regulation, 15*(4), 317-333.

75. Smith, C.W., Schneider, J., Minning, C., & Whitcher, S. (1981). Imagery and neutrophil function studies: A preliminary report. Unpublished manuscript, Michigan State University, Dept. of Psychiatry.

76. Rider, M.S., & Achterberg, J. (1989). Effect of music-assisted imagery on neutrophils and lymphocytes. *Biofeedback and Self-Regulation, 14*(3), 247-257.

77. Smith, G.R., & McDaniel, S.M. (1983). Psychologically-mediated effect on the delayed hypersensitivity reaction to tuberculin in humans. *Psychosomatic Medicine, 45,* 65-70.

78. Smith, G.R., McKenzie, J.M., Marmer, D.J., & Steele, R.W. (1985). Psychologic modulation of the human immune response to varicella zoster. *Archives of Internal Medicine, 145,* 2110-2112.

79. Smith, G.R. (1989). Intentional psychological modulation of the immune system. In J.V. Basmajian (Ed.), *Biofeedback*. Baltimore: Williams and Wilkins.

80. Tebecis, A.K., Ohno, Y., Matsubara, H., Sugano, H., & Takeya, T. (1976–77). A longitudinal study of some physiological parameters and autogenic training, *Psychotherapy and Psychosomatics*, 27(1), 8–17.

81. Ikemi, A. (1988). Psychophysiological effects of self-regulation method: EEG frequency analysis and contingent negative variation. *Psychotherapy and Psychosomatics*, 49(3–4), 230–239.

82. Morse, D.R., Martin, J.S., Furst, M.L., & Dubin, L.L. (1977). A physiological and subjective evaluation of meditation, hypnosis, and relaxation. *Psychosomatic Medicine*, 39(5), 304–324.

83. Fried, R. (1987). *The hyperventilation syndrome*. Baltimore: The Johns Hopkins University Press.

84. Barabasz, A.F. (1982). Restricted environmental stimulation and the enhancement of hypnotizability: Pain, EEG alpha, skin conductance and temperature processes. *International Journal of Clinical and Experimental Hypnosis*, 30(2), 147–166.

85. Duffy, F.H., Iyer, V.G., & Surwillo, W.W. (1989). *Clinical electroencephalography and topographic brain mapping: Technology and practice*. NY: Springer-Verlag.

86. Gellhorn, E., & Kiely, W.F. (1972). Mystical states of consciousness: Neurophysiological and clinical aspects. *Journal of Nervous and Mental Disease*, 154(6), 399–405.

87. Morgan, A.H., MacDonald, H., & Hilgard, E.R. (1974). EEG alpha: Lateral asymmetry related to task and hypnotizability. *Psychophysiology*, 11(3), 275–282.

88. Evans, F.J. (1982). Hypnosis and sleep. *Research Communications in Psychology, Psychiatry and Behavior*, 7(2), 241–256.

89. Bauer, K.E., & McCanne, T.R. (1980). Autonomic and central nervous system responding: During hypnosis and simulation of hypnosis. *International Journal of Clinical and Experimental Hypnosis*, 28(2), 148–163.

90. Raikov, V.L. (1983–84). EEG recordings of experiments in hypnotic age regression. *Imagination, Cognition and Personality*, 3(2), 115–132.

91. Tebecis, A.K., Provins, K.A., Farnbach, R.W., & Pentony, P. (1975). Hypnosis and the EEG. *Journal of Nervous and Mental Disease*, 161(1), 1–17.

92. Sabourin, M.E., Cutcomb, S.D., Crawford, H.J., & Pribram, K. (1990–91). EEG correlates of hypnotic susceptibility and hypnotic trance: Spectral analysis and coherence. *International Journal of Psychophysiology*, 10(2), 125–142.

93. Macleod-Morgan, C. (1982). EEG lateralization in hypnosis: A preliminary report. *Australian Journal of Clinical and Experimental Hypnosis*, 10(2), 99–102.

94. Bickford, R.G., Brimm, J., Berger, L., et al. (1973). Application of compressed spectral array in clinical EEG. In P. Kellaway, & I. Petersen (Eds.), *Automation in clinical electroencephalography*. NY: Raven Press.

95. Neher, A. (1961). Auditory driving observed with scalp electrodes in normal subject. *Electroencephalography and Clinical Neurophysiology*, 13, 449–451.

96. Walter, W.G. (1971). Physiological correlates of personality. *Biological Psychiatry*, 3(1), 59–69.

97. Banquet, J.P. (1973). Spectral analysis of the EEG in meditation. *Electroencephalography and Clinical Neurophysiology*, 35, 143–151.

98. Pagano, R.R., Rose, R.M., & Stivers, R.M. (1976). Sleep during transcendental meditation. *Science*, 191, 308–309.

99. Glueck, B.C., & Stroebel, C.F. (1978). Psychophysiological correlates of relaxation. In A.A. Sugarman & R.E. Tarter (Eds.), *Expanding dimensions of consciousness*. NY: Springer.

100. Jevning, R., Wallace, R.K., & Beidebach, M. (1992). The physiology of meditation: A review; A wakeful hypometabolic integrated response. *Neuroscience and Biobehavioral Review, 16*, 415–424.

101. Rugg, M.D., & Dickens, A.M.J. (1982). Dissociation of alpha and theta activity as a function of verbal and visuospatial tasks. *Electroencephalography and Clinical Neurophysiology, 53*, 201–207.

102. Freeman, W.J. (1983). The physiological basis of mental images. *Biological Psychiatry, 18*(10), 1107–1125.

103. Davidson, R.J., & Schwartz, G.E. (1977). Brain mechanisms subserving self-generated imagery: Electrophysiological specificity and patterning. *Psychophysiology, 14*(6), 598–602.

104. John, E.R. (1967). *Mechanisms of memory.* NY: Academic Press.

CHAPTER SIX

Sociospiritual Techniques and Physical Healing

Introduction

This chapter refers to the concept of spiritual techniques in the remediation of physical disorders, with specific emphasis upon the immune system. The term sociospiritual is adopted here to represent mechanisms of communication coming from outside of the patient's bodymind. In other words, higher powers or larger energy sources are being tapped into with these techniques. Not that these external sources were avoided with mental or emotional treatment processes, but they seem to be the primary component of the techniques discussed in this chapter.

Social support is one phenomenon that relies on external dynamics. It also utilizes components of physical, emotional, and mental treatments. The patient has to (physically) seek the support out. Then, either the patient's feelings are supported (emotional), or comfort is found (mentally) in knowing that others are going through similar problems, and in learning how to positively reframe one's plight. Yet, there is still a more mysterious quality of social support that beckons into the realm of the unseen power generated by any group with like-minded intention. One can experience this power in other media, for example, as an audience member at a concert, a performer in a musical or theatrical ensemble, or a participant in any other group with a common purpose and some allowance to "go with the flow" as opposed to an adherence to a rigid structure. (Don't expect to find this at your local city council meeting or even many churches which opt for preference of strict rules for conduction of agendas and ceremonial rituals instead of allowing subtle feedback from the audience to guide the process.)

A second technique to be discussed as a component of social support is "healing at a distance" or "intercessory prayer." This treatment form stands alone, however, due to its absence of the physical presence of a visible social support system. The mechanisms may in fact have less to do with the influences of a healer located some distance from the patient, than the channeling of some energy form located ubiquitously in the universe, very possibly what we consider the essence of many theologies.

Social Support

"No man is poor who has friends." This line from the movie *Its a Wonderful Life* exemplifies the survival potency of social support networks. I play constant witness to patients with catastrophic illness, emotional problems, or substance abuse who at some point in their therapeutic progress derive great benefit from the power of support groups. These patients are conveyed the knowledge in support groups that they are not alone. Furthermore, they learn through the feedback of others in the group what techniques have worked for them, and hence gain reinforcement for the compliance of healthy behaviors. Peers of different patient groups sometimes know what and how to confront other patients with, and the advice seems to be absorbed better at times from peers than from those with different relationships with the patient, such as family or doctor.

Support groups are not the only form of social support. Friends, families, co-workers, church members, professional colleagues, and even one's relationship with God, or a higher power, make up this complex network of social support. Each is important in its own way, and there is some evidence that problems within one social sphere are best supported by those within that same domain. For example, family problems, up to a limit, may best be handled when kept in the family. If the problem gets too stressful, an objective source like a therapist can help mediate the situation, but the support will still remain most powerful from within the family. All the therapy in the world has proven to be only slightly successful if the patient is going back into a dysfunctional family. For a patient with dysfunctional family issues, I often engage key members of the family, such as the parents or spouse, to help "support" the patient by simply acknowledging their feelings. This dynamic often improves the situation much more so than if the patient had only expressed their feelings to me. Likewise, work problems have been found to be best supported and relieved when expressed to peers on the workplace rather than by family members. However, when it comes to physical, sexual, or mental abuse, having just one close ally of any kind while one was experiencing the abuse while growing up, seems to significantly buffer the deleterious effects of these traumas.

Social support has thus far in the literature been evaluated primarily on a two-dimensional scale, with quantitative and qualitative factors[1], or, as others describe them, structural and functional ones.[2] Quantitative or structural support refers to the sheer number of supportive persons or resources in one's life. This could reflect one's marital status, membership in church and clubs, wealth, education, and so on. On the other hand, qualitative or functional support involves the perceived availability and satisfaction of one's resources.

My extensive work in running support groups for patients with both catastrophic illness and psychiatric problems has taught me some important insights on the nature of social support. Just as we have seen in the preceding chapters, the value of social support as a treatment intervention is perhaps of more use when the patient has attained certain criteria within the physical, emotional, and mental domains. I usually choose to work consciously on spiritual techniques when patients have 1) taken some responsibility for instituting healthy physical behaviors, 2) allowed themselves to feel and express repressed feelings, and 3) worked on mental techniques of quieting and self-affirmation. When the lower levels of intervention have not been attended to, patients will be inadequately prepared to engage in appropriate support-seeking behaviors. They may seek the support in unhealthy ways, through overattached or enmeshed relationships. These are the times when social support can act in a negative fashion, as in self-destructive relationships or when peer pressure serves to increase unhealthy behaviors, as demonstrated in the drug-use, violence, and other criminal behavior associated with certain urban gangs.

Therefore, when moving a patient into a support group, a certain readiness is needed to insure that the patient is going to obtain the desired benefits. In addition to the other techniques on lower levels, I utilize a mental technique to test the patient's readiness in gaining support from external resources. I call this exercise one's "spiritual image," or the image one receives when the patient is asked to visualize his connection with the rest of the universe. If the image comes back empty or blank, then it is a sign that the patient may have additional work to do on a previous level before healthy support can be solicited. It harkens of the adage, "go into a relationship because you want one, not because you need one."

I have experienced the need for this developmental approach to spiritual connectedness with many clients. Even though a religious membership has added support to some of my patients' lives, the sanctions imposed by their church when they felt they needed to leave a dysfunctional marriage caused immobilizing guilt and psychiatric symptoms due to the fear of being excommunicated and having their support taken away.

A Native American patient of mine made the comment that a part of the spiritual beliefs he had learned in his tribe demanded that mental validation (techniques belonging to the level developmentally preceding the spiritual) be minimized for fear that narcissism would detract from spiritual communalism. And while I would agree that our country's emphasis upon the self and individualism has probably helped in our own anglicized spiritual starvation, this patient had developed severe problems with alcoholism and relationships due to his inability to love himself. Thus, he felt good only within the rituals of his tribe, but rather unable to function in a healthy way outside of these ceremonies.

Humans have an interesting need to feel self-important and in control on the one hand, and also to be humbled and to experience being a small part of something much larger, on the other hand. This paradoxical shift reflects the homeodynamic nature of treatments within the last three chapters. The physical and emotional domains group together in their sensed effects upon the body. Physical techniques seem to utilize a higher degree of self-control whereas the emotional level demands more of a spiritual component of releasing and letting go. Likewise, the mental level involves more self-control in complying with the practice necessary for cognitive therapy or meditation. The spiritual level requires, again like the emotional, a certain release and letting go of control, before the healthy benefits are accrued.

In other words, a dynamic rhythm of health can be found in the alternation between techniques utilizing control versus those which demand release. The "serenity prayer" comes best to describing the periodic flow between the two poles of control and release. And, because the mental and physical levels bear so much resemblance to each other for their similarities of control and exercise; and, because the emotional and spiritual levels share the commonalities of inward attending and letting go, a resonant structure apparently exists among all the treatment interventions, suggesting a homeodynamic organization of all of the treatment tools for health.

For an overview of research on the effects of social support on physical healing, see Table 6-1.

TABLE 6-1.   *SOCIAL SUPPORT AND PHYSICAL HEALING*

1st Author	Date	Results
Reed	1983	Greater social integration associated with a lower prevalence of myocardial infarction, angina pectoris, and coronary heart disease
Kaplan	1988	Socially isolated individuals at a 2- to 3-fold increased risk of death from ischemic heart disease over 5–9 years
Thomas	1979	Precursor study found cancer to be associated with a lack of family closeness
Goodwin	1987	Marriage found to be associated with lower cancer incidence at all stages of cancer
Snyder	1993	Lymphocyte proliferation was lower in subjects reporting lower social support
Comstock	1972	Mortality rates of churchgoers over non-church-goers lower when all other factors controlled
Friedman	1980	Survival following heart attacks greater for those returning home to pets than without
Sagan	1988	Mortality rates of military servicemen lower than nonmilitary people of same age
Coe	1987	Monkeys separated from mothers had reduced antibody responses to viral challenge; familiar peers or familiar surroundings eliminated this reduced effect
Laudenslager	1985	Maternal or peer separation caused reduced T- and B-cell proliferative responses in monkeys
Seeman	1987	Patients with more available social support and who felt more loved had less atherosclerosis
Berkman	1992	Lack of emotional support predicted 6-month mortality rate in patients hospitalized for myocardial infarctions

(continued)

TABLE 6-1. *SOCIAL SUPPORT AND PHYSICAL HEALING (continuation)*

1st Author	Date	Results
Thomas	1985	Good social support in the elderly associated with lower serum cholesterol and uric acid, and higher indices of immune function
Kiecolt-Glaser	1984	Psychiatric patients who reported greater loneliness also experienced lower natural killer cell activity and T-cell pro liferation
Levy	1990	High natural killer cell activity in stage I and II breast cancer patients predicted by 1) high social support from spouse, 2) high social support from physician, 3) estrogen receptor-negative tumor status, 4) excisional biopsy as surgical treatment, and 5) actively seeking social support as a major coping strategy
Kennell	1991	Supportive companion during labor shortened labor & reduced need for C-section, forceps deliveries, epidural anesthesia, oxytocin use, prolonged infant hospitalization, and maternal fever.
Edens	1992	Social support in the form of friends was more effective than strangers or touch in modulating cardiovascular reactions to mental stress.
Ornish	1990	Group support, meditation, diet, and exercise reversed coronary artery blockage
Radojenc	1992	Behavioral intervention with family support superior to behavioral therapy without family support and control group in reducing swelling severity and number of swollen joints in rheumatoid arthritis patients
Fawzy	1993	6-week support group intervention increased natural killer cell cytotoxic activity and numbers of large granulocyte and natural killer cells in melanoma patients; 6-year follow-up found lower mortality rate in treatment group
Spiegel	1989	1-year support group intervention (including self-hypnosis for pain) with breast cancer patients led to twice the survival duration in breast cancer patients at 10-year follow-up

The mechanisms of social support seem to operate in a couple of directions. First, social support acts in a preventive, or health- boosting way. Individuals who have indicated a high degree of social support or social integration have been found to have a lower incidence of myocardial infarctions[3] and three times lower risk of death from heart disease[4] as compared to those who reported lower social support before disease onset. Premorbidity studies have also linked later onset of cancer with lower quality of support within the family.[5] Just being married has been discovered to confer partial immunity from cancer.[6] The immune system in general has been found to respond more quickly in those who report more adequate social support.[7] While family is an important form of social support, other types which have demonstrated protective influences include participation in church[8], involvement with pets[9], and military affiliation.[10]

Second, social support acts as a buffer in attenuating the detrimental effects of stress and/or ongoing disease. Animal studies have demonstrated that the stress-induced immune suppression caused by maternal or peer separation can be lessened or even reversed once these animals have been returned to their litters.[11-12] In humans, feeling loved by and connected with a large social network has been found to reduce the amount of atherosclerosis in patients undergoing angiography.[13] In patients hospitalized for myocardial infarctions, emotional support was found to significantly offset mortality after six months.[14] Negative effects on the immune system, especially on natural killer cell activity, have been found to be mitigated by strong social support in individuals exposed to the stresses of aging[15], psychiatric hospitalization[16], and cancer.[17]

Also considered part of the stress buffering role of social support is the effect of strategic social support as an intervention with medical disease or procedures. The continuous presence of a supportive companion during labor and delivery has been found to shorten labor, reduce maternal fever, and reduce the need for C-section or forceps deliveries, epidural anesthesia, oxytocin usage, and prolonged infant hospitalization.[18] When comparing the use of a friend's presence versus physical touch in buffering the cardiovascular reactions to mental stress, only the friend's presence was found to have a beneficial effect.[19] With regard to cardiovascular disease, Dean Ornish's now famous study demonstrated that a comprehensive program of group support along with diet, meditation, and exercise not only reduced cholesterol levels and symptoms of heart disease, but actually reversed coronary artery blockage as well.[20]

Social support interventions have also been quite effective in the treatment of immunological diseases. As expected from the model presented in this book, there is evidence that sociospiritual mechanisms are more powerful and longer-lasting than the previous three categories of techniques (physical, emotional, and mental). In a comparison study of different treatment approaches with rheumatoid arthritis patients, cognitive behavioral treatments which included family support were more effective than the cognitive behavioral interventions alone in significantly reducing joint pain and swelling.[21]

Two studies of cancer patients have yielded promising results in lengthening survival through support groups. In one, only six weeks of support group intervention with malignant melanoma resulted in increased natural killer cell cytotoxic activity and numbers of large granulocyte and natural killer cells.[22] Treatment also included education and stress management. The most exciting result was at the 6-year follow-up, which revealed a significantly lower mortality rate in the treatment group over the control group. In another now famous study of longevity in breast cancer patients, one year of support group intervention, including self-hypnosis for pain, led to twice the survival duration at the 10-year follow-up.[23]

Transpersonal Healing

Perhaps the most controversial of all of the treatment techniques involves the method of sending healing messages to someone not physically present with the healer. Sometimes called "intercessory prayer" and "transpersonal healing," controlled studies have now been conducted on these techniques which have moved it out of the area of phenomenology and into the laboratory (see Table 6-2).

TABLE 6-2. *TRANSPERSONAL TREATMENTS AND PHYSICAL HEALING*

1st Author	Date	Results
Barry	1968	Subjects demonstrated fungal growth inhibition through conscious intention
Nash	1982	Subjects able to both retard and accelerate bacterial growth in culture through conscious intention
Braud	1979	Psychic individual was able to inhibit in vitro cancer growth at a distance
Grad	1961	Mental intention significantly speeded up the healing of artificially created surgical wounds in mice
May	1992	Mice given lethal ionizing radiation dose manifested nearly half the mortality of controls if mentally healed
Braud	1989	"Calming" or "activating" transpersonal imagery found to elicit expected changes in electrodermal activity of isolated, "blind" subjects
Byrd	1988	Coronary patients who were prayed for had 1/5 antibiotics usage, 1/3 pulmonary edema rate, and less than 1/10 rate of endotracheal intubation as compared to non-prayed-for patients
Wirth	1994	11 of 16 diabetics decreased insulin usage following transpersonal healing
Booth	1973	Intercessory prayer evidenced medically documented regression in a case of pancreatic cancer
O'Regan	1993	Intercessory prayer induced medically documented cure in a case of neuroblastoma
Braud	1990	Subjects demonstrated psychokinetic effect of transpersonal shielding of red blood cells from hemolysis

The interactions studied thus far seem to suggest that transpersonal healing phenomena can be rendered between people, plants, animals, bacteria, and even individual cells in vitro. Transpersonal cognitive activity has also been demonstrated to modify subatomic events, as for example the experiments in which radioactive decay rates have been influenced.[24] This data supports the hypothesis that imagery and transpersonal phenomena such as intercessory prayer operate via quantum mechanisms. Mental-spiritual activity has even been found to be responsible for certain computer malfunctions, previously thought to be random electrical phenomena affecting miniaturized circuit boards. In these experiments, subjects were able to influence the electrical activity of a computer microchip through intentional thought.[25] This phenomenon of the elicitation of microcomputer failures was also reported by a large number of patients suffering immunological dysfunctions that we interviewed during our brain mapping study.

Transpersonal healing has been demonstrated with a variety of living organisms. In one experiment, subjects inhibited the growth of fungus cultures in the laboratory by consciously focusing on them for fifteen minutes. After several more hours of incubation, over three-fourths of the culture dishes evidenced retarded growth.[26] Another experiment demonstrated that the growth rates of bacterial cultures could be both accelerated and retarded with conscious intention.[27]

Some researchers have studied the healing abilities of psychic healers. In one, the British psychic Mathew Manning was able to inhibit the growth rates of cultured cancer cells while either holding the containers or from a distance.[28] Studies of the healer Estebany demonstrated that two weeks of mental intention significantly speeded up the healing of artificially created surgical wounds in mice.[29] In an experiment reported on in a review of psychic healing research from Russia, mice were psychically healed before, and/or after, lethal exposures to radiation.[30] Results indicated that most of the mice healed both before and after radiation lived whereas all or most of the controls died. Interestingly, the healer who experienced the most success did so from a distance of 800 miles.

Studies of conscious intention upon human physiology have also been fruitful. In subjects who were unknowingly focused upon by a person isolated in a distant room, transpersonal imagery to either "calm" or "activate" the physiological reactions (electrodermal activity) of these subjects was demonstrated to have the desired effect.[31]

Transpersonal imagery in the form of intercessory prayer has been studied in a couple of cases. In the most famous of these, nearly 400 patients admitted to a coronary unit were divided into two groups. In one, each patient was prayed for by up to seven people each, while the other group served as a control. Results overwhelmingly corroborated the influence of prayer as this group witnessed five times less antibiotics usage, three times less pulmonary edema, and ten times less endotracheal intubation as the unremembered group.[32] In another study of diabetics who received two weeks of both intercessory prayer and Non-Contact Therapeutic Touch, no significant group differences were found in insulin usage although 11 out of 16 diabetics in the treatment group did show a reduction in insulin dose levels.[33]

Several case studies have been medically documented on the power of intercessory prayer in the remission of cancer. One was of a sixty year-old woman who developed inoperable pancreatic cancer. Her daughter, who had been on bad terms with the woman, prayed for the recovery of her mother. The woman made a complete recovery and the tumor was later verified during another surgery to have regressed significantly.[34]

In one of the many miraculous cures documented by the International Medical Commission at Lourdes, a neuroblastoma was diagnosed in a 12 year- old girl. After a significant amount of intercessory prayer by the villagers at Lourdes, the girl was cured of her cancer.[35]

Homeodynamic mechanisms are implicated in the findings by some of these researchers that resonance between organisms enables stronger links of communication. William Braud conducted a study of the effect of subjects' intents to retard the rate of hemolysis in human red blood cells in vitro.[36] Subjects were blind as to whose cells were being focused on. Resonance was demonstrated in some subjects in their increased abilities to influence their own cells over those of other subjects. This is somewhat analogous to the quantum experiment of Einstein, Podolsky, and Rosen (or the EPR effect), in which a subatomic particle with two electrons is split in such a way that the electrons are emitted in opposite directions. The EPR effect demonstrated that if a force is applied to one of the electrons so that its spin or angular momentum was changed, as if by magic the other electron was equally effected, even though no force was directly applied! Objects or organisms which bear some resonance among each other, can most easily affect each other, regardless of the distance. This is what "non-local" refers to in quantum experiments.

This non-locality also seems to be present in the resonance effects phenomenologically reported by humans connected by genetics. For example, the mother who reports a pain in her body, only to find out later that her child had been hurt. This communication link has not only been found to circumnavigate the globe, but seems to defy the normal constraints of time as well. In telepathic sender-receiver experiments, sometimes the receiver has been known to sense the object as much as several days before that same object was even viewed and "sent" by the sender.

This implies that some universal, ubiquitous, intelligent energy (perhaps God) is present which we may channel into for information, as well as to utilize it for potential healing. Spiritual healing may be the manifestation of some cosmic, homeodynamic healing event which was pre-destined to occur anyway. Some validation of this notion comes from the Spindrift experiments.[37] These experiments evaluated the effects of prayer on germination of seeds. One of the interesting results was that non-directed prayer ("let thy will be done" or "what is meant to be") had a significantly greater effect on seed germination than did directed prayer, in which specific outcomes were visualized. LeShan and others have described this quality to the visualizations of those who experienced spontaneous remissions of cancer.[38] Theirs was not a desparate attempt to plead for a specific outcome, but rather a more quiet strength to make the most of life and accept the consequences.

Homeodynamic Shifting and Spiritual Healing
        Very few studies have been conducted on the response of the brain dur-
ing social support or support group interventions. Nevertheless, there appear to
be identical features involved in the two processes underlying both support
groups and transpersonal healing—simply the conscious focus upon other matter,
whether living or inanimate. The studies of Braud and Byrd reported on above
demonstrated that normal "senders" can induce the desired effects. Therefore,
even though neurophysiological data on psychosocial phenomena exists only on
situations involving a healer, or sender, and one healee, or receiver, there is no
reason to believe that the same physiological mechanisms aren't happening in
normal social support milieus. For an overview of research on homeodynamic
shifts involved with sociospiritual healing, see Table 6-3.

TABLE 6-3.   *HOMEODYNAMIC MECHANISMS OF*
                     SOCIOSPIRITUAL TREATMENTS

1st Author	Date	Results
McDonough	1989	Telepathy and clairvoyance tasks yielded EEG slowing into theta and delta
Targ	1974	Alpha-blocking demonstrated in one of six subjects in "transfer" evoked potential study
Grinberg-Zylberbaum	1992	"Transfer" evoked potential study yielded evoked potentials in receivers only when preceded by period of telepathy between receivers and senders
Grinberg-Zylberbaum	1982	Interhemispheric coherence was increased between analyst and patient as the degree of empathy increased during the session
Fahrion	1992	EEG recordings of healer and healee indicated increased beta and alpha activity and increased intra- and interpersonal synchrony

        Psi experiments have, for instance, demonstrated EEG downshifting into
the delta and theta bands during telepathy and clairvoyance tasks.[39] In addition to
a significant amount of alpha blocking in these experiments, greater involvement
of the right hemisphere was also observed. Alpha blocking was also observed in
another experiment in which "receivers" were informed that "senders" were in a
distant room looking at light flashes (typical of the photic-driving EEG experiments). Results indicated that information was obtained by one of the six subjects
as manifested by alpha blocking occurring in the receiver simultaneously when
flashes were presented to the sender.[40]

In another "transfer" evoked potential study as just described, senders and receivers first spent 20 minutes in a darkened, sensory- deprived room with instructions to establish "direct communication" with each other through telepathy.[41] The experimental pairs of subjects were then separated before testing, but asked to maintain their state of direct communication. Control pairs were also tested but never allowed to experience direct communication. Results indicated that receivers who had experienced direct communication with their paired senders also manifested a transferred EEG evoked potential, even though they never viewed any flashes. In contrast, the receivers who were prevented from experiencing direct communication had no such transferred evoked potential.

Another fascinating conclusion of this study is the finding that when three senders simultaneously viewed the flashes which were subsequently sent to a fourth (when all four people had previously experienced direct communication), the cumulative effects of the transferred potential were even greater than in the paired condition. In other words, the implication for the enhanced healing powers of a group (as in a support group or network) become more explainable.

What is being led up to in this discussion is that, not only are brain shifts responsible for health, but that with sociospiritual interventions, these brain shifts may be transferred from healer to patient. This has been documented in a study of EEG activity during a psychotherapy session. As the degree of empathy increased between the analyst and patient during the session, the amount of interhemispheric coherence increased and became more similar between the two individuals.[42]

In another study of the relationship between the brainwave activity of healer and patient, frequency activity and EEG coherence were recorded during four conditions: relaxation, meditation, healing with the client present (actually non-contact therapeutic touch), and healing-at-a-distance.[43] Two types of homeodynamic phenomena were observed in this study.

First, unusually high alpha and beta rhythms were detected during all conditions by the healing practitioner. The increased alpha production was consonant with the relaxation literature reported in Chapter 5. The high beta activity was more prolific during the meditation and healing conditions, probably indicative of imagery and nonverbal intentional activity as many of the electrode sites of activation were more frontally located. Dynamic shifts to primarily right hemispheric activity occurred during all conditions as well.

The second homeodynamic observation was that of increased periods of brainwave synchrony. Intrapersonal brainwave synchrony was noted at all frequencies for the healer, but foremost so in the upper beta frequencies. For the patient, intrapersonal coherence occurred primarily in the theta and alpha bands for all conditions. Interpersonal brainwave resonance between healer and patient was also quite high during all conditions, particularly during the healing-at-a-distance condition, and consistently at low beta and theta frequencies.

The fact that healing-at-a-distance brainwave resonance was highest suggests the power of certain mechanisms operating at the sociospiritual level which may transcend those of lower levels. Non-local, quantum-type dynamics are suggested by these data. The possibility of cumulative building of healing potentials may be provided during healing-at-a-distance conditions. The increased resonance of multiple brains, especially with some prior direct communication, may enhance the potential for many brains acting as one.

References

1. Sarason, I.G., Levine, H.M., Basham, R.B., & Sarason, B.R. (1983). Assessing social support: The social support questionnaire. *Journal of Personality and Social Psychology, 44*(1), 127–139.

2. Cohen, S. (1990). Social support and physical illness. *Advances, 7*(1), 35–47.

3. Reed, D., McGee, D., Yano, K., & Feinleib, M. (1983). Social networks and coronary heart disease among Japanese men in Hawaii. *American Journal of Epidemiology, 117*, 384–396.

4. Kaplan, G.A. (1988). Social contacts and ischemic heart disease. *Annals of Clinical Research, 10*, 131–136.

5. Thomas, C.B., Duszynski, K.R., & Shaffer, J.W. (1979). Family attitudes reported in youth as potential predictors of cancer. *Psychosomatic Medicine, 41*, 287–302.

6. Goodwin, J.S., Hunt, W.C., Key, C.R., & Samet, J.M. (1988). The effect of marital status on stage, treatment, and survival of cancer patients. *Advances, 5*(4), 12–17.

7. Snyder, B.K., Roghmann, K.J., & Sigal, L.H. (1993). Stress and psychosocial factors: Effects on primary cellular immune response. *Journal of Behavioral Medicine, 16*(2), 143–161.

8. Comstock, G., & Partridge, K. (1972). Church attendance and health. *Journal of Chronic Diseases, 25*, 665–672.

9. Friedmann, E., Katcher, A.H., Lynch, J.J., & Thomas, S.A. (1980). Animal companions: One-year survival after discharge from a coronary care unit. *Public Health Reports, 95*, 307–312.

10. Metropolitan Life Insurance Company. (1982). Mortality among United States service personnel. *Statistical Bulletin, 63*, 8–12.

11. Coe, C.L., Rosenberg, L.T., Fischer, M., & Levine, S. (1987). Psychological factors capable of preventing the inhibition of antibody responses in separated monkeys. *Child Development, 58*, 1420–1430.

12. Laudenslager, M., Capitanio, J.P., & Reite, M. (1985). Possible effects of early separation experiences on subsequent immune function in adult macaque monkeys. *American Journal of Psychiatry, 142*(7), 862–864.

13. Seeman, T.E., & Syme, S.L. (1987). Social networks and coronary artery disease: A comparison of the structure and function of social relations as predictors of disease. *Psychosomatic Medicine, 49*, 340–353.

14. Berkman, L.F., Leo-Summers, L., & Horwitz, R.I. (1992). Emotional support and survival after myocardial infarction: A prospective, population-based study of the elderly. *Annals of Internal Medicine, 117*, 1003–1009.

15. Thomas, P.D., Goodwin, J.M., & Goodwin, J.S. (1985). Effect of social support on stress-related changes in cholesterol level, uric acid level, and immune function in an elderly sample. *American Journal of Psychiatry, 142*(6), 735–737.

16. Kiecolt-Glaser, J.K., Ricker, D., George, J., Messick, G., Speicher, C.E., Garner, W., & Glaser, R. (1984). Urinary cortisol levels, cellular immunocompetency, and loneliness in psychiatric inpatients. *Psychosomatic Medicine, 46*(1), 15–23.

17. Levy, S.M., Herberman, R.B., Whiteside, T., Sanzo, K., Lee, J., & Kirkwood, J. (1990). Perceived social support and tumor estrogen/progesterone receptor status as predictors of natural killer cell activity in breast cancer patients. *Psychosomatic Medicine, 52*, 73-85.

18. Kennell, J., Klaus, M., McGrath, S., Robertson, S., & Hinkley, C. (1991). Continuous emotional support during labor in a U. S. hospital. A randomized controlled trial. *Journal of the American Medical Association, 265*, 2197-2201.

19. Edens, J.L., Larkin, K.T., & Abel, J.L. (1992). The effect of social support and physical touch on cardiovascular reactions to mental stress. *Journal of Psychosomatic Research, 36*, 371-382.

20. Ornish, D., Brown, S.E., Scherwitz, L.W., Billings, J.H., Armstrong, W.T., Ports, T.A., Mclanahan, S.M., Kirkeeide, R.L., Brand, R.J., & Gould, K.L. (1990). Can life-style changes reverse coronary heart disease? *Lancet, 336*, 129-133.

21. Radojenc, V., Nicassio, P.M., & Weisman, M.H. (1992). Behavioral intervention with and without family support for rheumatoid arthritis. *Behavior Therapy, 23*, 13-30.

22. Fawzy, F.I., Fawzy, N.W., Hyun, C.S., Elashoff, R., Guthrie, D., Fahey, J.L., & Morton, D.L. (1993). Malignant melanoma: Effects of an early structured psychiatric intervention, coping, and affective state on recurrence and survival 6 years later. *Archives of General Psychiatry, 50*, 681-689.

23. Spiegel, D., Bloom, J.R., Kraemer, H.C., & Gottheil, E. (1989). Effect of psycho social treatment on survival of patients with metastatic breast cancer. *Lancet, Oct. 14*, 888-891.

24. Radin, D.I., & Nelson, R.D. (1989). Evidence for consciousness- related anomalies in random physical systems. *Foundations of Physics, 19*, 1499.

25. Radin, D.I. (1990). Testing the plausibility of psi-mediated computer system failures. *Journal of Parapsychology, 54*, 1.

26. Barry, J. (1968). General and comparative study of the psychokinetic effect on a fungus culture. *Journal of Parapsychology, 32*, 237-243.

27. Nash, C.B. (1982). Psychokinetic control of bacterial growth. *Journal of the American Society for Psychical Research, 51*, 217-221.

28. Braud, W.G., Davis, G., & Wood, R. (1979). Experiments with Matthew Manning. *Journal of the American Society for Psychical Research, 50*, 199-223.

29. Grad, B., Cadoret, R.J., & Paul, G.I. (1961). The influence of an unorthodox method of treatment on wound healing in mice. *International Journal of Parapsychology, 3*, 5-24.

30. May, E.C., & Vilenskaya, L. (1992). Overview of current parapsychology research in the former soviet union. *Subtle Energies, 3*(3), 45-67.

31. Braud, W., & Schlitz, M. (1989). A methodology for the objective study of transpersonal imagery. *Journal of Scientific Exploration, 3*(1), 43-63.

32. Byrd, R.C. (1988). Positive therapeutic effects of intercessory prayer in a coronary care unit population. *Southern Medical Journal, 81*(7), 826-829.

33. Wirth, D.P., & Mitchell, B.J. Complementary healing therapy for patients with type I diabetes mellitus. *Journal of Scientific Exploration, 8*(3), 367-377.

34. Booth, G. (1973). Psychobiological aspects of spontaneous regressions of cancer. *American Academy of Psychoanalysis. Journal, 1*(3), 303-317.

35. O'Regan, B., & Hirshberg, C. (1993). *Spontaneous remission*. Sausalito, CA: Institute of Noetic Sciences.

36. Braud, W. (1990). Distant mental influence of rate of hemolysis of human red blood cells. *Journal of the American Society for Psychical Research, 84*(1), 1-24.

37. Dossey, L. (1989). *Recovering the soul*. NY: Bantam Books.

38. Horrigan, B. (1995). Larry LeShan: Mobilizing the life force, treating the individual. *Alternative Therapies in Health and Medicine, 1*(1):63-69.

39. McDonough, B.E., Warren, C.A., & Don, N.S. (1989). EEG analysis of a fortuitous event observed during the psi testing of a selected subject. *Journal of Parapsychology, 53*(3), 181-201.

40. Targ, R., & Puthoff, H. (1974). Information transmission under conditions of sensory shielding. *Nature, 251*(5476), 602-607.

41. Grinberg-Zylberbaum, J., Delaflor, M., Arellano, M.E.S., Guevara, M.A., & Perez, M. (1992). Human communication and the electro- physiological activity of the brain. *Subtle Energies, 3*(3), 25–43.

42. Grinberg-Zylberbaum, J. (1982). Psychophysiological correlates of communication, gravitation and unity. *Psychoenergetics, 4,* 227–256.

43. Fahrion, S.L., Wirkus, M., & Pooley, P. (1992). EEG amplitude, brain mapping, and synchrony in and between a bioenergy practitioner & client during healing. *Subtle Energies, 3*(1), 19–52.

CHAPTER SEVEN

Homeodynamic Hypothesis I: Symptom as Metaphor

As we have seen, homeodynamism hypothesizes that mind, brain, and body are organized harmonically, and contain cells that allow communication flow to occur quickly and precisely between the nervous and immune systems. This chapter deals with some interesting clinical possibilities that are suggested by homeodynamism. Specifically, the idea of "disease as metaphor" contains the notion that symptoms, especially those of a chronic or long-term nature, represent a harmonic linkage with the energy patterns being generated by the mind/brain. Homeodynamism not only accounts for the associations among general personality types and disease, e.g., cancer and Type-C personality, and cardiovascular disease and Type-A personality, but also suggests that specific conscious or unconscious maladaptive thought patterns can lead to isomorphic symptoms which are dynamically related to the same thought pattern.

Earlier this century, Dunbar[1] and Alexander[2] proposed that many chronic diseases had constellations of personality factors which were distinguishable from one another. Alexander's "nuclear conflict theory" proposed that unconscious conflicts and the concomitantly produced emotions elicited a cascade of autonomic and endocrine responses that predisposed one to certain diseases. Other researchers found associations between specific attitudes and psychophysiological disorders.[3] This "specificity of attitude" theory held for example that asthmatics feel left out and ignored whereas hypertensives feel threatened. As we shall see later in this chapter, it was about this time when psychodynamic explanations for different types of cancer fully bloomed.

Although the specificity of attitude theory experienced some validation, this theory gave way to "individual-response stereotypy," which suggested that individual programming (both genetic and behavioral) determined the mode of disease expression regardless of the stressor or resulting set of emotions. This concept finally evolved into the "diathesis-stress" theory in which psychophysiological stress causes autonomic responses which if chronic or intense enough cause disease patterns which the person has become predisposed to.[4]

There is even some data which throws some ambiguity over which factor—genes or stress—may be the predecessor of the other. One study was carried out on monozygotic twins, one of whom died from myelocytic leukemia while the other did not.[5] Results indicated that symptoms of leukemia developed during periods of major stress, usually involving losses which were significantly greater for the twin who subsequently became ill. However, these twin studies also documented a histological marker separating the normal from the affected twin—the presence of the Ph1 chromosome. Could this chromosomal mutation have been responsible for the development of a personality which was more vulnerable to stress? Or, could the genetic difference have accounted for attitude-specific differences of the type which have become associated with certain diseases?

One such specific difference which has become highly popularized in both the lay and scientific literature has been the development of the Type A and Type C personality constellations. This research has led to the association of Type A and Type C personalities with incidence of cardiovascular disease and cancer, respectively. Type A persons tend to overreact to stimuli with hostility, competitiveness, and impatience. These persons have been found to have an "overactive cardiovascular response" making them twice as likely as non-Type A's to develop coronary heart disease.[6]

On the other hand, persons found to be Type C are overcontrolled and underactive in situations expected to elicit more emotional responses. These persons tend to get cancer more than non-Type C's and psychologically appear to be less defended and more depressed than those without cancer.[7] As we saw in Chapter 6, lack of family closeness has become a valid predictor of the incidence of cancer later in life.[8]

BodyMind Isomorphism...The "As If" Phenomenon

Homeodynamic resonance, discussed in Chapter 2, dealt first with the structural and functional similarities between organs and mechanisms of the mind and body. This resonance was established to demonstrate how easily energy and information could be transferred between mind and body. In fact, because there is now known to be almost total integrity between the two, it may be time to drop the Cartesian axe which cleaved the mind and body into two separate entities over 200 years ago. As Jeanne Achterberg suggested, simply call it the bodymind.[9]

The homeodynamic concept of bodymind is that our behavior and thoughts are implicitly and explicitly expressed in our body and vice versa. Our mental and physical symptoms are feedback that have a literal translation within the bodymind. To suggest isomorphism, or the idea that, for example, a physical symptom can be translated directly into information regarding a psychosocial mechanism, is to commit scientific blasphemy. Some have suggested that specific psychological meanings correspond to a wide compendium of ailments.[10] On the other hand, why do patients seem to experience significantly better disease management or even healing if they treat their symptoms as a metaphor for their own individual psychologies.

In other words, treating one's pain or disease as if it were a direct reflection of the way one views the world, facilitates recovery from these symptoms. Enacting this "as if" strategy serves to reconnect mind and body from a dissociation which occurred as a result of ineffective coping strategies to stressors. An analogy is that the mind and body transmit at the same frequency on the body's radio band. When physical or emotional trauma/neglect becomes too difficult to deal with due to inadequate resources, the mental radio frequency changes slightly in one direction. I suggest that the mental signal changes because the body usually reflects the true way things are, in other words, it doesn't lie. These two slightly out-of-phase signals enable less information to be transferred between the two. If one has ever heard two radio signals with similar power broadcasting at nearly the same frequency (a phenomenon the FCC usually prevents) the communication goes back and forth between the two signals, rendering the message incomprehensible.

Because the bodymind does actually operate via the previously discussed electrical mechanisms (documented in Chapter 2), it is not implausible to suppose that these electrical connections are made more congruent by assuming the symptom as a metaphor. In a sense, the electrical loop becomes closed enabling two-way communication between body and mind. To say that this receptiveness to feedback empowers the patient would be a metaphor in itself, because the patient is not only psychologically empowered, but if he/she is operating as a bodymind (both body and mind at the same frequency) then the literal amplitude of electrical power is increased as well. In brain mapping studies of patients with immunological disorders, decreases were consistently found in global field power, or the overall amplitude of voltage generated by the brain.

Tuning-In To Disease Metaphors

The rest of this chapter will focus on some of the more common chronic medical conditions. Case studies will be used to demonstrate the learning power of considering the metaphorical meaning of symptoms. Homeodynamic theory does not suggest that there is a consistent, specific behavioral message associated with each type of disease. This approach would be too reductionistic and avoidant of the patient's own highly individualized meaning derived from the disease process. Every catastrophic disease is a wake-up call designed to have the patient ask the right question. I, as a psychologist and healer, cannot tell the patient what the right answer to his or her medical dilemma is. However, if the patient with a chronic disease is able to ask the question, "what am I supposed to learn from this illness," and attain some resonance with an answer which adds to one's quality of life, then the patient has discovered his or her own right answer. These "right answers" subsequently lead to major behavioral changes, increases in psychophysiological resonance, a more highly internalized health locus of control, and usually improvement of symptoms.

Cancer

Cancer is a disease in which the cells proliferate at a rate which is beyond that normally regulated by the body. These cells multiply at such a high rate that they invade and/or destroy healthy tissue, causing pain, malfunctioning, and even death. Often the cancer tissue seems to be an autonomous tissue or tumor, separate from the rest of the normal functioning body. However, many agree that cancer is still part of the same cellular structure as the rest of the body, only in a more dedifferentiated form.[11-12] That is, cancer cells are really just more primitive versions of the surrounding, now-differentiated, normal cellular tissue. More primitive cells tend to grow much more rapidly, thus accounting for the faster growth rates of cancer.

It is interesting that cancer has been described as the oldest of all diseases, predating the dinosaurs.[13] Something that old must have some adaptive value or else it would have become extinct itself. There is the possibility that cancer can be viewed for its capacity to keep life and evolution on an ever-shifting, dynamic course. Afterall, it would be difficult for a species to evolve if it never died. Otherwise it would die out from overpopulation and over-utilization of the resources, without a chance to experiment through trial and error with genetic mutations with greater chances for survival.

The causes of cancer are related to many factors including genetics, environmental toxins, and viruses, as well as emotional and mental aspects. Each of these stressors has been found to induce oxidative changes in the DNA of target organs. Even emotional stress has now been demonstrated to elicit an overabundance of free radicals in these organs.[14] Free radicals are chemical agents possessing one or more unpaired electrons, which also causes oxidative damage within the cell nucleus. Oxidation produces DNA lesions, which if remain unrepaired before the cell divides, can cause mutations and ultimately malignancies.

This book will focus primarily on the emotional and mental attitudes. Prospective studies of individuals have determined that personality variables were much more predictive of death from cancer or cardiovascular disease than was smoking.[15] Attitudes of learned helplessness and the hopelessness of depression have been found to add significantly to one's chances of developing cancer at an earlier age than expected. These feelings and attitudes have been determined to have been precipitated by loss or life-change which the individual was not resilient enough to handle. One could even say the same thing about the causal mechanisms of cancer caused by radiation. The cells which developed cancer were not resilient enough to withstand the incoming high frequency energy. The cancer metaphor which is developing is a lack of resilience to change, or a reduced ability to shift. This psychogenic rigidity has been confirmed in psychoanalytic investigations into the nature of the cancer personality.[16]

When changes are encountered by us, feelings and emotions are created within us. If not expressed, a secondary energetic loop continues to affect the body as if some kind of radiation were being emitted, only from the inside of our body. Expressing the repressed emotion, such as in a normal grief response, discharges the energy and reduces the total stress load on the body. This phenomenon was observable in both the interviews of patients with cancer as well as in their EEG brainmaps.

One important way of discharging this internal energy is through adequate social support mechanisms. However, the literature has revealed that psychosocial alienation is one of the most common features of the premorbid cancer personality.[8,17] Cancer has even been found to be cultivated in vivo through the elimination of cellular contact. This was accomplished by inserting semipermeable capsules into the peritoneal cavities of animals, thus allowing the passage of body fluids but cutting off cell-to-cell contact.[18] Apparently, on a microscopic level, cellular alienation can induce malignancy. Just as homeodynamic theory predicted, social alienation seems to be more than a metaphor for cancer, but rather an isomorphic characteristic of the bodymind.

There is evidence that cancer may not be an immunological disorder, at least in a primary way. Lewis Thomas's controversial immune surveillance theory suggested that because transplantation patients given immunosuppressive drugs later had higher incidences of certain cancers, that the immune system must somehow be involved in eliminating precancerous cells. However, immune dysfunctioning has yet to be discovered in cancer patients. Secondly, pathologists and immunologists have confirmed that spontaneously arising cancers provoke little or no immune response.[12,19] Therefore, cancer will be treated medically and metaphorically in this book as a disease which is characterized primarily by cellular alienation, and secondarily by weakened immunity.

Another common facet of many of those patients who have developed cancer is a denial of anger.[20] As described in the beginning of this chapter, cancer patients often exhibit an overcontrolled personality style in which strong emotions are typically pushed below the surface of one's consciousness. As another example of the denial system, the cancer patient has also been discovered to have the lowest number of stress symptoms than any other disease group.[21] This physiological denial system was demonstrated elegantly in a study of the sensory thresholds of cancer patients and normals to thermal and vibrational stimulation.[22] Results of the study indicated that cancer patients exhibited significantly higher thresholds to both types of stimulation, suggesting that they are more cutoff from these internal signals.

An intriguing discovery along these lines has indicated that not responding to certain internal physiological signals predicates individuals to neoplastic disease. Frustration of a strong desire to stimulate a particular organ has been found to be highly correlated with the consequential development of cancer in that organ.[16] For example, cervical cancer occurs most frequently in women highly motivated for, but prevented from achieving sexual orgasm. Likewise, the same sexual frustration in men has been found to lead to higher rates of prostate cancer. Breast cancer, on the other hand, has been linked with lower incidences of the nursing function.

One might also say that these sexual/nursing behaviors produce a homeodynamic shift that is responsible for the increased competence of the immune system to fight off cancer. Orgasm undoubtedly produces a minor seizure of sorts. I have interviewed many clients who have acknowledged that foot twitches often accompany orgasm. It just so happens that the region of the brain homunculus on the motor cortex associated with the genitals is adjacent to that of the foot, indicating that an electrical discharge is occurring in the brain as well as in the body. On the other hand, nursing often produces feelings which mothers describe as relaxation, another homeodynamic behavior associated with brain wave shifts.

A further example of the psychophysiological denial of the cancer patient involves what I described in Chapter 5 as "organ neglect." Mental denial of an area of the body associated with abuse or inferiority, can sometimes evolve into malignancy in that area. I have worked with several patients who developed cancer in the genital areas following rape or molestation.

Stomach cancer has been highly correlated with poverty levels, suggesting that basic nutritional neglect leads to the development of tumors in that part of the gastrointestinal tract. On the other hand, a different metaphor is relegated to lower sections of the GI tract. Colon and rectal cancers have been found to occur almost six times more frequently in individuals reporting severe on-the-job aggravation as opposed to those not under such stress.[23] The symptomatic isomorphism seems appropriate in describing this particular workplace stress as a "pain in the ass."

Rorschach studies of cancer patients have yielded some intriguing metaphors themselves. Cancer patients have been found, for example, to exhibit an unusually high use of "whirling" imagery in describing the Rorschach inkblots.[24] This fact seems somewhat symbolic of the rapid and chaotic growth of the neoplastic disease itself. Another interesting phenomenon I have observed quite consistently in conducting health imagery among both group and individual settings is the increased activity of one's imagery when alone as compared to the group environment. This feature, when applied to the cancer patient, may be symbolic of the reduced social support system generally found with this type of patient.

Cancer and Unresolved Grief: Case Studies

Cancer, like most physical and mental diseases, has an onset usually preceded by major life changes such as loss of a family member. Any major life change is eventually resolved with completion of the grieving process. Most diseases having psychological roots involve the inhibition of dynamic flow through the various stages of the grief process. The need for this dynamic process speaks to the very essence of the homeodynamic language of health. The connections of one's social support system often provide the means for the continued movement through the grief process.

Kubler-Ross identified stages of the death and dying process as occurring in the following order: denial, anger, bargaining, depression, and acceptance.[25] In my own clinical experience, I have found that these stages are very similar to the grief process engaged in by every individual upon encountering a major life change. These stages, Denial— Bad (Fear)— Mad— Sad— Glad (Acceptance),   include the four basic feeling states discussed in Chapter 4. The difference from Kubler-Ross's stages is that fear is another stage which occurs after denial, but before anger, and bargaining has been eliminated from this new sequence. What I have found in many cancer patients is that due to their often diminished support network, they are often stuck in the denial stage. This was witnessed in the earlier reported research on cancer patients' denial of psychosomatic symptoms and their higher thresholds of pain.

The course that many of my own cancer patients have experienced is that when a significant loss or major life change is encountered by these individuals, the inadequacy of their social support networks immobilized them during the beginning stages of their grief process. These patients were often parentalized at very early ages and learned how to deal with emotionally taxing situations on their own. Consequently, they often repress or even deny many of their feelings, always looking strong and in control on the outside.

However, because of the unavailability of a close support system, these individuals can deny their loss so completely that it finally becomes introjected inside their bodies—mind into matter—as cancer. In many ways, cancer is like newborn life in that the cells are undifferentiated and rapidly proliferating, just as fetal tissue is. A good example of the relationship between fetal and cancer cells is in the condition called molar pregnancy. This condition can arise when a fetus spontaneously aborts and instead of being sluffed off, the fetal cells continue to grow, forming a malignant tumor.

I have had several patients diagnosed with molar pregnancies. Each of these cases were marked by an inadequate support system coupled with a cessation of the grief process. Even with chemotherapy, there was difficulty in reversing the growth of the cancer. However, once these patients were able to say goodbye to their unborn children and, with support, complete the grief process, the tumors began responding to the treatments and eventually regressed.

Endometriosis is not neoplastic but is similar to molar pregnancy because it is undiscarded menstrual tissue which begins to grow ectopically on the uterus, causing pain. One patient of mine had an elective abortion which, due to poor social support, she had never grieved over. Over the years her physical pain intensified until one day in psychotherapy all the emotions from her abortion came flooding back. Suddenly she realized metaphorically that she had been hanging on to that tissue (endometriosis) which she had been unable to let go of (her never-born child) or forgive herself for years ago. The physical pain was a somatization of her guilt. As she began to grieve over this lost dream and let this child go, she found it easier to forgive and love herself, especially in her pelvic area. Within days, her constant and intense physical pain began to subside on a permanent basis.

Another patient named Mary developed thyroid cancer as a young adult. The tumor was localized to the left thyroid gland and was subsequently removed along with the thyroid. The patient's psychological family history included the report that she never saw her parents get angry. Mary was in denial of her own anger and inability to set limits for herself when she developed cancer the first time. Mary reported that she learned to assert herself more in her marriage and her cancer remained in check for over 10 years.

Mary suffered a crisis several months before her cancer reappeared. Her mother died, also of cancer. Although her death was not untimely, due to unresolved issues of emotional abandonment and internalized guilt, Mary went into denial about her mother's death. This was marked by the collection of her mother's belongings into a room in her house. When she entered counseling, Mary was most interested in using imagery as her intervention. It was recommended that she work on resolving her grief issues. However, she was unable to comply with any of the exercises which involved letting go of her mother. In some ways, it was as if Mary's cancer were a way of keeping her mother alive. The thyroid gland is involved in feeding (metabolic) and warmth (temperature control), which may have been the metaphorical somatization of these unmet psychological needs as a child.

Her EEG brain map during imagery seemed to reflect this unresolved grief issue. As seen in Figure 7-1, a predominant and complete set of harmonics in one "key" is present with delta at 2 Hz, theta at 6 Hz, alpha at 11 Hz (not quite twice theta), and beta at 22 Hz. Another partial set of harmonics, which I suspect is related to the repressed and unresolved emotions, appears to have an alpha at 8 Hz and a beta frequency at 16 Hz.

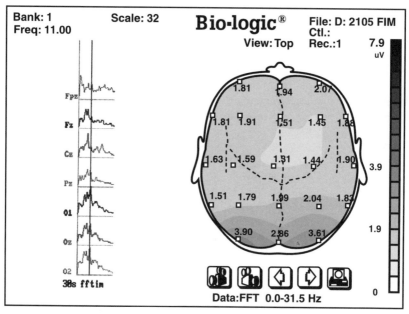

Figure 7-1.
Spectral analysis and alpha brain map of cancer patient during ineffective imagery.

Homeodynamic theory postulates that the presence of two different energy centers distributes the electrical activity over a wider portion of the frequency band, preventing the individual from experiencing enough high voltage activity necessary for activation of the immune system. These two energy centers would also create interference patterns which would add and subtract electrical energy in the bodymind. As Becker has discovered, cancer grows in places in the body where there is the least amount of electrical current.[11] Therefore, the thyroid may have been the site of this decrement of electrical activity in Mary's case.

Mary's cancer returned following treatment. Interestingly, there seemed to be a correlation between her medical deterioration and her difficulty with her imagery. She visualized color changes occurring at the cancer site, although the vividness and duration of her imagery were low. This was also reflected in her brain maps, as the presence of a single harmonic pattern was never observed during her imagery exercises.

On the other hand, Brenda was another cancer patient (breast cancer) who had not experienced any further tumor progression following medical treatment. When she had visualized health, her brainmap evidenced only one harmonic pattern (See Figure 2). She too had utilized color changes in her imagery of her body being cancer-free. However, two major differences distinguished Brenda from Mary. First, the vividness and perceived effectiveness of Brenda's imagery was stronger and also lasted for longer time periods during meditation than Mary's. Secondly, Brenda had not had any unresolved grief issues which were still jamming her bodymind communication system as Mary had. Even though Brenda had had a mastectomy, her support system was sufficient enough to buffer the stress of this potentially stigmatizing loss.

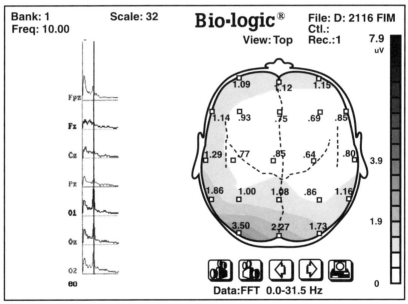

Figure 7-2.
Spectral analysis and alpha brain map of cancer patient during effective imagery

Another patient of mine had lung cancer which had been treated surgically years before, but was beginning to recur. Frank had experienced an emotionally constricted childhood with very little affection. He had worked for the same company for many years and although performing successfully, had experienced very little reward or acknowledgment for his services. Frank was interested in utilizing imagery as a complementary treatment for his cancer. His initial attempts were fairly ineffective as he imaged his own army being much smaller than the cancer. Then one day he came in and said that he had decided to accept an offer his company had made to send him overseas to work for a year or two. I was somewhat concerned that his departure might throw him into an environment of loneliness. On the other hand, the shift might also break up his current static condition of ennui.

About two years later Frank returned back to America and his old job. He indicated that his cancer was in remission and that he had never been happier in his life. His colleagues overseas had treated him with appreciation and he remarked that he had never felt so supported. Frank also said that he had continued his imagery and that now his defense system was large in number and acted as a surveillance system against any cancer cells. He had also incorporated elements of his new overseas environment into his visualizations as a reminder of his support.

This environmental change that Frank had made acted as a homeodynamic intervention against the childhood emotional abandonment he had never grieved over. The dynamic quality was the shift toward an increased support system. The resonance was exhibited in the increased quality and perceived effectiveness of his health imagery. Frank was able to stay disease-free for about five more years. He learned how to build and utilize a support network at his job and lived beyond his retirement.

LeShan has reported on the case of a man who, as an adolescent, had witnessed his father murder his mother.[26] Through the ensuing trials, he had encountered grave fear at the thought of having to testify against his father. Later he repressed everything he had witnessed and questioned his father's guilt entirely. As a young adult, he developed a pain in his throat which upon examination revealed a tumor. The repressed memories could not be eliminated completely, and thus became metaphorically crystallized at the site of his psychogenic stress—the throat. Very possibly, this unresolved grief issue which he had repressed caused a second harmonic electrical pattern in his brain waves. This pattern would have additive and subtractive effects in the electrical energy depending on where the two harmonic patterns intersected. Homeodynamic theory suggests that in this case the subtractive nodes of electrical activity were localized at the site of the throat either directly, through the perineural system, or indirectly, at the site of the sensory-motor cortex corresponding to the throat. During a psychotherapy session the day before his scheduled surgery, he recalled the entire incident of his mother's death complete with all the accompanying emotions. This catharsis apparently provided a major homeodynamic shift as his tumor vanished four days later and his surgery was cancelled.

Autoimmune, Infectious, Allergic, and Inflammatory Diseases

This section will address a wide variety of diseases and their metaphorical analyses based on case studies. There are two reasons for including these diseases together. First, unlike cancer, immune mechanisms have been confirmed in these diseases. Second, patients who develop chronic problems with these types of diseases appear to have progressed beyond the denial stage of their grieving processes. The stage that many are stuck in is fear/anxiety. Hence, this group expresses much more neuroticism and anxiety in coping with stress.

Autoimmunity

Autoimmune disease is a cluster of disorders in which the immune system has developed a flaw in discriminating self from nonself and has begun to attack itself. In each of the particular autoimmune diseases, different organ or tissue sites are attacked. For example, in diabetes, the body forms autoantibodies against the insulin- producing islets of Langerhans in the pancreas. In Graves disease, or hyperthyroidism, antibodies attach to the receptor cells of the thyroid, causing an overproduction of thyroid hormones. Other autoimmune diseases include, but are not limited to myasthenia gravis, multiple sclerosis, Crohn's disease, rheumatoid arthritis, systemic lupus erythematosus, and ulcerative colitis.

As in cancer, genetic predisposition and possible exposure (in this case, to viruses) are implicated in the etiology of autoimmune diseases. However, since the immune system manufactures antibodies as a learned response to encounters with foreign antigens, behavioral factors would seem to have a logical place in the genesis of autoimmunity. Psychological factors have indeed been linked to autoimmunity as well as in cancer. These are a history of chronic exposure to stressful circumstances, usually involving the loss or separation from a significant relationship.[27] In my own clinical experience, this loss can also happen through incidents of early childhood physical and sexual abuse, especially when the perpetrator's abuse simultaneously represented a loss of social or familial support. For example, if the abuse was committed by a family member, then that person was then lost as any potential support resource. Other personality dimensions attributed to autoimmune patients were over- conscientiousness, self-sacrifice, and high anxiety.

In my own experience with patients with cancer and autoimmunity, parental abuse seemed to play a more predominant role in the latter, causing more stress and anxiety. Cancer patients, on the other hand, have been found to deny stress, anger, and anxiety. Families-of-origin for the autoimmune groups tended to be more enmeshed whereas the cancer families were more distant. This possibly explains the different degrees of interest in support groups that I have seen expressed by cancer and autoimmune patients. I have conducted many support groups as part of the American Cancer Society, through hospitals, my own private practice, and at research institutions. I have found much more interest by patients with autoimmunity to participate in support groups than by cancer patients. The severity or life-threatening nature of cancer over autoimmunity wouldn't appear to explain this difference in interest because even AIDS patients have been demonstrated to exhibit extremely high concern for support group participation. The difference then, seems to be accounted for by the higher degree of alienation experienced by cancer patients.

As with cancer, autoimmune diseases are often triggered by the stress caused by the non-resolution of grief issues. However, compared with cancer patients, persons with autoimmunity have been found to have less denial, but on the other hand, more anxiety.[21] This fact suggests that autoimmune patients have sometimes progressed beyond the denial stage and are perhaps more locked into the fear/anxiety stage of the grieving process. This would explain the high prevalence of repressed anger with both groups. Neither group with a chronic history of unsuccessful management of either disease has effectively resolved issues relevant to the anger stage, such as in asserting oneself, although the autoimmune group has perhaps gone further than the cancer group as evidenced by their lack of denial and increased neuroticism.

General Metaphors of Autoimmunity

Autoimmune patients that have sought some type of behavioral or supportive therapy typically have been anxious and overachieving individuals. These personality characteristics also seem to characterize in a metaphorical way the immunological dynamics occurring inside the body—that is, an overactive immune system. The self-sacrificing characteristics of the autoimmune patient (mentioned above) also appear to represent the sacrifice made by the body to the immune system. It is as if the autoimmune patient says "I am going to overwork so that you will recognize me, even if it costs me something." The autoimmune patient's immune system likewise appears to declare that "I must maintain my vigilance and not let my guard down, even if I wear out some of my own soldiers."

Therefore, the metaphors of high-stress, over-conscientiousness, overwork, and self-sacrifice seem isomorphic with the immunological hypervigilance found in these patients. When autoimmune patients have been asked to describe their disease and health imagery, almost always images of heat become associated with the disease and symbols of coolness likewise with healing. Cancer is visualized most often as cold and dark.

In patients who have attempted visualization of health, but have not been properly educated about the role of the immune system in their particular autoimmune disease, their mental imagery often consists of a powerful immune system attacking some foreign disease. While I would suggest that their spontaneous, uncontaminated imagery is probably more likely some accurate feedback about what is actually happening inside the body (immune system attacking the body), it is interesting to compare these patients with cancer patients, whose initial, natural imagery often consists of little or no internal defense system—the so-called "black or blank" image.

Specific Autoimmune Case Studies
Rheumatoid Arthritis and the "Immobilized Anger" Metaphor

Julie was a patient with rheumatoid arthritis. She had been taking prescription anti-inflammatories for several years, but had begun to experience stomach irritation due to these. Julie had noticed a connection between her stress level and the severity of her disease, so she sought out biofeedback to determine if she could manage her pain and reduce her need for medication.

Julie's initial brainmap was characterized by two alpha frequencies at 9 and 11.5 Hz and two theta frequencies at 4.5 and 5.5 Hz (see Figure 7-3). The presence of these two spectral or harmonic signatures suggested an area of emotional repression regarding some unresolved issue. An exploration of her predominant feelings toward her family-of-origin indicated that she had a great deal of ambivalent feelings toward men, which was overtly expressed as either anger or seductiveness.

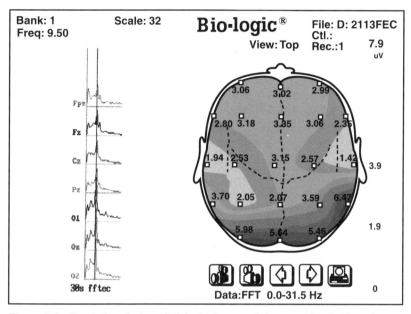

Figure 7-3. *Spectral analysis and alpha brain map of rheumatoid arthritis patient during ineffective imagery.*

When this emotional pattern was explained to Julie as a common behavioral manifestation of childhood sexual abuse, she became very tearful and began to reveal stories of sexual molestation by her natural father. As she began to experience the progression of feelings in the grief response, her imagery took on characteristics of these phases. In the initial denial phase, before she became aware of the abusive memories, Julie's imagery of her disease/health consisted of a dark, almost black, space, like a closed closet that she was inside. No movement or shifts in content or any other features of this imagery occurred during this phase.

Upon recollection of the abusive memories, her imagery became more prolific with red explosions representing the disease. Health to her simply became the quieting of these red explosions. This phase of the grief reaction was marked by increases in her expression of anger and sadness. She remarked that she had felt immobilized as a child to push her father away, fearing his reproach. To her, the anger had instead become mobilized into her body, which she now felt was "damaged goods." Her rheumatoid arthritis became a metaphorical manifestation of this.

At this point the work was only half done. The problem was that Julie's imagery of health was basically still ill-defined. To her it was the absence of illness. The path to health seems to require at least two stages. The first is to purge the secondary energy source by expressing the stress-inducing feelings which have been repressed. Next, however, is the stage of filling one's vessel with positive energy once the negative has been eliminated. In terms of imagery, one has to begin to formulate a visualization representative of self-love and acceptance.

To Julie, this phase was encountered by a second shift in health imagery, represented by cool water from a waterfall splashing over and through her body. This imagery seemed to connect her to the river-of- life which she visualized as flowing through her. This shift was accompanied by significant increases in her ability to manage her own pain without the continual use of anti-inflammatories. She only required the use of medication during occasional flare-ups of her disease.

Of further significance was the shift in her EEG brainmap while conducting her health imagery from a previous bitonal spectral pattern to one in which only one alpha frequency was present (see Figure 7-4).

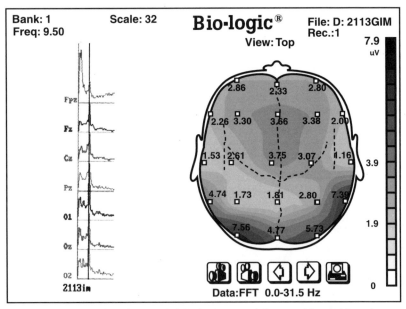

Figure 7-4. *Spectral analysis and alpha brain map of rheumatoid arthritis patient during effective imagery.*

The bitonal theta pattern was still evident, as she had yet to confront her father. However, notice also the much higher delta activity (artifact-free), which was reported on in Chapters 1 and 3 to have been found negligent in rheumatoid arthritis patients. The higher frontal beta activity is reflective of enhanced imagery.

Diabetes Mellitus and "Can't Buy Me Love" Metaphor

Diabetes is more often being considered an autoimmune disease because it is the body's own immune system which attacks the insulin- producing islets of Langerhans within the pancreas. Insulin is a protein hormone essential for the metabolism of carbohydrates. Complex carbohydrates are broken down more slowly, and can be metabolized without much problem by daily injections of insulin. Simple carbohydrates, or sugars, however, are more problematic for diabetics and usually have to be abstained from.

Betsy was a patient of mine with diabetes who had grown up in a family with a lot of conflict, compounded by an alcoholic father. The internalized messages of her self-esteem were often quite negative although I noticed that she was often "sugary sweet" to others. She tended to avoid conflict but would put herself in situations that created some emotional intensity. Betsy longed for love but sought it in some unhealthy ways. In other words, she was stuck within a grieving process about family-of-origin issues (emotional/mental abuse and abandonment). She was beyond the denial stage but unable to venture into assertiveness (limit setting and expression of anger).

As I do with many patients, I proposed to Betsy a "Cinderalla proposition"—a metaphor relating her psychodynamics to her diabetic symptoms that she "try on for size." If these suggested metaphors fit, or resonate with patients, they seem to know intuitively right away if it is the right one for them or not. Betsy's metaphor was that her diabetes represented an intolerance to "sugar" (symbolized as love), both from herself and others. Throughout the world, sugar, candy, and sweets are ritually used as tokens of affection and love.

In reality, Betsy had a family history for diabetes which was probably triggered by the stress of inhibiting the successful resolution of the grief process regarding her dysfunctional family. Yet, the metaphor homeodynamically resonated with her in such a way that as she began to love herself more, her blood sugar fluctuations decreased and she required less insulin in managing her diabetes.

Ulcerative Colitis/Crohn's Disease and the "I Can't Stomach It" Metaphor

Immunological factors have been now implicated in most of the gastrointestinal diseases. Autoimmune factors have been identified in the cases of Crohn's disease and ulcerative colitis. Bacterial infections are now considered the responsible culprit for stomach ulcers. Stress, however, definitely plays a role in precipitating the onset of symptoms, possibly through its detrimental influence on the immune system. Some of the personality traits which have been associated with disorders of the stomach and bowel include anxiety, neuroticism, and introversion.[28]

Although no attempt was made to stereotype metaphors of symptomatology, many of the patients of mine with ulcerative colitis have exhibited interesting consistencies. On the one hand there has been an almost universal softness of the voice which covered up a much more intense repressed anger inside. It was as if the patient with autoimmunity of the gut were needing to say something, but since they couldn't verbalize it, the message was communicated through the other end of the alimentary tract. Again, biology may govern the area of the body where the stress is localized. However, the source of the stress is often the same—the inhibited resolution of the grief process at the stage of anxiety and fear. Low internalized self esteem usually prevents one from continuing the grief resolution.

Another patient of mine named Diane had entered therapy to learn biofeedback and relaxation for her ulcerative colitis. She had the characteristic soft voice and was found to be "unable to stomach" critical remarks made by her mother and some of her co-workers. Her family-of-origin had been "uncomfortably" close, but was of little help in supporting any assertive behaviors on her part.

A curious phenomenon occurred one evening with Diane which led to a metaphorical consideration of her medical symptoms. My session with Diane had been my last session of the night and on my home I found myself waiting at the traffic light right behind her vehicle. As I continued home, she proceeded in my same direction, unaware of my presence. I happened to notice that she "tailgated" every car that she came up behind. As I knew this patient pretty well, I decided to confront her at our next session on her potentially dangerous driving habit, hoping to discover that she was just in a rush that particular evening in question. However, she answered forthrightly that she tailgated as a regular practice. As we pursued the matter in greater detail, we discovered that she was "on everybody else's ass" on the highway as a displacement of the anger harbored at people in her family and her workplace, who she perceived as always being "on her ass."

The amazing thing was that when I began to query my other patients about this tailgating behavior, I discovered that some of my other GI responders were also engaging in it. In essence, flirting with the possibility of rear-ending another vehicle acted as an expression of displaced anger toward those in the family who had been so critical when they were growing up. Yet, what they were accomplishing in a metaphorical way was a "rear-ending" of their own body through the irritable bowel symptoms.

When this one particular patient was confronted with this behavior, she remarked that she had never had the "guts" to confront those who really needed confronting. I was immediately struck by the reference to the body part where she lacked courage. Interestingly, she was neglecting the body part in her mind ("I don't have the guts") which was subsequently being eaten away with ulcers, in her body. Therapeutically, as she began to set more appropriate limits in her family and her work, this patient began to face the even more crippling fear that her family might reject her, or that she might get fired. When these events failed to occur and she realized that there was more support than she had thought was available, her colitis symptoms became much more manageable.

This course of treatment has been very similar with a number of other colitis or Crohn's patients of mine. These patients have all had an enmeshed family system who have been very critical. One might ask whether the organ-neglect of the "guts" couldn't just as easily precipitate colon or stomach cancer? Perhaps, except that the cancer patient's family is more often disengaged rather than being enmeshed. One might say that the GI responders are at least externalizing the anger, albeit on the highway. The cancer patient would more likely not ever externalize the anger.

Graves Syndrome and the "If You Can't Stand the Heat, Stay Out of the Kitchen" Metaphor

Graves syndrome, or hyperthyroidism, involves an increase in the production of thyroid hormones. These hormones are involved principally with metabolic rate and the conversion of fat and carbohydrates into energy. When the thyroid is producing excessive amounts of thyroid hormones, the typical consequences are decreased tolerance to heat (due to the increased metabolism), decreased weight, and increased tiredness.

Sylvia was a Graves syndrome patient I have worked with. Some of her symptoms included an intolerance for heat, finicky eating habits, weight loss, and fatigue. Sylvia's psychodynamics, like many other autoimmune patients, involved unresolved childhood abuse issues amidst an enmeshed family.

Unlike the more typical cancer patient, she had built up a rather substantial support network. Yet, each member of this system served a somewhat specialized role. She was always very conscious that she had made one member of her network upset, and then got on the telephone to access another friend to help her deal with her abandonment fears. Yet, her fear of intimacy kept her from using any one member of her social support system for any feelings which arose spontaneously. She particularly protected all members from her expression of assertiveness, or more importantly, in the healthy setting of limits as a way of preventing the need to get angry.

In essence, she was avoiding the "psychological" heat of both intimacy and abandonment and consequently building a physical intolerance to real heat through her hyperthyroidism. The organ of focus—the throat—is important here as one which is having to run overtime to appease the diametrically opposed fears of abandonment and intimacy. Attempts to reduce this tension served to "feed" the social support system, rather than "getting fed" from it, consequently leading to the metaphorical symptom of weight loss. By staying out of the psychological kitchen (because anger had been previously conditioned as abuse), she ended up starving. Another well-known result of hyperthyroidism is vitamin deficiency.

When I posed the metaphor that by avoiding the psychological heat, she was embroiling herself in the symptoms of the Graves disease, Sylvia suddenly realized that she really had nothing more to lose by going ahead and asserting herself with her family. By setting limits with her family, she found that they were not going to abandon her— her worst fear. After these confrontations, her imagery became much more effective at cooling what she visualized as her overheated thyroid. Symptomatically, Sylvia improved from this point on as well.

Allergies

Allergies are characterized by a reaction by the immune system to exogenous, or outside-of-the-body antigens. Pollens, dust, molds, foods, fungus, and other chemicals can often be the culprits in one's upper respiratory misery. While most individuals may not register symptoms upon exposure to these substances, in allergy sufferers a genetic component is turned on by a variety of stressors, leading to the following reaction. Immunoglobulin E, or IgE, molecules called antibodies are given an inaccurate message to bind to the antigens, forming an antigen complex. The message may in fact be the electrotonic signaling suggested by Becker, which is transmitted easily among the body's perineural cells (glia in the brain and Schwann cells in the body). Hypervigilance can also be transmitted through an increase in muscle tension as detected by higher electromyographic (EMG) readings. These same voltages are often negatively correlated with the brain's voltages. As was pointed out in a previous chapter, higher voltages in the brain are usually associated with both slower brainwave frequencies as well as lower EMG voltages.

Allergy-prone people also usually have a higher-than-normal level of immunoglobulin E. Next, these IgE complexes adhere to mast cells in the mucosa, acting like a key, unlocking the door to thousands of histamine molecules, which cause swelling and edema to occur. Hence the mucous membranes become swollen and effluent. Mast cells have been discovered in prolific numbers adjacent to neurons, suggesting their high responsivity with the nervous system.[29]

Allergies/Sinuses and the Pack-Rat Metaphor

Larry was a patient who was referred to me for upper respiratory allergy symptoms and recurrent sinus infections. As we began to explore his family, Larry reported that he was quite anxious around his family and that he felt that he could never measure up to them. At one point in therapy he had made the statement that "I feel bad about myself and always take criticism very personally. If someone says something good about me, I usually don't believe it." Larry's unresolved grieving issue which was causing him so much stress involved his inability to move beyond the irrational fear of losing his parents if he occasionally confronted them about their judgemental and critical statements.

One day Larry began to describe tendencies he had to accumulate objects and memorabilia, like a "pack-rat." This patient also had unresolved grief issues over a relationship that he couldn't say good-bye to. At this point I asked him to try on a Cinderella proposition, which went as follows: first, his allergies were a metaphorical representation of his psychological fears and hypersensitivities, and second, his sinus infections, characterized by congestion and poor drainage, represented the holding onto objects he feared losing.

Larry took no time in agreeing that these metaphors had a familiar ring to them. We developed a cognitive-behavioral therapeutic plan which involved biofeedback and relaxation training to reduce his fears and anxiety. During the relaxation process, Larry created some helpful images of his immune system not needing to be over-defensive to harmless invaders as well as his sinuses opening up and draining properly. Next, we constructed a list of positive affirmations which boosted his deflated self esteem. We also developed a reframing technique for him to utilize to fend off critical statements made by those in his family or love relationship. Finally, I had Larry participate in a brief individual ritual wherein he said as if his family and lover were present, that "he loved them but needed to say good-bye now." This ritual is very effective in assisting patients in completing the grief process with anyone, alive or deceased, that they are still psychologically enmeshed with.

Several years after his therapy terminated, Larry was reported to have much less problem with his allergies. At the last reporting, he had no further sinus infections. And, after completing his grief rituals (saying good-byes), he began to enjoy a more balanced relationship with his parents and even married his lover!

Asthma and the Breath-Holding Metaphor

John was an asthmatic patient who used daily steroidal bronchial dilation medication. On the surface, he appeared to have no major grief issues involving trauma, abuse, or loss. He had been raised in an intact family with which he still had frequent contact. However, there was one family-of-origin dynamic which I began to explore regarding the lack of emotions expressed in his family. John remarked that he had grown up in the perfect family and that his parents had never fought. (When patients make this statement, I have learned to investigate this issue more carefully.) Apparently what he meant by this was that his parents had gone "out of their way" to avoid family conflicts. In so doing, his parents became "suffocating" in their neurotic attempts to insure that everyone in the family was "happy."

When I asked John if he thought that his own asthma might not be an allergy to his parents, he made a sudden realization that his asthma always got worse when he was around them. I then asked if his asthma was perhaps a metaphor for his "holding his feelings in." In fact, he went on to explain that, like most asthmatics, exhalation was more difficult than inhalation, which created the sensation of constantly "holding his breath." He grinned as he became aware that living in his family meant always "holding your breath."

Therapeutically, we began a course of respiratory biofeedback to improve both his diaphragmatic breathing in addition to his forced expiratory volume. Psychologically, he began to learn how to express his feelings and not be afraid of the emotions of others. He learned that health was more a matter of a dynamic flow, both of emotions and breath, rather than the static condition of "keeping the peace." John's symptoms gradually became much more manageable and the use of his bronchial dilator was substantially reduced.

Dermatological Conditions and the "Thin-Skinned" Metaphor

Dermatological conditions involve a host of physiological mechanisms, from the immunological to the cardiovascular. The one I have had the most clinical exposure to is acne. It was serendipitous that following treatment of many teenagers with depression and adjustment disorders that I noticed that their acne had cleared up. Although the types and numbers of stressors facing these adolescents had not changed, their coping skills had. Probably the most commonly accepted metaphor for these kids' acne was that they were "thin- skinned" when it came to critical remarks from family or peers. In terms of the grief process, they had become stuck in the fear stage and didn't know how to assert themselves or set effective limits with others.

After therapeutic intervention including relaxation, confidence- building, and assertiveness-management training (usually with their parents), most of these youngsters who had chronic problems with acne found themselves becoming more clear-skinned. At the same time they had also become less hypersensitive to criticism.

Infectious Diseases

AIDS and the "Sacrificial Lamb" Metaphor

While there is doubt among some as to whether cancer is a disease caused by an ineffective immune system or rather one of a lack of communication among cells, there seems to be no question of the source of attack of the AIDS virus. This disease attacks the helper T-cells, disabling them so that they can not signal to killer T-cells and B-cells of the approaching foreign invader. With the body's own defense system rendered helpless, the AIDS virus can ravage the immune system and eventually the nervous system (due to the interconnectedness of the two), creating a ripe target for other foreign invaders.

Little data has been accumulated on personality characteristics of AIDS patients. While only considering the constellation of individuals who would participate in dangerous activities without complying with known preventive measures such as condoms or clean-needle usage, a predisposition for self-abuse and depression would seem warranted. Indeed, depression and stress have been determined to be factors related to the number of HIV-related symptoms[30] and to declines in CD4 lymphocytes in HIV-positive individuals.[31]

Most of the physicians who treat large numbers of AIDS patients have all remarked how an extraordinarily high percentage of these individuals have had addiction problems, especially with alcohol, drugs, food, and sex. If this characteristic is true, then issues of control would seem to be at the root of the behaviors which caused most of these patients to be infected. This feature is also highly suggestive of patients with autoimmune disease, with many of those having a difficulty managing their disease also being stuck in the fear/anxiety stage of their own unique grieving issue.

From my clinical experience, AIDS patients share two other features with autoimmune patients that seem quite distinct from cancer patients. On the one hand, my AIDS patients have had more of the family-of-origin enmeshment and abuse common to autoimmunity than the disengagement observed with cancer. Also, like autoimmune patients but different from cancer patients, victims of AIDS were much more comfortable in seeking out social support, regardless of how appropriate or inappropriate it was. The AIDS patients were the ones starting and attending their own support groups. The AIDS patients had their own support systems and thrived on complex communications networks. The point is that the AIDS patients were desparate for support and desperately afraid of being alone.

Unfortunately, most psychosocial and medical treatments for AIDS have only produced a great amount of hope without the results. No one seems to have been cured of AIDS, only delays in the seroconversion status from HIV-positive have been found with certain interventions. However, there is one group of patients who have been reported on recently who have demonstrated a possible cure. Some infants who have contracted the disease prenatally from their mothers have been shown to later test HIV- negative during their childhood. While no explanation has been determined, two homeodynamic mechanisms seem plausible. First, the cells in an infant, as discussed earlier, are more undifferentiated and have a much more dynamic metabolic and growth rate. Possibly this activity confers some adaptability and resilience on the part of the infant in combatting the AIDS virus. Secondly, babies spend much more time than adults in delta and alpha brainwave activity, two of the essential electrical patterns for both synchronous communication within the body and for the enhanced functioning of the immune system.

In looking at the use of metaphors in treating AIDS, several patients that I worked with individually had an almost-too-gentle spirit combined with a desperation for connection which led them into health-compromising situations. In a metaphorical way, their submission to psychological boundaries through their veils of nicety was to become a physiological boundary invasion which was to take their life.

One HIV-positive patient I worked with in individual therapy was always caving into the demands of others, while still bearing a grin on his face. Mike was so afraid of hurting someone's feelings that he allowed his psychological boundaries to constantly be invaded. Through the therapeutic process, he was able to form a more solid foundation for self-love so that he could more effectively establish healthy boundaries. Mike was also able to show his anger more freely regarding childhood abuse issues. He especially became irate at the fact that he had become the "sacrificial lamb," or scapegoat in his dysfunctional family, who took the heat in the family to take the pressure off of others. He also began to understand that perhaps the unfairness of his having been infected with the AIDS virus was a recapitulation of the earlier injustice of being the whipping post in order to maintain peace or protect others. As he realized this metaphor for his disease, he began to ask for what he wanted and allow himself to get angry when his limits got crossed over.

Mike was in the clinical process of developing AIDS when he initiated therapy, as his T-cell counts were dipping below 200. Perhaps through his metaphorical understanding of his illness his counts rose to well over 200 and he remained relatively symptom-free for another five years. Even though he eventually succumbed to Carposi's sarcoma, he was able to establish a quality of life for himself that he felt was far richer than the one he endured before becoming HIV-positive. Somehow, this most deadly of diseases was able to create an "emergency" which perpetuated healing on many levels, even though the physical body finally became exhausted.

The Common Cold and the "Inability to Say Something" Metaphor

The common cold is another infectious disease for which no cure has been found. However, the onset and degree of infection by cold viruses has been determined to be highly related to stress. In a well-controlled study of subjects given nose-drops with either placebo or one of five kinds of rhinovirus, psychological stress was highly correlated with the incidence of infection rates and clinical colds.[32]

Therefore, the use of metaphor as a healing intervention seems quite warranted in the case of the common cold. Bob was a patient of mine seeking counseling for marital problems. As part of a symptom checklist, Bob noted that he came down with four or five colds a year. His marriage, unlike his family-of-origin, had been very non-confrontational. Consequently, over the years he and his wife drifted apart until finally she began to bring up the idea of divorce because she felt disconnected from him. Fearful of letting go of the relationship, he jumped into therapy to try to "solve" the problem. Bob was unable to show any anger about his wife's withdrawal, just as he had been immobilized from confronting his parents about the rages and alcoholism that he had been exposed to as a child.

Once his wife filed for divorce, however, Bob came into our session one day steaming and irate. He also had a sore throat, and because he was not an allergy sufferer, felt assured that he was getting a cold or a "strep" throat. I suggested to Bob that he do some anger expression and not suppress his feelings. He unleashed a litany of grievances against her that stemmed back to the beginning of their relationship. The next day he called me to report that he felt a burst of energy following our session and that his cold had disappeared.

Although Bob's therapy ended several months later, I followed up on his progress for another two years. I found that he had learned how to assert himself in both personal and work relationships. Furthermore, he had contracted only one cold in the last two years. Thus, intervening with the homeodynamic technique of emotional expression had allowed Bob to progress through individual grief responses without getting stuck. This dynamic flow had increased his overall energy levels and evidently boosted his immune system.

Inflammatory Diseases
Chronic Fatigue, Hypervigilance and the "Touch-Me-Not" Metaphor

Chronic fatigue syndrome (CFS) is a constellation of symptoms which is still creating quite a controversy within the medical community. The symptoms can include fatigue, low-grade fever, sore throat, muscle weakness and pain, and the immunological abnormalities of lymphadenopathy, chronic infections, increased numbers of circulating immune complexes, and allergic sensitivities to a variety of substances. Chronic fatigue, sometimes called fibromyalgia, also bears some similarities to autoimmune disease, although there is usually not a presence of circulating antibodies with CFS which attack some organ within the body. Instead, the immune system seems to have been tripped on by some previous infection, but unable to turn off even after the infection subsided.

While the etiology of CFS is unclear, several of these patients that I have worked with have been victimized through sexual traumas such as childhood abuse or rape, which were still psychologically unresolved. The common personality characteristic of many of these individuals was the inability to get angry about the traumatic incidents. It was like their power had been completely taken away, resulting in a condition of physical fatigue. On the other hand, these patients became hypervigilant regarding their environment and their uncertainty about safety. Symbolizing this heightened sensitivity was the concurrent hypervigilance within the immune system. Inside the body was being waged the war that these patients felt immobilized to carry out. Consequently, they were being worn out through the constant utilization of resources. Furthermore, these patients could not engage in satisfactory deep sleep to replenish these resources or the immune system, lending to the presence of chronic infections, including pneumonia.

One of these patients, Sara, displayed muscular pain, fatigue, and skin sensitivity characterized by her extreme resistance to touch. She had been raped several months before developing symptoms of chronic fatigue syndrome. Her experience of pain to the touch was connected in therapy with her revulsion of anyone coming into physical contact with her. This was very likely a post traumatic symptom resulting from her rape. The only way Sara could protect herself in her eyes was to manifest a symptom which would make her inaccessible to everyone—a "touch-me-not." Unfortunately, this included her boyfriend as well. Sara was stuck in the fear stage of her grieving process regarding this trauma.

Over time, this patient began to participate in weight lifting as a way of increasing her physiological and psychological strength. She also found that after particularly exhausting exercise sessions, that she became irritable. I had a feeling that she was approaching some readiness in dealing with the feelings surrounding her trauma. One day in therapy Sara erupted angrily about having to repeat an incident about her parents that I had forgotten about. When I asked if there were perhaps something else that was also on her mind, she started pounding on the couch about the bastard that forced himself on her, alternately crying and yelling.

Following this catharsis, Sara began to manifest increasing levels of muscular strength and a gradual subsiding of fatigue and tactile sensitivity. The quality of her sleep also began to improve. Over time, with the help of special nonsexual touching exercises, she became increasingly more physically intimate with her boyfriend. She still has bouts of fatigue and/or rage from time to time, but as she explores these symptoms metaphorically as the emergence of a repressed emotion which is trying to "touch" her, she is able to maintain her sensitivity to the real world and stay "in-touch."

Headache Pain and the "Atlas Carrying the Weight on Your Shoulders" Metaphor

Headaches, whether migraine or tension, are almost always manifested as a result of constant high levels of muscle tension, as measured by surface electrode electromyography (EMG). Sometimes headaches can be caused by a wide variety of other reasons such as hypertension, repression of tears, sinus congestion, medication or food sensitivities (such as caffeine), etc. Nevertheless, even in a large majority of these cases, muscle tension can be secondarily elevated. The primary targets of this muscle tension are the postural muscles of the head, or those holding the head upright or holding the jaw together.

Inflammation is involved in two ways in migraine headaches. First, the immune system produces prostaglandins due to the micro-injuries of chronically tensed muscles. The immune system cannot distinguish internal from external injuries, and therefore sends protective defenders at the site of any injury to prevent infection. As in the case of practically all internal injuries, such as strokes, myocardial infractions, broken bones, etc., this immune response does more damage than good. Secondly, migraine headaches involve a vascular "inflammation" in which blood vessel walls become hyper-dilated. This is a rebound response due to the chronic vasoconstriction which often characterizes the peripheral vasculature of migraineurs.

Janice was a patient with a history of debilitating migraines which often sent her to the Emergency Room. Before conducting a psychophysiological evaluation, I palpated her shoulders to see if they were tender and she reeled in pain. She said that she had been working nonstop without a break and hadn't even noticed. Janice also made the comment that she felt that she was the only one who could do the work. When I suggested that she was like Atlas carrying the weight upon her shoulders, she replied, "who else is going to do it?"

Surface EMG indicated that her muscle tension levels were highly elevated, particularly at the trapezius (shoulder) and temporalis/masseter (jaw) sites. With EMG biofeedback, Janice was able to lower her muscle tension levels to within acceptable ranges. However, she would just as easily tend to block out her pain until a migraine ensued. This feature seemed to be related to childhood repression of anger toward her over- controlling mother, aggravated by her lack of having been modeled any assertiveness skills. She found that instead of fighting back with her mother, it was easier doing what she wanted to "keep her mother off her back." Consequently, her mother was still metaphorically "on her back" with the increased muscle tension and headache activity.

To assist Janice in preventing the buildup of muscle tension, we engaged in some expressive and cognitive techniques to grease the wheels of her grief process, which had been stuck at the anger stage. Once she felt more comfortable in setting limits, she subsequently developed a greater sensitivity in becoming aware of stress signals in the form of emotions or muscle tension. Janice also began to successfully utilize a technique which, when she felt her internalized critical parent "sitting on her shoulders," she would say out loud, "I love you mother, but get off my back."

Very shortly, the frequency and intensity of Janice's migraine activity decreased significantly. Her visits to the Emergency Room also terminated. Homeodynamically, she had allowed the grief process to become more dynamic through the use of a metaphor which integrated her body, thoughts, and emotions.

Lower Back Pain and the "Rear-Ending" and "Resisting the Urge to Kick the Living Daylights Out of Someone" Metaphors

Again, the majority of cases of chronic low back pain seems to involve functional, or muscular tension problems, rather than structural, or skeletal problems. Recent studies, in fact, have shown that most of us do have structural abnormalities, including lordosis, kyphosis, or some other misalignment, although most of us do not report chronic back pain. As with headache activity, chronic pain in other sites, such as the lower back, involves the immunological response of inflammation.

Two metaphors have surfaced in working with chronic back pain patients. First, I have had several patients who were rear-ended in automobile accidents. These patients' chronic pain became an issue when the accidents triggered previously unresolved traumas. The unresolved traumas in a way became localized at the site of injury from the accident. The "rear-ending" phenomenon seems almost diametrically opposed to the "tailgating" metaphor described in the Autoimmune section. The difference again relates to the particular phase of the grieving process that each group of patients was arrested. The rear-ended patients were in the stage of denial. However, it was a different type of denial than that found in cancer patients. This denial was precipitated through post traumatic stress instead of through disengagement. Furthermore, these rear-enders had a larger support system, albeit fraught with emotional intensity as distinguished from the lack of emotionality characterizing many cancer patients who had a poor progress with their disease. The reality of these patients being "hit-from-behind" also seemed to be a metaphorical recapitulation of earlier sexual and physical abuse.

Secondly, these chronic pain patients localized their muscular tension in their lower backs because they had been immobilized from kicking their offender off of them during the actual abuse. Hence, the back pain became a crystallization of the lack of dynamic flow through the grief process.

Conducting biofeedback on these individuals was extremely difficult at first, because when the leg, hip, and back muscles began to relax, memories (which had been locked into these muscles) of the sexual or physical abuse emerged. When these memories surfaced, these patients were encouraged to kick their legs, thereby dynamically unlocking the memories from these muscle groups. Once allowed to use their legs to symbolically remove the perpetrators from their bodies, they regained some of the muscle strength in their backs and legs and radically diminished much of their pain. Biofeedback was able to commence once these patients began to progress through the fear stage and show some evidence of assertiveness

Cardiovascular Disease
Hypertension and Unresolved Sadness

Essential hypertension, or high blood pressure of unknown origin, is usually the result of pathologies in the kidneys (previous disease, scarring, etc.) which affect the normal filtration of the blood. As part of the body's response to maintain the normal rate of blood filtration, hypertension often results. If normal blood pressure were to occur, the body would become uremic and waste products would be retained. So, the body puts high (blood) pressure on itself to filter out harmful products. Metaphorically, the hypertensive with problems managing his or her disease, may also have difficulty psychologically filtering criticism.

The personality type often associated with hypertension and coronary artery disease is type-A. The essential components of type-A are competitiveness, hostility, and impatience. In terms of the unresolved grief response, this patient has often moved beyond the fear stage and is stuck in the anger stage, unable to process sadness. This patient may interpret most remarks as threats, unable to filter the benign from the truly harmful.

Jerry was a hypertensive patient of mine who had been referred for biofeedback. He was currently taking three hypertensive medications. His personality was marked by a great deal of overtly expressed anger coupled with an inability to cry. Jerry felt threatened by many and competed with most. This was, of course, a wall protecting him from great wounds of abandonment in his childhood. Jerry had been fostered out to adoptive parents several months after his birth. His adoptive parents, however, were very strict on him while at the same time unaffectionate. Not surprisingly, his blood pressure was highly correlated with the amount of defensiveness he had to bolster each day.

Jerry made slight gains through biofeedback aimed at increasing both his diaphragmatic breathing and his heart rate variability. Particularly problematic, however, was his inability to increase his peripheral temperature. Jerry was trained in imagery although his attempts were met with his own criticism. When asked to visualize his cardiovascular system, he imaged a wall surrounding his heart. Changing course somewhat, I decided to work with him on his grief issues. Once he began to see that his parent's critical remarks were no longer threats and that they could not foster him out as his natural parents had done, Jerry let his "wall" down and learned how to cry. In his imagery, the wall began to come down as well, helping him see that many of his connections with people were supportive, not threatening. Consequently, his finger temperature began to rise, reaching criterion in several weeks.

Therapeutically, I challenged him to first begin to be more balanced with regard to his attribution of the source of negative versus positive comments. For example, he couldn't attribute the cause of all negative remarks to himself but ascribe the positive ones to others. He needed to become responsible for both negative and positive feedback, or for neither. Realistically, he began to show a more balanced reflection of each. This involved a combination of letting some negative comments role off his back and reframing others into compliments. Secondly, he made conscious efforts through cognitive therapy to love and respect himself more. This also led to his taking more time away from work to enjoy by himself or with his friends and family. As his ability to filter the comments from others and the introjected critical parent within, his hypertension eased to the point that one of his two blood pressure medications was ceased and the other cut in half.

These homeodynamic techniques allowed Jerry to progress through his inhibited grief process so that he could use his full array of emotions without feeling condemned or threatened. His metaphor to not put so much pressure on himself in filtering out the judgements of others and his internalized critical parents aligned his bodymind into resonance with the end result of his blood pressure dropping. .

References

1. Dunbar, H.F. (1943). *Psychosomatic diagnosis.* NY: Hoeber.

2. Alexander, F. (1950). *Psychosomatic medicine.* NY: Norton.

3. Graham, D.T., Lundy, R.M., Benjamin, L.S., Kabler, J.D., Lewis, W.C., Kunish, N.O., & Graham, F.K. (1962). Specific attitudes in initial interviews with patients having different "psychosomatic" diseases. *Psychosomatic Medicine, 24*:257–266.

4. Lacey, J.I. (1967). Somatic response patterning and stress: Some revision of activation theory. In M.H. Appley & R. Trumbull (Eds.), *Psychological stress.* NY: Appleton-Century-Crofts.

5. Greene, W.A., & Swisher, S.N. (1969). Psychological and somatic variables associated with the development and course of monozygotic twins discordant for leukemia. *Annals of the New York Academy of Sciences, 164*(2), 394–408.

6. Rosenman, R.H., Brand, R.J., Jenkins, C.D., Friedman, M., Straus, R., & Wurm, M. (1975). Coronary heart disease in the Western Collaborative Group Study. *Journal of the American Medical Association, 233,* 872–877.

7. Shekelle, R.B., Raynor, W.J., Ostfeld, A.M., Garron, D.C., Bieliauskas, L.A., Liu, S.C., Maliza, C., & Paul, O. (1981). Psychological depression and 17-year risk of death from cancer. *Psychosomatic Medicine, 43,* 117–125.

8. Thomas, C.B., Duszynski, K.R., & Shaffer, J.W. (1979). Family attitudes reported in youth as potential predictors of cancer. *Psychosomatic Medicine, 41,* 287–302.

9. Achterberg, J., & Lawlis, G.F. (1980). *Bridges of the bodymind.* Champaign, IL: Institute for Personality and Ability Testing.

10. Hay, L.L. (1987). *You can heal your life.* Carson, CA: Hay House.

11. Becker, R.O. (1985). *The body electric.* NY: William Morrow & Co.

12. Dermer, G.B. (1994). *The immortal cell.* Garden City Park, NY: Avery.

13. Klein, J. (1982). *Immunology.* NY: John Wiley.

14. Adachi, S., Kawamura, K., & Takemoto, K. (1993). Oxidative damage of nuclear DNA in liver of rats exposed to psychological stress. *Cancer Research, 53*(18), 4153–4155.

15. Eysenck, H.J. (1988). Personality, stress, and cancer prediction and prophylaxis. *British Journal of Medical Psychology, 61,* 57–75.

16. Booth, G. (1969). General and organic-specific object relationships in cancer. *Annals of the New York Academy of Sciences, 164*(2), 568– 576.

17. Bennette, G. (1969). Psychic and cellular aspects of isolation and identity impairment in cancer: A dialectic of alienation. *Annals of the New York Academy of Sciences, 164*(2), 352–364.

18. Harris, M. (1964). *Cell culture and somatic variation.* NY: Holt, Rinehart, & Winston.

19. Nossal, G.J.V. (1993). Life, death and the immune system. *Scientific American, September,* 53–62.

20. Wirsching, M., Hoffmann, F., Stierlin, H., Weber, G., & Wirsching, B. (1985). Prebioptic psychological characteristics of breast cancer patients. *Psychotherapy and Psychosomatics, 43,* 69–76.

21. Thomas, C.B. (1988). Cancer and the youthful mind. *Advances, 5*(2), 42–58.

22. Lipton, R.B., Galer, B.S., Dutcher, J.P., Portenoy, R.K., Pahmer, V., Meller, F., Arezzo, J.C., & Wiernik, P.H. (1991). Large and small fiber type sensory dysfunction in patients with cancer. *Journal of Neurology, Neurosurgery, and Psychiatry, 54*(8), 706–709.

23. Courtney, J.G., Longnecker, M.P., Theorell, T., Gerhardsson de Verdier, M. (1993). Stressful life events and the risk of colorectal cancer. *Epidemiology, 4*(5), 407–414.

24. Thomas, C.B., & Duszynski, K.R. (1985). Are words of the Rorschach predictors of disease and death? The case of "whirling." *Psychosomatic Medicine, 47,* 201–211.

25. Kubler-Ross, E. (1975). *Death: The final stage of growth.* Englewood Cliffs, NJ: Prentice-Hall.

26. LeShan, L.L., & Gassmann, M.L. (1958). Some observations on psychotherapy with patients with neoplastic disease. *American Journal of Psychotherapy, 12,* 723–734.

27. Moos, R.H., & Solomon, G.F. (1965). Psychologic comparisons between women with rheumatoid arthritis and their non-arthritic sisters; I.Personality test and interview rating data. *Psychosomatic Medicine 27,* 135–149.

28. Robertson, D.F., Ray, J., Diamond, I., & Edwards, J.G. (1989). Personality profile and mood state of patients with inflammatory bowel disease. *Advances, 6*(4), 18–19.

29. Theoharides, T.C. (1990). Mast cells: The immune gate to the brain. *Life Sciences, 46*, 607–617.

30. Rabkin, J.G., Williams, J.B.W., Remien, R.H., Goetz, R., Kertzner, R., & Gorman, J.M. (1991). Depression, distress, lymphocyte subsets, and human immunodeficiency virus symptoms on two occasions in HIV-positive homosexual men. *Archives of General Psychiatry, 48*, 111–119.

31. Burack, J.H., Barrett, D.C., Stall, R.D., Chesney, M.A., Ekstrand, M.L., & Coates, T.J. (1993). Depressive symptoms and CD4 lymphocyte decline among HIV-infected men. *Journal of the American Medical Association, 270*, 2568–2573.

32. Cohen, S., Tyrrell, D.A.J., & Smith, A.P. (1991). Psychological stress and susceptibility to the common cold. *New England Journal of Medicine, 325*, 606–612.

CHAPTER EIGHT

Homeodynamic Hypothesis 2: Rituals and the Preservation of Culture

Periodically in the remote mountains, deserts, or shores of North America, I have led and participated in workshops focusing on the power of rituals in the healing process. In some of the most powerful of these rituals, participants may gather on the floor of our meeting place, lying down in a circle much like spokes of a wheel with our heads facing outward. With very little instructions given except to use the voice in an exploratory manner to merge and diverge from the total group sound, we begin. No one has any idea of what will happen and because of our own cultural pressure to not use our voices unless professionally trained, we start out very timidly. Several of us begin to make breathy wind-like sounds and others are heard softly creating up and down glissandos like sirens in the distance. Then someone starts laughing and, as if given permission to raise the decibel level of the group sound, everyone is laughing at full volume. Laughs you could not even imagine are spontaneously erupting from all around. Suddenly, animal sounds like wolves and screeching vultures are erupting with total disinhibition. Noises from a lifetime, to be sure, but perhaps sweeping into a more primitive, phylogenetic consciousness as well, are flowing freely like some lifeline into the evolution of the universe has just been tapped.

Eventually, the cacophony drowns out and gives way to more gentle sighs of relaxation. Slowly, however, more tonal melodies start to emerge. Unfamiliar lullabies begin to rock in the air while others center on a single tone, chanting over and over in a mantra-like style. More and more the vocalizing blends, forming ethereal chords which take on a power greater than that of any single individual's sounds. Like an aural aurora borealis, it hovers there in the air above us, then glides across the room to another location. A second peak is reached, only harmonic this time. People will remark later that this was the point in the choral improvisation that they were "taken out of themselves and connected with some energy or power much larger than themselves." After a total duration of anywhere from fifteen to fifty minutes, the vocalizing begins a decrescendo, drifting off finally into silence.

Although individual physical healing often occurs with some of the attendees, an integrating effect upon the group as a whole always occurs on a more mysterious, higher power or level. This transformation has a deep consciousness or awareness, and yet it can rarely be verbalized. Phenomenologically, we may speak of some sort of "spiritual" experience we have just witnessed. People feel electrified and energized, some with energy they have not experienced in many years. Warmth reaches into our extremities until our hands and feet become almost hot.

What we have experienced time and again is the power of ritual, not only to heal individually, but more importantly to perpetuate our connection with higher powers, our community among the participants, and the self-preservation of our culture. All rituals serve to preserve groups, communities, and cultures through this recreating process. Individuals are stripped of their self-possession and reinserted back into the spiritual matrix of the culture. In the example above, an entire "creation story" unfolded before our ears, without any prior discussion or expectations. Through the creation of our vocal improvisation, we recapitulated the creation and evolution of humankind. This allowed us to accomplish healing on an individual basis, as well as to preserve our group membership for as long as it took to reconvene.

What will be considered in this chapter is the use of ritual as a homeodynamic technique to help ensure the survival of a culture. Instead of occurring only on the individual level, these cultural shifts happen on a group level. Furthermore, resonance is manifested through the like-mindedness of all of the group members.

Rituals and Individual Healing

Cultural and religious rituals have long been a form of transpersonal medicine due to the homeodynamic shifts generated through the mechanisms of social support. Feelings of interconnectedness, whether to one's family, one's culture, or to one's God perpetuate a homeodynamic environment necessary for healing.

In her excellent review of the use of rituals in transpersonal medicine, Jeanne Achterberg traced the importance of repetitive behaviors in different examples of survival.[1] On the lower phylogenetic end of the spectrum, animals conduct ritualistic behaviors to reduce the physical symptoms of anxiety. She also comments on the survival of an Alaskan woman, who after being trapped for months in an avalanche while pregnant, "filled the days ceremoniously tanning an otter skin for her baby's birthday gift and writing on every scrap of paper she could find." With only the help of her rituals, this woman remarkably survived the winter and delivered her own child. She also discusses the survival of women from the Holocaust, whose accounts have attributed their perseverance to the ongoing observance of religious ceremonies and personal rituals such as birthdays.

The power of rituals has also been documented in a study of mortality among Chinese before and after the Harvest Moon Festival.[2] Death from all causes dipped by 35% the week before the Festival and peaked by the same amount during the week after. Presumably, the social and religious interest generated by the ritualistic observance of this holiday brought a dynamic shift in both mental and spiritual consciousness as well as a consensus, or resonance, among its celebrants. These factors produced a marked alteration in the normal pattern of life expectancy.

The healing power of rituals relates to the function of symbolic representation. The chant improvisation reported at the beginning of this chapter symbolically represents phylogenetic evolution from the sounds of animals to the formation of melodic patterns, and the ontogenetic development of humans from the lullabies to the more chordally complex theme and variations which culminated our composition.

Symbolic representation also occurs in the highly evolved forms of dress regalia at ceremonies, as well as in the use masks. Masks are intended to evoke specific spiritual powers through the identification process. However, the identification mechanism has been found to induce healing on its own through the various trance states produced.[3] Mask rituals, also called symbolic penetration techniques, activate neural structures not ordinarily accessible to normal consciousness. These techniques have been found to contain two main properties: the potential to (a) bypass inhibitions and constraints on neural models, and (b) expand and alter systems of transformations comprising neural models.[4] In so doing, mask rituals can alter psychophysiological organization and its consequent effects upon healing.

Rituals and Cultural Preservation

Cultural preservation is similar to individual healing, only on a grander scale. However, the homeodynamic hypothesis remains the same: a population will preserve its culture through the participation in communal rituals. This hypothesis has validity in looking at examples of cultures or sects whose strength has been due to the practice of rituals and whose demise was contingent upon the cessation of such rituals.

One such culture was the Mayas of Central America. This group flourished from roughly 2000 B.C. until the mid 17th century. Time-passage within the Mayan culture consisted of ritualistic feasts and their preliminary periods of fasting and continence, which succeeded one another almost without break.[5] In other words, hardly a Mayan day was spent without either preparing for or participating in one of its various rituals. Consequently, this culture aspired to some of the greatest heights in intellectual, artistic, and medical progress in all of the Americas.

The fall of the Mayas has been attributed to several cofactors, including increases in both the wealth and population. As materialism spread, however, spiritualism fell in favor of more secular and militaristic interests. Crucial to this transition was the abandonment of the great ceremonial centers in favor of secular housing developments. Then, as the rituals began to dwindle, so did the Mayas, until it was finally absorbed into the Mexican culture. Thus, ritual was an integral part of identity.

The modern Native Americans serve as another example of cultures which have been in existence for thousands of years. Even though the individual tribes have been continually removed from their own land until their country was virtually replaced, the Native Americans have somehow survived remarkably well in spite of poverty, alcoholism, racism, etc. It wasn't until I began to spend increasing amounts of time in Northern New Mexico that I realized that the

Pueblo Indians there marked time with the continual procession of feasts, festivals, and dances. And, so it goes in other tribes across America. Very likely, the preservation of these cultures has depended on the tradition of ceremonies in which homeodynamic bodymind shifts occur simultaneously in all members of the tribe, creating an environment ripe for both individual, and more importantly cultural healing.

A Native American patient of mine described his difficulty in complying with cognitive therapy tasks involving affirmations about his self esteem. He felt that this approach would be considered narcissistic by Indian tradition. Self was given over to the tribe and thus the tribe preserved. Individuality was something foreign to his cultural indoctrination. He returned to his tribe regularly for rites and festivals. And, he felt a closer bond to his culture than many of us who have forgotten our own rituals and have blended into the "melting pot." One of the last great Euro-American "tribal" rituals is the family reunion.

Another example comes from the 12-step tradition known as Alcoholics Anonymous. This sixty-year old grassroots treatment approach to addictions has generated one of the most far reaching and successful interventions ever introduced. The recidivism rate on the chemical dependency units at many psychiatric and rehabilitation hospitals is somewhere between 30 and 60%, depending on whether it is your 1st or 2nd hospitalization. However, those who attend AA on a regular basis have a recovery rate well over 90%. This is because AA involves a ritualistic approach very similar to ceremonies practiced by cultures all over the world in which one is stripped of their self-possession (through the anonymity) and reinserted into a spiritual matrix (by turning one's will and life over to the care of God as he or she is understood). For one hour a day each of over thousands of AA groups practice this ritual and maintain their sobriety for another 24 hours, and in so doing, the preservation of the organization for many years to come. It is now practiced for a wide variety of addictions including drugs, sex, gambling, and overeating.

Our own modern-day culture in America poses some threat to disintegration due to the loss of rituals and spirituality. Joseph Campbell has remarked about the fall of American civilization into drugs, gangs, and crime due to the lack of initiation rituals required to become an adult member of civilized society.[6] Furthermore, with their frustration with organized religion and its outdated and moralizing attitudes on certain topics, today's youth are increasingly turned off to "spiritual" practices. As a result, we have all become spiritually starved and in search of the rituals which we have thrown out with the bathwater. This ceremonial cessation combined with the focus upon individuality, freedom, and "it's your thing, do what you wanna do" stand to undermine the very fabric of our entire culture.

Another of the important rituals that Campbell indicates are gradually being lost is marriage.[6] In some cultures, he describes, the premarital and marital rites take months. And, for better or for worse, these marriages survive longer. However, in the land of the Las Vegas wedding, the bride can wake up the next day astonished to find that she is now Mrs. Groom. Because too little in the way of preparator rituals often precedes the marriage vows, the ritual of lifelong marriage may soon go the way of the dinosaurs.

If pre-marital rituals are important for the sustenance of marriages, then relationships themselves have a dynamic way a reenergizing families. Physicists have discovered that if something changes or shifts in a periodic way, then it has frequency. If it has frequency, then it has energy.[7] Rituals, then, can be viewed as ways of creating energy. In other words, the circadian (daily) shifts we encounter in our bodies, in addition to all the other mental, emotional, and social shifts, are nature's way of counteracting the universal trend toward entropy, chaos, and death, so that we can reenergize ourselves for another day in the life on this planet. Shifts involve a movement between two polarities such as rest and work, pleasure and discomfort, right-brain vs. left- brain, and hearing vs. vision.

One can see these laws of physics enacting themselves in relationships and families. Perhaps the old adage "opposites attract" could be further revised to say "opposites create energy." Two individuals in a relationship, each possessing a trait representing a different polar end of a continuum (e.g., relaxed/anxious), might subconsciously experience an opportunity through their relationship to create energy between themselves. Thus, the relationship is recreated. Often, this is the case. Couples find each other attractive not only through conscious criteria such as looks, interests, and values, but probably moreso based on subconscious attempts to resolve old unhealed wounds from one's family-of-origin. From the dynamic perspective, similar looks, interests, and values shouldn't be enough to provide the life-sustaining energy a couple needs to survive. Years of private practice with families however has convinced me that couples are attracted to the energies created by the differences (fostered by old, unresolved issues) existing between them. For example, one is a "fuser" and the other is an "isolator," or one is emotional and the other is overcontrolled.

And if relationships aren't enough to convince the reader of the energy yielded through complementary forces, children have an amazing propensity to grow in just the right ways to provide whatever unconscious forces the couple may have lacked. But, like spokes in a wheel, these different energies serve to propagate families into further generations.

In a more macroscopic view of the human race, longevity of our species would be propagated (according to homeodynamism) through our racial diversity. If Hitler, or any number of other racial purists, had succeeded, our (human) race might have found itself particularly short- lived, in comparison to the alternatives. Immunologically, we have known that our offspring are better protected from disease if we mate with those whose immune systems are most complementary to ours, thus the sanctions against incestual marriages. Some animals have the ability to smell pheromones on potential mates that represent the make-up of their immune systems. More importantly, the animal chooses the immune system of the mate immunologically most diverse from himself!

Hence, we return to our immune system as the fundamental definer of our bodymind and what we know as our "selves." We wear our immune systems on our sleeves, although, probably more through our emotions than through smell. The emotional processing part of the brain, the limbic system, was where Candace Pert found the most prolific concentrations of immune modulators, or lymphokines.[8]

In essence, we are musical instruments playing the song of our immune systems. The homeodynamic rituals we create serve to protect us on many different levels. As the threat of cold war subsides, the one danger that we seem to be unable to quell at present is that posed by new antibiotic-resistant strains of bacteria and deadly viruses. And yet, the threats will probably shift back and forth to insure our adaptability in dealing with a variety of forces. As long as we keep shifting to the beat of the Cosmic Drummer, we may yet survive

References

1. Achterberg, J. (1992). Ritual: The foundation for transpersonal medicine. *Revision, 14*(3), 158–164.

2. Phillips, D.P., & Smith, D.G. (1990). Postponment of death until symbolically meaningful occasions. *Journal of the American Medical Association, 263*, 1947–1951.

3. Rouget, G. (1985). *Music and trance.* Chicago: University of Chicago Press.

4. Webber, M., Stephens, C., & Laughlin, C.D. (1983). Masks: A re-examination, or "Masks? You mean they affect the brain?" In R. Crumrine & M. Halpin (Eds.), *The power of symbols.* Vancouver: University of British Columbia Press, 204–218.

5. Thompson, J.E.S. (1954). *The rise and fall of Maya civilization.* Norman, OK: University of Oklahoma Press.

6. Campbell, J. (1988). *The power of myth.* NY: Doubleday.

7. Wolf, F.A. (1986). *The body quantum.* NY: Macmillan Publishing.

8. Pert, C.B. (1986). *The wisdom of the receptors.* Advances, 3(3): 8–16.

INDEX